FLORENCE NIGHTINGALE,
AVENGING ANGEL

Florence Nightingale
Avenging Angel

Hugh Small

Constable · London

First published in Great Britain 1998
by Constable and Company Limited
3 The Lanchesters, 162 Fulham Palace Road
London W6 9ER
Copyright © Hugh Small 1998
ISBN 0 09 479010 8

The right of Hugh Small to be identified as the author
of this work has been asserted by him in accordance with
the Copyright, Designs and Patents Act 1988

Set in Monotype Garamond 12pt by
Servis Filmsetting Ltd, Manchester
Printed in Great Britain by
St. Edmundsbury Press Ltd
Bury St. Edmunds, Suffolk

A CIP catalogue record for this book is available from the British Library

To my wife

NORMA

Contents

List of Illustrations

Acknowledgements

I would like to thank Radcliffes & Co., who administer the Henry Bonham Carter Will Trust, for permission to publish letters of Florence Nightingale and her family. Extracts from three letters in the Greater London Record Office are printed by courtesy of the Florence Nightingale Museum Trust, London. Sir Ralph Verney has kindly allowed me to print letters from the Nightingale papers at Claydon House. My thanks are also due to the Director of Special Collections at the Boston University Library and the librarian of the Woodward Medical Library at the University of British Columbia for permission to publish letters in their collections. I am grateful to the Earls of Pembroke for permission to print extracts from letters at Wilton, and to Lady Buccleuch for permission to use extracts from Sir John McNeill's papers. I would also like to thank the Head of Archives at the National Army Museum for permission to quote from the correspondence of Lord Raglan.

I must mention a number of individuals who helped me enormously by facilitating my researches. They include Alex Attewell, Curator of the Florence Nightingale Museum, and Lynn McDonald of the University of Guelph. My editor Carol O'Brien has made very important contributions to my text. The staffs of the National Army Museum, the British Library, Durham University Library, the

Scottish Record Office, the Wellcome Institute, and Claydon House all helped me to locate material. Finally I would like to note the extremely important role played by the London Library.

1

Resolving the mystery

FLORENCE NIGHTINGALE is one of history's most famous invalids. At the age of thirty seven, twelve months after returning from the Crimean War, she took to her bed and stayed there for more than ten years. Many theories have been advanced to explain her mysterious illness. Suggested causes have included stress due to conflict with the War Office or with her family, and numerous real or imaginary ailments. Most recently, medical science has attributed her symptoms to brucellosis, an infection carried in dairy products which she may have contracted during the war.

While she was ostensibly a bedridden invalid Nightingale worked intensively for military and civilian hospital reform. This is one of the contradictions that have puzzled her biographers. Another supposed contradiction is that despite her advanced and sensible views on nursing she refused to recognise new discoveries about the spread of infection through germs. It may seem unlikely that a new study could resolve these and many other contradictions when no major new source material has entered the public domain since her death in 1910. This book tries to do so by exploring for the first time in depth an area of her life that has received little attention.

Although her name is as famous as those of England's best-known admirals and generals and the amount of archive material on her is immense, Nightingale has had few biographers. None of them has felt the need to explore Nightingale's own claim that while she was Superintendent of Nursing in the hospitals of the Crimean War 14,000 soldiers died in hospital because she and the medical staff neglected elementary sanitary precautions. It would be pointless to explore this subject with a view to judging the people involved by today's standards, and this book will not do so. What it will do is to examine Nightingale's own theories. Her previous biographers, by choosing not to do so, have ignored the subject that was dearest to Nightingale's heart, and which she came to believe gave meaning to her life. If she was brave enough to confront the truth, why should we avoid it? Not only did she seek out the facts at great personal cost, she went to enormous trouble to reveal them as widely as possible and to preserve the evidence for the historical record, despite an official cover-up that involved leading politicians and Queen Victoria herself. Most remarkable of all, she used the truth to push Victorian England into a burst of social progress that may justify a claim that the pioneering National Health Service was born on the floor of the Scutari Barrack Hospital.

If we listen carefully to what Nightingale says on this subject, we can correlate it with the contemporary archives of leading political figures to understand why they entrusted Nightingale with an investigation into hospital conditions and then suppressed her findings. This gives not only a new perspective on social reform in Britain, but also a new view of many of the leading political figures of the time. We see men of great political power choosing to do good by stealth, and a concerned young Queen opposing the transfer of power to an incompetent House of Commons. If we try to gloss over Nightingale's account of the tragedy in her hospital we miss these insights as well as depriving ourselves of any possible happy ending.

Some of Nightingale's previous biographers imply vaguely that the death rate subsided when she took control of nursing in the army's hospitals. But Nightingale herself tells us that it soared, only beginning to decline four months later. In their understandable reluctance to delve too deeply into her claims – claims that medical authorities have denied, though never disproved – the biographers have failed to ask a key question: when did Nightingale herself develop her theory that the men died because of poor hygiene? If Nightingale knew from the start why so many thousands of men were dying, why did it take four months to introduce what she later claimed was a simple remedy? And if she did not know then, when exactly did she find out, and what effect did that discovery have on her?

Some previously unused letters, not in the Nightingale Papers, allow us to answer these questions for the first time. They show beyond any possible doubt that Florence Nightingale would not accept until twelve months after the war was over that bad hygiene had killed thousands of patients in her hospital. When she discovered what she believed to be the proof, she suffered a complete mental and physical collapse. This was when her 'illness' began, and when her life changed direction in a way that has appeared so contradictory to her biographers.

The change in her was so dramatic that it is as if there were two different women. When she arrived home in August 1856, she was quietly proud of her achievements. Her demonstration that respectable women could nurse men in hospital had made her the most popular figure in England. After some hesitation, she joined the movement for army reform, planning to make use of her wartime experience. She thought that her popularity, though embarrassingly exaggerated, would help her to succeed in improving conditions for the common soldier where others had failed. After that, she planned to return to nursing, becoming the matron of a military or civilian hospital where she would supervise and train hospital nurses using the fund that a grateful public had subscribed in her name during the war.

Twelve months later, after she had discovered the real reason for what she called the 'loss of an army', all these dreams lay in ruins. It was not only her state of health that had changed. She had abandoned all thought of continuing her nursing career, had lost interest in hospital administration and in the Nightingale Fund for training nurses, and had turned against the medical profession. She had also broken off all contact with her family. When she recovered her mental faculties after her breakdown, she was obsessed with the hygienic state of buildings. Her obsession afterwards diminished and her interests broadened, but during the rest of her long and productive life she remained a reclusive invalid. And she never afterwards spoke of her Crimean War service with pride.

These changes become much easier to understand in the light of her post-war discovery and her remorse at having agreed to a public cover-up. The apparent inconsistencies become guides to understanding Nightingale and her times rather than obstacles. Although she was literally crippled by her feelings of guilt her humbling experience seems to have sharpened her judgement of other people and of events. And in view of the fact that her painful search for the truth reveals a capacity for open-mindedness and honesty, it is worth re-examining her later attitude to new ideas such as the discovery that germs cause infection. On careful analysis, the widespread allegations that she refused to accept the germ theory turn out to be false.

This story may resolve some old mysteries about Florence Nightingale. But it creates a new, more profound, mystery. The unanswered question is: did she complete her self-imposed task of paying back many times over her imaginary debt of human lives, and has she finally earned the reputation that she came to hate?

2

Early Life

IN HER YOUTH FLORENCE NIGHTINGALE dreamed of a life of heroic action, and by strange chance her dream was realised during the Crimean War. But then, unlike most women who were attracted to nursing, she was not satisfied with action alone. She had to step back and analyse the conduct of the war and her own role in it, with the unexpected but perhaps inevitable result that she found plenty to criticise in both. Her need for both intense action and profound analysis came from the circumstances of her education and family life.

She was the younger of two sisters, born in quick succession while their wealthy parents were travelling the Continent on an extended honeymoon. Her sister was born at Naples and named Parthenope, after one of the Sirens who was said to be buried there. Florence was born one year later, in 1820, and was named after the city of her birth. Her father had been an indolent but intelligent and reflective youth who had inherited great wealth from an uncle. Her mother was a socially active woman of great beauty, who married her father for his wealth after realising that the minor aristocrat with whom she had fallen in love did not have the means to finance her extravagant life-style. Once the children were born Nightingale's father spent his time avoiding his wife's attempts to integrate him into society, hiding in the Athenaeum Club in London or studying with Florence in his library. Florence, like her father, found society activities trivial and meaningless.

Affluent families of that time were usually highly religious and Florence Nightingale's family had a strong Unitarian tradition. A Unitarian is a Christian who does not accept the doctrine of the Trinity, a doctrine that was a basic test of adherence to the official established Church of England. The Unitarians' refusal to accept this creed was due to their reluctance to follow rules handed down by authority rather than a claim of superior insight into the nature of God. Another common Unitarian technique for provoking the Church of England was to deny the divinity of Christ. Until 1813 it was a criminal offence to do so in England. The Member of Parliament who persuaded that body to repeal this section of the criminal law in 1813 was Florence Nightingale's maternal grand-father.

It is hard to know whether Florence actually considered herself a Unitarian, because members of the sect are difficult to categorise and she herself is particularly elusive. But the strength of the tradition in both her mother's and her father's family must have influenced her and some of her medical attitudes are easier to understand when their Unitarian overtones are taken into account. The Unitarian religion is described as based on 'deeds not creeds'. Unitarians were fond of pointing out that the Trinity and other creeds did not come from the bible but were invented by earthly rulers who wanted to suppress independent thought. Nightingale herself claimed to be unqualified to guess at such details as whether God was one being or three, details which she called His *essence*. She could, she said, deduce what kind of *character* He had from the way He had created the world, and that was enough for her to be able to do His work. This is a Unitarian position. To our more cynical ears it may sound as though Unitarianism was a cunning camouflage for atheism, but Nightingale's most private writings show that she was a devout Christian.

Florence's independence of thought made her relationship with

[6]

her mother and sister difficult. She was most attached to her father who devoted much of his wealth to intellectual pursuits for himself and his daughters. Florence was very close to him when young, much closer than her older sister Parthenope had been. Their father had educated both of them himself at home, and Florence had been the apter pupil. But as Florence grew up under his wing and began to yearn for a life of useful activity she came to look on her father with a mixture of pity and contempt. One of her autobiographical notes written while she was still living at home reads: 'My father is a man who has never known what struggle is. Good impulses from his childhood up, having never by circumstances been forced to look into a thing, to carry it out. He has not enough to fill his faculties – when I see him eating his breakfast as if the destinies of a nation depended upon his getting done, carrying his plate about the room, delighting in being in a hurry, I say to myself how happy that man would be with a factory under his superintendence – with the interests of two or three hundred men to look after.'[1]

She was not doing justice to her father when she said he had never 'carried anything out'. One – perhaps the only – important achievement of his life was too close for her to see. This was the education of Florence, an ambitious project that he completed single-handed at home and on educational trips abroad to France, Italy and Switzerland. He accomplished far more than was necessary or considered desirable for a lady, training her in French, German, Italian, Latin, Greek, History, and Philosophy. Her father might, in different circumstances, have had a brilliant career as a teacher. Florence's assessment of him as a frustrated would-be factory superintendent does not show much insight into his character, but it may reveal more of her own yearnings and ambitions, projected onto him when she found they were unsuitable for herself.

A certain amount of managerial competence was normal in a gentlewoman, responsible as she often was for managing a large staff of servants. But when at the age of twenty Florence asked if she could study mathematics, and began to talk about accomplishing something in the world, her father was uneasy and he seems to have regretted having awakened an appetite for action that could not be fulfilled. There was no useful role for highly educated ladies in Victorian society; Florence was already over-qualified for the family duties that awaited her. After much argument she was allowed to study mathematics under a tutor.

Her sister Parthenope was, for Florence, a kind of *alter ego* which she struggled desperately to distance herself from; a distorted image of herself which she feared. It is possible, too, that Parthenope resented Florence's anti-social traits because Parthenope recognised them as latent in herself. There had been continual friction between the two of them as Parthenope tried to correct what she saw as Florence's unnatural desire to build a life outside home and marriage. When Florence, in her late twenties, developed an interest in hospitals Parthenope's anxiety was so intense that her family thought she was unbalanced. Not that they thought Florence's interest in hospitals and nursing was 'normal', either. 'It was as if I had wanted to be a kitchen-maid,' she said in later life. Predictably, the family split along religious lines under the strain. Florence and her father remained loyal to the Unitarian tradition while Parthenope and her mother reverted to conventional Church of England doctrines more in keeping with their mission of amiable socialising with the ruling class.

Nightingale's father owned two large country houses: Lea Hurst in Derbyshire, and Embley Park, an ornate Elizabethan-style mansion near the New Forest. From July to October each year the family occupied Lea Hurst, and from then until March they wintered at Embley. Referring to Embley, Florence described her sister's vocation as 'to make holiday for hard working men out of London, who come to enjoy this beautiful place.' In March the family went to London for the 'Season,' staying usually at the Burlington Hotel in Mayfair. It was an apparently busy life of itinerant socialising, but like many similar Victorian ladies Florence recognised the incongruity of such a gilded existence in the midst of poverty, and devoted some of her time to good works in the villages surrounding her father's estates.

The family's energetic socialising brought Florence into contact with many of the ruling class, in particular with Lord Palmerston, the future Prime Minister. Palmerston's country house of Broadlands was only a couple of miles from the Nightingales' winter home. Palmerston was a rising young politician in his late thirties when the Nightingales first became his neighbours in 1825. In 1830, when Florence was ten years old Palmerston became Secretary of State for Foreign Affairs. He was later to rise to unheard of heights of popularity and success as Home Secretary and then Prime Minister during the Crimean War and after. In later life he was balding and cherubic, with dyed mutton-chop whiskers and badly fitting false teeth. He looked like a quintessential Englishman of the *Punch* cartoon variety, but his air of jovial humbug disguised a politician of great genius, whose power was heightened by his skill in concealing his true intentions. Florence's father had seconded the nomination of Lord Palmerston as a successful Parliamentary candidate for their local constituency of South Hampshire in the general election that followed passage of the Reform Bill in 1832. Florence, barely in her teens, accompanied her father to hear their friend Palmerston speak at public meetings nearby, and pronounced herself satisfied with his foreign policy. William Nightingale unsuccessfully tried to enter Parliament himself at the same time, now that reform had made politics compatible with his principles, and his failure was another disappointment to himself and to Florence.

The Palmerstons and the Nightingales often dined together informally. Florence shone in such company, where her erudition made her the conversational equal of the most distinguished men. The notoriously poor quality of the quadrilles that she rendered on the pianoforte may have increased the men's respect for her, as also the fact that she was graceful but fairly plain. In her twenties Florence formed another close friend in the world of politics. Sidney Herbert, the second son of the Earl of Pembroke, was ten years her senior. As a political contact Herbert complemented Lord Palmerston to perfection because the two belonged to different parties and one or the other of them was a Cabinet Minister almost continuously from

1830 to 1865. Each of them, at the time Florence first met them, was widely believed to be a future Prime Minister, although Sidney Herbert did not live long enough to achieve it. He and his wife Elizabeth, known as Liz, were a golden couple – he was tall and slim with delicate features, wavy hair and a sincere manner; she was one of the great beauties of the era. They adored each other; they were very wealthy and, like Florence, were interested in providing hospitals for the poor. Florence met them in Rome through mutual friends in 1847, and on her return to England she went with Mrs Herbert to visit a hospital that she and her husband had set up. Sidney and Liz Herbert were eventually to be responsible for overcoming the resistance of Florence's family to her leaving home to take up hospital work.

Florence Nightingale had heard God call her to his service in 1837, when she was 17. In a different society she would no doubt have entered a convent. Seven years later she discovered that God wanted her to work in hospitals; again, in France or Germany it would have been quite normal for her to become a Sister of Mercy in a religious order dedicated to such work. But in England women were not encouraged to find such outlets for their humanitarian and managerial urges, and Nightingale spent most of her youth dreaming up imaginary scenarios under which she could achieve her goal. Her private writings indicate that daydreaming occupied so much of her time that she fought against it as a dreadful affliction. In these reveries she escaped from the stifling trivialities of the drawing-room to perform heroic humanitarian feats in hospital under the gaze of a beloved leader. The daydreaming was her secret and loathsome vice, and she carefully noted her success or failure in trying to suppress it. It is likely that the affliction was common throughout Victorian England.

By the time she reached the age of thirty she was desperate at not having any outlet for her ambitions. In a letter to her parents she claimed that women were driven to madness by the type of imprisonment that she had to suffer: 'I see the numbers of my kind who have gone mad for want of something to do'. The only time she felt satisfied was when she visited the sick poor and taught their children in the humble village schools near the family home in Derbyshire. 'Oh happy, happy six weeks at Lea Hurst', she wrote, 'where I had found my business in this world. My heart was filled. My soul was at home. I wanted no other heaven. May God be thanked as He never yet has been thanked for that glimpse of what it is to *live*.' The attempts of her class to combine social activity with good works repelled her. 'In London there have been the usual amount of Charity Balls, Charity Concerts, Charity Bazaars, whereby people bamboozle their consciences and shut their eyes . . . England is surely the country where luxury has reached its height and poverty its depth.'[2]

She longed to work in a hospital but whenever the word was even mentioned her mother and sister fainted and had to be revived with smelling-salts. She tried to convert to Catholicism but the Catholic Church refused her because Cardinal Manning believed with some reason that she only wanted the support and hospital training that it gave to its nuns, and not its beliefs. She had been prepared to set up a Catholic religious order dedicated to training nurses.[3] Unlike the Church of Rome, the Church of England had no provision for training women in good works as it did men. There was actually no provision in England for training women to do anything at all. Her Unitarian tradition would have made it quite easy for her to convert opportunistically to Catholicism: during the Middle Ages some Unitarians even converted to Judaism to avoid persecution by other Christians.

She railed against the poor quality of a woman's life as compared to a man's in an autobiographical tract called *Cassandra* in which she described the middle class unmarried woman as being a slave to her relatives. A woman was always expected to be available to entertain parents or their guests, and could not even retire to her room for study as a man had the right to do. 'Passion, intellect, moral activity,' she wrote, 'these three have never been satisfied in woman. In this cold and oppressive conventional atmosphere, they cannot be satisfied. To say more on this subject would be to enter into the whole history of society and of the present state of civilisation. Women long to enter into some man's profession where they would find direction, competition (or rather opportunity of measuring the intellect with others) and, above all, time.'[4] She resented having to accompany her father when he went to the spa town of Malvern for the fashionable water treatment. Cynically she defined the activity thus: 'The water-cure: a highly popular amusement during the last few years amongst athletic individuals who have suffered from the tedium of life, and from those indefinite diseases which a large income and unbounded leisure are so well calculated to produce'.

It began to dawn on her that the chains that bound her to such futile occupations were in her own mind. Why could she not just walk out? Her father was far from being an ogre; she must have known he would give her an allowance even if he could not, for fear of upsetting her other relatives, approve her departure. Why could she not, in short, simply become a man? Not *disguise* herself as a man as many women had done, but just refuse to acknowledge the supposed differences between men and women. 'Why cannot a woman follow abstractions like a man?' she asked her father. 'Has she less imagination, less intellect?' No, she answered, women had simply acquired the habit of thinking about nothing but their own experience. It may have occurred to her that in describing so minutely and egocentrically her pointless life in *Cassandra*, she had fallen into the trap of conforming to the female stereotype.

There were some bridges that she needed to burn if she was to really get out of the trap. One was her relationship with Richard Monckton Milnes, who had been trying to persuade her to marry him for nine years. The indecision was preventing Milnes from getting on with his life, and he finally demanded that she make up her mind. She refused him, and he immediately married someone else. 'I don't agree at all that a woman has no reason for not marrying a good man who asks her,' she wrote, 'and I don't think Providence does either. I think He has as clearly marked out some to be single women as He has others to be wives.' When she had made the break with Milnes she knew she had to find her direction: 'Today I am thirty – the age Christ began his Mission. Now no more childish things, no more vain things, no more love, no more marriage. Now, Lord, let me only think of Thy will.'

She realised that her disappointment lay in her failure to make her family understand her ambition to work in a hospital, and this disappointment was caused by her own misguided attempts to enlist their sympathy for her ambitions. 'I must expect no sympathy nor help from them. I have so long craved for their sympathy that I can hardly reconcile myself to this. I have so long *struggled* to make myself understood . . . I must not even try to be understood. It must be only for fun that I try to make them understand me – because I know that it is impossible'.[5]

The break finally came when she was thirty-two years old. Liz Herbert was on the committee of a charitable institution in Harley Street which looked after sick governesses, and she arranged for Nightingale to become the superintendent. Nightingale stayed twelve months at Harley Street, from August 1853 to October 1854. Her work consisted largely of organising supplies of goods and services after the recent move from other premises. For example, she terminated the arrangement under which the grocer's boy would call up to three times a day, and bought supplies in bulk on a monthly basis. She brought the dispensary in-house, and reduced the staffing costs. It was similar to the work she had done at Embley and Lea Hurst, but in a medical context. Surgeons performed a few operations on the premises, which she often attended, and the only one that she records ended in failure when the removal of a cataract led to inflammation and blindness. In describing this postoperative complication at the time Nightingale made no comment about its possible causes – an interesting omission in the light of her later concerns.

When she gave notice after twelve months it was on the grounds that the patients were not interesting enough. They were nearly all either hypochondriacs or incurable cancer sufferers.[6] Nightingale told the committee that she was looking for a position where the medical and surgical treatment offered was more appropriate for instruction of the students in a nursing school. After the first twelve months of her career, therefore, Nightingale had some practical experience of hospital nursing and administration. She was looking for a position where she could set up nursing school in a large London teaching hospital. She and Sidney Herbert (who was by now a Cabinet minister) had already conducted several surveys of hospitals, examining the defects in the pay, organisation, and accommodation of nurses. They believed that the obstacle to improving the opportunities for women in nursing was the perception that nurses in hospital were exposed to grave dangers of immorality (sexual harassment, we would call it) and drunkenness. It was these fears, more than the medical horrors, that had made Nightingale's mother oppose her daughter's initial attempts to work in a hospital. Overcoming them would enable other women with less powerful friends to escape from the trap that Nightingale had found herself in.

Her experience with supplies and her knowledge of best practice in managing female staff in hospital made Nightingale an obvious choice to lead a party of nurses to the Crimean War. So did her mental outlook. She had a sort of towering optimism and confidence, based not just on self-esteem but on a deep religious belief that the universe is fundamentally on the side of mankind. She was even able to look back on her long imprisonment in the family, immediately after she had made the break, and see that it had served its purpose. It had been a gestation period, while she learned how to create herself individually as mankind must create itself collectively. She wrote to her father on her thirty-second birthday, thanking him for his support in breaking free 'I am glad to think that my youth is past, and rejoice that it never, never can return – that time of follies and bondage, of unfulfilled hopes and disappointed inexperience, when a man possesses nothing, not even himself. When I speak of disappointed inexperience I accept it, not only as inevitable, but as the beautiful arrangement of Infinite Wisdom, which cannot create us gods, but which will not create us animals, and therefore wills mankind to create mankind by their own experience'.[7]

This philosophy of 'mankind creating mankind' was her father's.

At this time, she tried to explain this philosophy in a monograph addressed *To the Artizans of England*. She had entered into religious discussions with some of the working men in the villages surrounding Lea Hurst, and found that they had no respect for traditional religion, and she wrote this monograph hoping to convert them to a rational religious philosophy devised for the manufacturing age. The artisans of Derbyshire must have had a rather pessimistic view of human nature, because her 1852 tract is a justification of the belief that human nature is innately good, despite the historical evidence to the contrary. The history of human nature appears to be a history of evil, and Nightingale finds the solution to this problem in the explanation that our awareness that the past is evil is precisely what makes our nature good: we recognise improvement. To make the point that the disappointments of the past are necessary for the triumphs of the future, she used a metaphor that linked her age of industrialisation with ancient times: '"The vessels of Pompeii all speak one language – look out for steam!" The human mind, struggling for assistance in moving from one place to another, was unconsciously pursuing the course leading to the discovery of the use which might be made of steam for this purpose'.[8]

Her tract shows that in 1852 she had already studied the work of the Belgian statistician and social scientist Alphonse Quetelet, although she does not mention him by name. She says that the number of murders in a particular social group can now be foretold, and the variations between groups can be used to find out and alter the circumstances that cause a high murder rate. This was a reference to Quetelet's approach of using statistics to explore social trends. The comprehensive registration of births, marriages, and deaths which started in England in 1837 allowed socio-economic statistics to be collected for the first time. The proportion of people able to sign their name on a marriage certificate, for example, gave a crude index of the education level in a particular area, and it soon became apparent that crime was lower in counties with higher education, even when the level of income was the same.[9] Such evidence was eagerly seized upon by social improvers.

[15]

There is no evidence that Nightingale at that time considered statistics useful for day-to-day hospital management or for public health. Her 1852 tract also shows that her interest in disease was rather superficial. She writes in the *Artizans* that, contrary to popular belief encouraged by the clergy, cholera is not God's way of punishing sin, rather it is 'incident on certain states of body under certain circumstances.' By the time she went to the war two years later, she had begun to associate cholera with lack of cleanliness.

After her breakdown in 1857, Nightingale revised *To the Artizans of England* and incorporated it into a much longer book entitled *Suggestions for Thought*. We shall see in due course that a comparison of the two texts shows how the war and its aftermath changed her ideas. Meanwhile, it is remarkable that in 1852 Nightingale already counsels her artisans that, just as mankind must do badly in order to do better, so must individuals inevitably make serious mistakes. 'A healthy moral nature, having on an occasion erred', according to Nightingale, 'should regret the error, even though it was inevitable in God's scheme of things, but should not feel remorse'. Two years later, a few weeks before leading a party of nurses to the Crimean War, Nightingale commented in a letter to her sister on the unfortunate case of a Mother Superior who accidentally poisoned one of her nuns: 'your mistakes are a part of God's plan'.[10] It seems that she believed that God needed people with good intentions who were prepared to take risks. This may have been a more common belief in those days of personal philanthropy than it is today. It was to stand her in good stead. Indeed, it is as though the history and private thoughts of Florence Nightingale before the Crimean War, to paraphrase her own metaphor in a rather macabre way, seem 'to cry out with one voice: "Look out for Scutari!"'

In October 1854, one month after Nightingale gave her notice at Harley Street, a crisis erupted in the new general hospital that the British Army had established at a safe distance from the war zone in the Crimea. The first important battle was in early September, and when the wounded arrived at the hospital they found it bare of supplies. The male orderlies who were supposed to look after the patients had been badly recruited and proved incapable. It was inevitable that Sidney Herbert and his wife should conceive the idea of sending Florence Nightingale to the East.

At the time, Sidney Herbert was trying to find a way to use his position in the Cabinet to help his wife solve the problems of female nursing in English teaching hospitals and create career opportunities for people like her friend Florence Nightingale. Then the newspapers began to report the disastrous state of the British hospital at Scutari, and to praise the superior female nursing provided by the nuns in the French hospitals. 'Why have we no Sisters of Charity?' cried *The Times* plaintively. It seemed an ideal opportunity to try out the new kind of highly disciplined and organised nursing proposed by Liz and Florence. If it could be shown that a party of English nurses could survive contact with a horde of soldiers in the field, then the horrors of a London teaching hospital and its dissolute medical students would no longer prevent the introduction of intelligent women into an environment where they could be taught to be of real use. This desire to use the army for social experimentation was typical of the time, and we will see many instances of it in the Crimea.

Sidney Herbert's job in the Cabinet was a junior one. It created so much confusion in managing the war that it was abolished four months later when the Government was overthrown largely because of this confusion. His title was Secretary at War. The job was so unimportant that it had not always carried a seat in the Cabinet. A different Cabinet minister, the Duke of Newcastle, was responsible for operational conduct of the war. Sidney Herbert's job was to oversee only the finances of the army. He used his position to persuade the Duke of Newcastle that his friend Florence Nightingale was the only person who understood the real problem of introducing female nurses in a high-risk environment like a military hospital. The real problem, which had caused Nightingale's family to oppose her plans, was the fact that English female nurses could not defend themselves against the sexual advances of the medical staff and patients. Nightingale and Herbert believed that draconian disci-

pline could solve this problem and could also stop the nurses inca-
pacitating themselves with alcohol. The problems were less serious
with women who were members of a religious order, but there were
not many of those in England. Mixing a number of orders together
was certain to lead to sectarian strife.

Lord Newcastle therefore allowed Herbert to write inviting
Nightingale to lead a party of nurses to Scutari. The letter shows that
Herbert was most concerned about the problems of discipline, and
that Nightingale's advantages over rival candidates such as Lady
Maria Forrester lay in her ability to impose 'strict obedience to rule'.
He wrote: 'Nor would those Ladies probably ever understand the
necessity, especially in a Military Hospital, of strict obedience to rule
etc. Lady Maria Forrester is incapable of directing or ruling the
nurses. There is but one person in England that I know of who would
be capable of organising and superintending such a scheme, and I
have been several times on the point of asking you.' Sidney Herbert's
letter also reveals that he was sending Nightingale to the war to
promote the idea of female hospital nursing as well as to serve the
sick. 'If this succeeds, an enormous amount of good will be done,
now, and to persons deserving everything at our hands, and a prejudice will have been broken through, and precedent established,
which will multiply the good to all time.'

Nightingale's skill in managing the supply of goods and services,
developed in her father's large country houses and further refined at
Harley Street, would be an added advantage on her mission. *The Times*
was criticising the lack of supplies, even of bandages, at Scutari:
'When the wounded are placed in the spacious building where we
were led to believe that everything was ready which would ease their
pain or facilitate their recovery, it is found that the commonest appliances of a work-house sick ward are wanting.'[11]

The world's most powerful industrial nation was filling its steam-
ships with unheard-of quantities of supplies for despatch to the hospitals – bandages by the ton, and 15,000 pairs of sheets according to
Herbert's letter to Nightingale – but for some reason none of it was
arriving at the right place. It was ending up in Varna which the army

[18]

had left months previously, or supplies destined for Constantinople were going to the Crimea instead. Some supplies were even being brought back to England because nobody would take responsibility for them at the destination. The Government was prepared to give Nightingale unlimited authority to spend money on its behalf, and Herbert appeared to have solved the problems of Scutari at a stroke. And so on 21 October 1854, aged only thirty four and at the head of a little band of thirty eight nurses, Florence Nightingale set off for Constantinople on a P&O steamer under the admiring gaze of an anxious nation. It was as if one of the fantastic heroic daydreams of her youth had come true.

3

War

WHAT CAUSED the Crimean War? It is sometimes claimed that it resulted from the theft of a cross in a church in Bethlehem in 1847, aggravated by a chain of trivial incidents including a storm in Besika Bay in the Dardanelles in 1853. Looking for something more substantial, historians have invoked economic and demographic trends, commercial imperatives, and superpower relationships. But however many layers of analysis are added, the explanation is never satisfactory. According to Professor Asa Briggs, the Crimean war would probably never have happened if Palmerston had remained as Foreign Secretary. He had been dismissed from that post in 1851 at the request of Queen Victoria who was annoyed that he was bypassing her on matters of foreign policy. Without Palmerston, the country drifted into what has been called 'the most unnecessary war in modern Europe' under a vacillating coalition Government led by Lord Aberdeen as Prime Minister.[1]

The war began early in 1854 after the Russian navy destroyed the Turkish fleet at Sinope in the Black Sea, and Russia invaded some Turkish provinces in the Balkans. Britain, which had long feared Russian expansionism, suspected that the Russians planned to seize Constantinople. In alliance with the French, Britain landed an army in what is now Bulgaria and tried unsuccessfully to engage the

Russians there. Then Britain and France decided to attack and destroy the naval base at Sebastopol in the Crimea, home of the Russian fleet that had won the victory over the Turks at Sinope. A British army numbering 20,000 men was landed in the Crimea in September 1854, and with its French allies fought its way to Sebastopol. There, they settled down to a siege that was to last for twelve months.

The Crimea is a lozenge-shaped peninsula that hangs down from the top of the Black Sea. The entrance to the Black Sea is above Constantinople (now Istanbul) through the narrow strait of the Bosphorus about three hundred miles south of the Crimea. The Bosphorus is about twenty miles long, from one to three miles wide, and flows between wooded cliffs backed by distant mountains. This unusual geographic feature divides Europe from Asia, European Turkey from Anatolian Turkey, and the old part of Constantinople known as Stamboul from the elegant suburb of Uskudar on the Anatolian shore. The British name for Uskudar was Scutari. Constantinople lies about fifteen miles south of the point where the Bosphorus enters the Black Sea. Below Constantinople, the Bosphorus widens into the Sea of Marmara which then narrows again at its southern end before entering the Mediterranean. As the Bosphorus enters the Sea of Marmara at Constantinople, it is joined by a horn-shaped body of water, the Golden Horn, which bisects the European part of the city. Opposite the Golden Horn on the Anatolian shore, standing on a clifftop, is the vast Turkish barracks which the British in 1854 decided to borrow for use as a military hospital.

From the windows of the Scutari Barrack Hospital, the view down over the Bosphorus to the Golden Horn and the old city of Stamboul was superb. According to Florence Nightingale, who had travelled to some exotic spots in the Mediterranean, it was the best view in the world. She liked to watch the sun set directly behind the domes and minarets of that 'great market by the sea'. Scutari itself was a quiet backwater of rich merchants' houses whose vast square, formerly an assembly point for the caravans that set off on the pilgrimage to Mecca, had been deserted by the camels and not yet invaded by the motor-car.

The British occupied the Scutari barracks early in 1854, using it at first as a depot on the way to Bulgaria and only later as a hospital. It was only after the invasion of the Crimea, and the battle of the Alma in September, that large numbers of patients began to arrive there by ship from the Crimea. When Florence Nightingale arrived at the beginning of November 1854, Scutari was already full of patients, and more were arriving daily. A few days after she arrived, the battle of Inkerman took place and shiploads of casualties streamed in. Within three weeks there were 2,300 patients in the Barrack Hospital. The hospital supplies still had not materialised. Shiploads of chamber pots had disappeared into thin air; dysentery was rife among the prostrate casualties. There were no basins, no towels, and no soap. Only thirty patients a day could be cleaned in the few hip baths available. The officials in charge of the stores were hoarding the supplies they had, and the medical officers were so frightened of making trouble that they refused to write requisitions and claimed that they had everything they needed. Nightingale and a Mr MacDonald from *The Times* scoured the bazaars of Constantinople for basic necessities, often using money given by the readers of that newspaper instead of Government funds.

Ten days after Nightingale arrived in Constantinople, there was a terrible hurricane in the Black Sea. Dozens of British supply ships sank including a modern steamship that contained most of the army's winter clothing and tons of supplies for Scutari that had not been unloaded when the ship called there because they lay underneath the ammunition destined for the Crimea further on. The army camped outside Sebastopol crouched helpless as the wind tore away the tents from around them in the night. When dawn broke the men found themselves marooned on a bleak plateau six miles from the only harbour through which supplies could be landed. The Russians had captured the road from the harbour to the camp during the battle of Balaclava in October, and the only way to bring in supplies was now over a muddy track up the mountainside. It seemed as if even

Brunel's marvellous modern steamship the *Great Britain,* one of the wonders of the world, could not help the British army now. The world's most advanced industrial state could not protect its troops from the onslaught of winter. A fortune in supplies piled up in the tiny port of Balaclava. An opposition MP pointed out in the House that the Minister of War had transported a full complement of supplies a distance of three thousand miles, but unfortunately the distance to the camp was three thousand and six.

There were no more battles until the spring, but the men kept coming into Nightingale's hospital because the British army in the Crimea had begun to die. Scurvy, dysentery, frostbite, and starvation was spreading through the camp on the plateau above Sebastopol. Throughout the winter a steady stream of sick men trickled down the hillside to Balaclava harbour, mostly on mules provided and driven by the efficient French ambulance corps, in a contrivance called a *cacolet* – a pair of chairs slung on either side of the mule's back. In the harbour they were loaded slowly onto ships for a voyage of several days across the Black Sea to Scutari. Many died on the track, in the harbour, or on the transports, and others died while waiting to be brought ashore in small boats at Scutari, where the ruined landing pier was unusable. The survivors staggered or were carried up to Florence Nightingale's Barrack Hospital.

The hospital was an enormous rectangular building of three floors with a tower at each corner, built around an enclosed quadrangle or parade ground. On each floor, a single corridor ran around all four sides of the building. The corridor was on the inside, next to the enclosed quadrangle, between four and five metres wide and high-ceilinged. Leading off the corridor on the outside of the building were barrack rooms used as wards, more than a hundred of them on each floor and each about seven metres square. In these wards a low wooden bench barely ankle-high ran around the room, upholstered and stuffed with uncomfortably hard material. On the side of the room next to the corridor, there was a wooden gallery below the ceiling. The floors of the rooms were of wood, often rotten; the corridors were paved with broken unglazed tiles.

[23]

At first, Nightingale was the only nurse allowed inside the hospital at night. She used to walk the length of the corridors before going to bed, a distance of more than 800 yards around the four sides of the rectangular building. Then she would go to the other floors and walk a similar distance again, in the dim half light of crude oil-dip lamps. The corridor was lined with beds – most of them simple straw-filled mattresses on the tile floor. The men lay with their heads towards the wall, with only a metre or so separating their feet from the opposite mattress and barely half that separating each mattress from the one next to it. In the barrack rooms the separation was similar, and if every available space was taken the whole building could theoretically have held around 3,000 patients. At its peak there was a patient population of 2,500. The death rate was then at its peak, too – up to seventy in a single day.[2] Few soldiers could be found strong enough to carry a load, and Turkish labourers carried away the corpses as well as bringing the new arrivals up from the landing pier. At night the patients hardly ever spoke, and lay in deathlike silence as Nightingale passed alone between the endless lines of beds in the corridor. Most of them had been admitted suffering from sickness, starvation, or frostbite; those wounded in battle were more often sent to another hospital nearby.

During the first four months after Nightingale arrived, there was hardly any ventilation in the hospital. The windows were small and low down so that a stifling volume of foul air would have remained trapped above them even if they had been open. But they were shut tight against the cold, with broken panes stuffed with rags. Heating was by iron stoves whose chimneys led out through holes in the windows. The wall separating the corridor from the rooms prevented any possibility of a through draught. The filth and infestation in the wards and corridors cannot be adequately described.

Either the medical staff or Nightingale herself initially barred nurses from the hospital at night. Some doctors refused to have nurses on their corridors or rooms even during the day, but after a while, some of the medical officers wanted nurses to help them visit patients during the night and the prohibition was relaxed. Those medical officers who preferred a callous approach had ways to justify it. One was the fact that the soldiers were there by individual choice. Unlike those of Continental Europe where conscription was almost universal, this army was a volunteer one. The soldiers could have investigated the terms of service before they chose to enlist; for example, they could have found out that it would be their own responsibility to obtain fuel even where there was none available except for a dwindling supply of roots clawed out of the frozen ground. When the Commander-in-Chief Lord Raglan belatedly ordered Commissary-General Filder to issue fuel, the troops continued without it during the Crimean midwinter while Filder raised objections to Raglan's order on the grounds that no fuel had been issued during the Peninsular War. Filder's use of precedent seems to indicate that there were no written regulations and he presumably expected volunteers to have looked into this before enlisting. It was not surprising that they had not had this foresight – it only proved how unsuitable they would have been for any other occupation.

A litany of the horrors of Scutari quickly becomes tedious. Descriptions of the reactions of nurses, doctors and patients to these conditions are more interesting. It is dangerous to rely on some independent contemporary accounts by visitors to Scutari because of the humanitarian propaganda, the frenzied sentimentality, and the self-censorship of those who faced social death if they failed to grovel before the nation's heroine. Nightingale herself, being immune to some of these influences, is a useful informant. Her letters home show that she believed that the common soldier was being deprived of the basic necessities of life, even in hospital, by lazy or incompetent officials. According to her, artificial shortages went unreported by frightened medical officers whose career could be ruined by writing requisitions that they knew would not be filled.[3] Patients were left in the care of drunken orderlies who were often malingering soldiers, thieves avid for the savings of the dying, or pensioners who had foolishly volunteered to come out of retirement to accompany the army and who were rapidly succumbing to disease and delirium tremens.

Some of the accounts written by the nurses who worked for Nightingale also seem reliable, especially those that were not written for publication. These accounts show that the nurses quickly identified the doctors who were susceptible to moral pressure, and enrolled them in a conspiracy to cheat the lazy officials and get more food for their patients. Nightingale did the same thing on a broader and more organised scale. She too was impressed by the meekness and simplicity of the common soldier in the hour of his trial. 'I have never been able to join in the popular cry about the recklessness, sensuality, and helplessness of the soldiers. Give them suffering and they will bear it . . . Give them work and they will do it. I would rather have to do with the army than with any other class I have ever attempted to serve.'[4]

Her innovations were at first of a very basic nature. Ten days after arriving, she wrote to a surgeon she admired in England telling him: 'I am getting a screen now for the amputations, for when one poor fellow, who is to be amputated tomorrow, sees his comrade today die under the knife it makes an impression – and diminishes his chance.'[5] Before that, the surgeons operated in full view of the other patients in the ward, because there was no operating room. Nightingale's screen, despite her optimism, made no difference to the mortality from amputations which she later estimated at 82 per cent. But it may have done something for human dignity.

The army doctors, most of them young and very inexperienced, reacted to the horrors that surrounded them in different ways. The nurses found that even the kindly doctors became exasperated and unreasonable when the newly-arrived patients proved to be too far gone to recover. A nurse reported that one of the doctors seldom appeared in the wards at all but remained in his own quarters, smoking. Another junior surgeon wrote furious letters home criticising the nurses, including Nightingale. He claimed that she had made a patient wait for fifteen minutes because she insisted on being present at all operations. Worse, he claimed that Nightingale dressed the wounds of a soldier while his genitals were exposed in a way that 'must have been hurtful to his feelings'. This young surgeon wrote of

Nightingale: 'She may be a lady, but I don't think she has the modesty of anyone deserving to be a woman'.[6]

Body lice swarmed on the emaciated patients, 'as thick as the letters on a page of print', and the genitals of a wounded soldier who had been months in the trenches without washing would not have been a pretty sight. Nor would the wounds themselves, but Nightingale sometimes described them with something like admiration in her letters home: 'The Surgeons pass on to the next, an excision of the shoulder-joint – beautifully performed and going on well – bullet lodged just in the head of the joint, and fracture starred all round'.[7]

Her sister Parthenope became Florence's enthusiastic public relations officer in England during the war. She lobbied home officials on Florence's side in her disputes with other officials in the East. She also copied out Florence's letters home for wide circulation, but she was careful to suppress the descriptions of wounds and other aspects of Florence's perverse habit of dwelling on things that ordinary people did not find interesting. A senior army officer who visited Scutari was appalled that Nightingale 'seems to delight in witnessing surgical operations, with arms folded.'[8]

Some nurses who had thought that they would contribute to the men's recovery wanted to go home when they found it was not to be. Most of them, though, were satisfied to make the men's last hours more pleasant, to give them a little dream of home before the end. They schemed to extract more food from the officials, convinced that at least this prolonged life. When these schemes failed, the nurses were sometimes so distressed that the dying patients had to comfort them.[9] The nurses scared the visiting wife of the British Ambassador by telling her that the doctors were deliberately starving the patients and the gullible Lady Stratford began to send up delicacies. One nurse was carrying Lady Stratford's latest delivery when a callous doctor asked her contemptuously: 'Are you giving calves' foot jelly to *soldiers*?' The nurse defiantly replied: 'To dying men.' A nurse wrote after the wounded came in from the battle of Inkerman:

One night as Sister Elizabeth and I were returning through a long dark corridor, we met a tall soldier staggering along as if unable to walk, bent down and actually crying like a child. We spoke to him, and found that he had landed that night with a number of sick, but not being able to keep up with the others had fallen behind, had lost his way, and now knew not where to lay his aching limbs. We took him from ward to ward until we found him an empty bed. On returning to our quarters, we found ourselves shut out, as the nurses had retired to rest. However, on our ringing, Miss Nightingale herself opened the door, and on hearing our story she searched out some provisions and sent us back with them to our poor exhausted friend, and waited up to let us in on our return. She looked, I thought, very sweet and kind, though delicate and worn out.

Both nurses and patients remained passive as the death toll mounted. 'It seems strange that we could witness such scenes and sufferings calmly' wrote a nurse 'but to us and to the poor sufferers there seemed granted a calm and quiet temper and a sort of stunned feeling, because had we realised all their sad sufferings we could not have borne it. Daily we missed some pale face we had just learned to know and love, and who loved us, and daily we watched some solitary pilgrim pass peacefully through the dark waters of death. In the course of a few days all who had been entrusted to us had gone, and were succeeded by others who equally seemed doomed to die.'[10]

Nightingale wrote hundreds of letters to bereaved families: 'Dear Mrs. Hunt, I grieve to be obliged to inform you that your son died in this hospital on Sunday last. His complaint was chronic dysentery – he sank gradually from weakness, without much suffering. Everything was done that was possible to keep up his strength. He was fed every half hour with the most nourishing things he could take, and when there was anything he had a fancy for, it was taken to him immediately. He sometimes asked for oranges and grapes, which quenched his thirst, and which he had, whenever he wished for them. He was very grateful for whatever was done for him, and very patient.' In Florence Nightingale's room at her sister's house, amid the relics that have accumulated there from the descendants of that vanished army, there is one pathetic orange, shrivelled to the size of a walnut, which the recipient would not eat because Miss Nightingale had given it to him.

The nurses had no understanding of *why* the man were dying, even though they suspected that the death rate at Scutari was worse than elsewhere. A nurse wrote: 'The amputations which took place in the hospital were, as far as I knew, mostly unsuccessful. The patient sunk and died under the operation, or soon after it, while those amputated on the field mostly recovered. The reason of this was, I think, that on the field the men were in the full vigour of life, and able to bear the pain and exhaustion, while those operated on in the hospital were worn out by suffering.'[11] Several healthy discharged soldiers, on their way back to England made the mistake of lodging in the wards of the Scutari hospital while they waited for their ships home. Also a perfectly clean English railway workman, in a Sunday-best top hat, came in feeling a little unwell. He had come out to the East on a contract for the army, to make a little money, because his savings bank had gone bankrupt and he had orphaned grandchildren to support. He thought that if he earned a little money from the army he would not have to worry that his wife and companion of forty years might end up in the workhouse. But discharged soldiers and elderly workman alike were tumbled in to a common grave with the human wrecks from the trenches, and at home the workhouse opened its cheerless arms to their loved ones.[12]

In Scutari, the Angel of Death was always efficient. One night two nurses were told to stay up to look after eight patients whose lives were in danger, with instructions to call two more nurses to replace them at midnight. But the second shift was never needed; all eight patients died well ahead of schedule, 'and when all were at rest we returned to our quarters and went to bed'.[13] Those simple nurses were haunted by the experience for the rest of their lives. 'One lad asked me for a drink, and then to read to him,' remembered one of them, 'and then at his request I wrote for him to his friends in

Oxford. He said 'It has pleased the Lord to take my comrade in the night, but I am spared a little longer,' but in passing in the evening I spoke to him and, getting no answer, I found he was gone. He asked me to kiss him before he died, and I am sorry I did not.' These must have been very difficult words for this woman to write so many years later.

One night the same young nurse followed Nightingale to the dead-house, where the day's corpses from her hospital lay. 'It was an awful place to visit at any time, and as I waited at the door and saw Miss Nightingale calmly uncover the faces of the dead, and look on them as they lay far from wife or mother in that dreary place, it seemed strange to see one so frail, graceful, and refined standing at the dead of night alone amid such sad scenes of mortality.' Nightingale was going to have reason to remember those faces of the dead.

Six weeks after her arrival at Scutari at the head of her party of thirty-eight nurses, another party arrived containing 'ladies' as well as working-class nurses whom Nightingale had not agreed to receive. She was furious with Sidney Herbert for sending them and threatened to resign. She did not think she could impose discipline by herself on such a large number of women, especially because there was not enough room in the hospital to lodge them all. Putting women in lodgings outside the hospital would make it even more difficult to stop them fraternising with the soldiers or getting intoxicated. 'The ladies come out to get married, and the nurses come out to get drunk' she wrote.[14] She slept with the key to the nurses' quarters under her pillow.

Lord Raglan wanted to bring the extra nurses to the Crimea to staff new hospitals closer to the front. The risk that the Russians would overrun the port at Balaclava now seemed more remote, and it would therefore be safe to open hospitals there. But Nightingale opposed Raglan's wishes. One of the newly arrived nurses, Elizabeth Davis, went to see Nightingale and told her she wanted to go to the Crimea because she would be more useful there. Her description of

Nightingale's hostile response is remarkably vivid: ' "Before I go any further" said Miss Nightingale "I want to impress one thing particularly on your mind. If you do go to the Crimea, you go against my will". This she repeated over and over again. I persevered in my intention of going to Balaclava, and she observed, "Well, Mrs Davis, I can't let you go without someone to over-look you. If you do go" she added, joining her open hands sideways together, and then forcibly dividing them and spreading out her arms by her sides, "I have done with you and your new superintendent *entirely*." '[15]

This shows that it was not for lack of a superintendent that Nightingale did not want the nurses to go to the Crimea. She obviously did not want to delegate that role for one reason or another. Even her supporters said that she found it difficult to delegate responsibility during the early months of the war. There was also the fact that her authority in the hospitals in the Crimea was not clearly defined. Her original letter of instructions said that she was in charge of nursing at hospitals in Turkey – and at that time there were no others. Eventually the War Office sent an order clarifying her status as General Superintendent of the hospitals outside Turkey as well, but before then she was naturally concerned that trying to supervise nurses in the Crimea would lead to arguments with the medical authorities there.

The only way Nightingale could see of controlling nurses at this time was by centralising both nurses and patients physically under her gaze. Lord Panmure, the new Minister of War, was in favour of centralising control and thought that Nightingale was the appropriate leader, but he eventually had to instruct her how to exercise this control in a distributed fashion by appointing nursing superintendents in the other hospitals, reporting to her. This helped eliminate unnecessary movement of patients and reduced the death rate. But before this many of the nurses who did 'desert to the front' unsupervised and disowned by Nightingale, showed extraordinary heroism and devotion. It is surprising that the Dictionary of National Biography contains no entry for Jane Shaw Stewart, for Mary Seacole, or for the unruly Martha Clough who disobeyed all the Nightingale rules and installed herself in a primitive regimental field hospital where she could indulge her weakness for claret to the full.

In later life Nightingale was ashamed of having received the credit that was due to these nurses. 'I often think, or rather do not like to think' she wrote in 1888 'how all the people who were with me in the Crimea must feel how unjust it is that all the "Testimonial" went to me. I don't think Sister Bertha is without this feeling – how could she be? – though she never expresses it'.[16] Sister Bertha Turnbull, one of the first nurses to rebel against Nightingale's iron rule at Scutari and go up to the front, had turned up unexpectedly on the sixty-eight-year-old Nightingale's doorstep after a lifetime of good works as far afield as Honolulu.

Nightingale never even tried to establish control over the hospitals that existed at Koulali five miles north of Scutari, between January and October 1855; eventually she officially resigned from them to avoid disputes with her rivals Miss Stanley and Mother Bridgeman who had taken up residence there after they had brought out the second party of nurses. Rather than encourage new hospitals nearer the front Nightingale acted to increase the size of her own hospital. She persuaded some of the medical officers to join her in a plan to renovate some disused parts of the building, and when the construction ran into funding difficulties she paid for it herself. This increased the approved capacity from 1,220 to 1,600 beds, but the actual number of patients was higher; the hospital was permanently overcrowded.

Nightingale knew that she could safely act on her own initiative because of the trust the Government placed in her. But in late January of 1855, when she had been in the East for nearly three months, the Government in which her old friend Sidney Herbert was a Cabinet Minister fell from power when the House of Commons voted to conduct an enquiry into its mismanagement of the war. Lord Palmerston, who had been Home Secretary in the disgraced Government, formed a new Government with himself as Prime

Minister and at first kept Herbert in the Cabinet. But when Palmerston failed to make the House of Commons desist from its plan to conduct an enquiry, Sidney Herbert resigned because of his previous involvement as Secretary at War. Florence Nightingale had lost her most important supporter in the previous Government, but she had gained Lord Palmerston who was perhaps even more supportive in his unobtrusive way.

The House of Commons Committee began to listen to evidence on 5 March, and their report, known as the Sebastopol Report, shows that the confusion in the supply arrangements for the army was their most important preoccupation. Britain's unique industrial strength seemed to count against her in the struggle because everything the army did now required stores of complex manufactured items to be in the right place at the right time. The Duke of Wellington would never have allowed this dependency – he had opposed the introduction of percussion rifles to replace the old flintlock system for which the igniting device was a piece of stone that could be found on the ground. The manufactured percussion caps were technically superior but the Duke reasoned that they would be one more thing that could go missing, leaving the soldier helpless. The deceased Duke's worst fears were proved right in the Crimea. Vast quantities of prefabricated huts were sent out for the winter, but all the nails to put them together went missing. The sick could not be moved without Messrs Smith and Clarke's patent folding stretcher, but the legs and the transverse bars which kept them stretched were put on a different ship and the rest of the gadget was useless without them.

Florence Nightingale's hospital at Scutari came in for a good deal of criticism in the Sebastopol Report, again because of the chaotic supply arrangements there. Bandages, brushes and mops, kitchen utensils, beds and clothing all seemed to be in short supply despite the millions of pounds' worth of goods sent out from England. But she was also extensively praised for rectifying the shortages using the funds at her disposal. On the day that the Sebastopol Committee first heard evidence in London, Nightingale was visited at Scutari by the ghost of a dead owl that she had once kept as a pet. She wrote to her family the next day, describing the apparition:

> Dearest people,
> I saw Athena last night. She came to see me. I was walking home late from the General Hospital round the cliff, my favorite way, and looking, I really believe for the first time, at the view – the sea glassy calm and of the purest sapphire blue, one solitary bright star rising above Constantinople, our whole fleet standing with sails idly spread to catch the breeze which was none, the domes and minarets of Constantinople sharply standing out against the bright gold of the sunset, the transparent opal of the distant hills (a colour one never sees but in the East) which stretch below Olympus always snowy and on the other side the Sea of Marmara, when Athena came along the cliff quite to my feet, rose upon her tiptoes, bowed several times, made her long melancholy cry, and fled away . . .[17]

It was an exhilarating view and Nightingale loved to walk along the cliffs at sunset. But what message was the ghostly owl bringing her that evening, and from whom? Was it a message from the Crimea, or from London? In the Crimea, 300 miles away across the Black Sea, the authorities had begun to wonder why the sick soldiers sent into Nightingale's hospital were not coming back. At about this time the correspondent of *The Times* was writing from the front: 'It is strange we have got up so few convalescents from Scutari. The hospitals there seem to swallow up the sick forever'.

In London, the new Government did not believe that a committee sitting in the House of Commons could solve problems 3,000 miles away on the Black Sea. Palmerston had his own ideas about what was wrong and immediately on becoming Prime Minister despatched men to investigate and take action on the spot, technically qualified civilians whom he could trust. The splendid British fleet becalmed in front of the Golden Horn that evening, on which Nightingale stood gazing down while she listened to a ghostly owl at her feet, included a vessel containing Palmerston's five trusted commissioners. They disembarked the next day at Scutari. They were men of unrivalled experience in their fields, examples of the best that Britain produced in that era of remarkable achievement. The youngest one of them, and possibly the most talented, would be dead within six weeks. The four survivors would all become lifelong friends of Florence Nightingale. Their mission in the East was to save the British army – the second British army to be sent there. The first army had already been lost.

Palmerston's decision to send civilian commissioners to intervene in army matters was to bring him into conflict with Queen Victoria, not for the first time in his long career. Eventually Florence Nightingale was to become a pawn in this conflict, as Palmerston used her to thwart the Queen's attempts to exert royal control over the army.

The control of England's army had been a bone of contention since the time of Charles I. The Revolution Settlement of 1688 had not clearly defined the military roles of Parliament and Ministers. In the time of the Crimean War disputes were common over whether the Commander-in-Chief in London's Horse Guards took orders from the Queen herself or from her Ministers. In the Duke of Wellington's time the question never really arose. Because of the enormous prestige he carried as the victor of Waterloo, as Commander-in-Chief he had almost absolute power over the army. But when Wellington died in 1852, it appears that the old problems came to the surface. Recent historical studies at the Royal Military Academy at Sandhurst have revealed a hitherto unsuspected conflict as Queen Victoria and her husband Prince Albert tried to turn back the constitutional clock and re-establish special royal control over the army.[18]

At the beginning of the war, Victoria had been on the throne for seventeen years but was still only 35 years old – one year older than Florence Nightingale. In her youth Victoria was a very unpopular monarch, due to her continental ancestry, her choice of a foreign husband, and the widely-reported unfair treatment of one of her

[35]

ladies-in-waiting who died after Victoria and her doctors diagnosed
a tumour as an illicit pregnancy. After he became Prime Minister in
1855, Palmerston handled Victoria with respect, trying not to repeat
the error that had led her to insist on his dismissal as Foreign
Secretary in 1851. He sometimes encouraged her interest in military
affairs. For example, he allowed her to change the design of the
Victoria Cross. She threw out many cheap-looking and inferior
designs proposed by civil servants for this 'all ranks' bravery medal
and rejected their suggested motto *For the brave* because it implied
that anyone who didn't have it wasn't brave. That is why this most
coveted and rare decoration, of all times and all countries, bears
Victoria's own words: *For Valour*.

Both Queen Victoria and her husband were military enthusiasts
who followed army affairs closely and felt qualified to interfere. The
Army High Command, which had been severely criticised in
Parliament, had everything to gain by encouraging this interest and
persuading the Queen that ancient, unwritten, constitutional principles required her to exert her nominal authority as head of the army
more forcefully than Lord Palmerston would like. When Lord
Palmerston became Prime Minister early in 1855, after Nightingale
had been in the East for three months, the prestige of the Queen's
army had fallen to a low ebb. It would be hard to imagine anybody
less likely than Palmerston to be impressed by obsolete constitutional
arguments for allowing the sovereign to control the army. His first
government appointment had been as Secretary of State at War no
less than forty five years previously, and as long ago as 1812 he had
argued that ministers could issue orders to the army independent of
the Sovereign.

Palmerston's new Minister of War was Lord Panmure. Although
the army saw Panmure as a typical civilian meddler, he had some military experience: in his youth he had served as an army officer. His
army career had been the result of a row with his father, a man of
legendary brutishness who cut the young Panmure off with £100 a
year and an army commission. Panmure, who was heir to his father's
barony had also served as a junior minister at the War Office in a pre-

vious Government. Lord Panmure was a taciturn man, a somewhat overbearing Scotsman. He did not have the air of sincerity of Sidney Herbert, nor the disarming affability of Lord Palmerston. He was not a handsome man to look at: he was stocky, with an oversized head and clumsy appearance. He already had a reputation for independent action and he now had a very personal reason for wanting to impose his own authority on the army despite the claims of the High Command that they did not have to take orders from him.

When his famously eccentric and cruel father threw Panmure out of their home, Panmure and his two brothers had entered into a pact of loyalty to each other in defiance of their father's orders that the younger sons should never speak to the heir again. The second son joined the army, as second sons often did, and went away to the war. On its way to the Crimea, the army camped at Varna, in Bulgaria. It was through his brother's letters home from Bulgaria that Panmure first learned of the chaotic state of the army's supply arrangements.

At that time, as Nightingale's Royal Commission would later demonstrate, nobody in the army had the official responsibility for ensuring that the choice of campsite for the army was a healthy one. It was by now well known in civilian circles that cholera, a disease of which the cause had not yet been proved, tended to associate itself with particular locations, and soon this would be recognised to be a consequence of the drainage and water supply. The army had not learned this lesson and camped at a site that was already well known to the local population as prone to cholera. The disease broke out. Many hundreds of soldiers died, among them Panmure's loyal brother. Panmure had his body brought back for burial in Scotland.

Within days of taking office under Palmerston Panmure deeply offended the army High Command by writing a confidential letter ferociously rebuking the Commander-in-Chief in the Crimea for the filthy state of his camp and his failure to use his supplies to relieve the suffering of the troops. Shortly afterwards, Panmure and Palmerston dispatched their five commissioners to the Crimea to investigate and remedy these two matters. Panmure's instructions to the commissioners clearly extended into areas where the Army High

Command might dispute his authority, a fact that Panmure was obviously aware of because he kept part of their instructions secret from the army and from the Queen. Two of the commissioners (Sir John McNeill and Colonel Alexander Tulloch) were supplies experts sent to investigate why food and clothing were not being issued to the troops. The other three were Sanitary Commissioners, with instructions to clean up the camps and hospitals in the Crimea and Turkey. Florence Nightingale's biographers have frequently claimed that she encouraged the sending of this Sanitary Commission. This claim, which she herself repeatedly denied, has had the paradoxical effect of understating the political importance of the support that she later gave, because the Commission was in reality the dying gasp of one of the most important social movements of modern times. The true instigator of the Crimean Sanitary Commission was a figure who at that time was unpopular throughout England for his dictatorial approach to public health: the eclipsed would-be sanitary reformer Edwin Chadwick.

Chadwick's movement to clean up London and other cities in England, which had begun with the passing of the Public Health Act in 1848, had run out of steam in 1854 at about the same time that Nightingale went to the Crimea. That summer, after bitter arguments, Parliament abolished the first General Board of Health created by the Act of 1848. The Board of Health had been led by Chadwick, who was Secretary of the Poor Law Commission, and Lord Shaftesbury, President of the Health of Towns Association.[19]

Chadwick despised medical science. He believed that sanitary administration was a matter for engineers and lawyers. 'Sanitary science' according to Chadwick, was 'a subsidiary department of engineering, a science with which medical practitioners could have little or nothing to do.'[20] Not surprisingly, the medical profession joined with many other vested interests to oppose the spending of public money on Chadwick's expensive sewerage and water supply schemes. After Chadwick's Board of Health was abolished, mainstream medical professionals took charge of public health expenditure and ran it their way. Chadwick's proposal to recycle human excrement from the cities as fertiliser in suburban market-gardens may not have caught on, but most of his other controversial ideas have worked to perfection. At the time, though, his plan to force people to be clean by law was seen as both dictatorial and impractical. In 1852 Lord Derby as Prime Minister encapsulated the mood of the people when refusing to support legislation on burials and water supply: he stated that it would be impossible ever to enforce cleanliness by legislation.

Chadwick's strongest supporter in Parliament had been Lord Palmerston, who was Home Secretary in the Government which dismissed Chadwick and which in turn was dismissed because of its mismanagement of the war. In the crucial debate that led to Chadwick's dismissal, Palmerston had strongly defended him, arguing that the personal criticisms of Chadwick – that he was overbearing, dictatorial, and a centraliser – were unjustified. However, the Prime Minister's representative Lord John Russell, cast blame on Chadwick in his closing speech, saying that 'Many persons were financially interested that the plans of the General Board of Health should not be adopted, and it was very probable that Mr Chadwick has not observed towards these classes of persons the most conciliatory tone possible'.[21] The House voted Chadwick's board out of existence, and the long official involvement of Chadwick and Lord Shaftesbury in public health was ended.

Chadwick's downfall was greeted with general satisfaction throughout the country. *The Times* voiced the people's relief: 'Mr Chadwick has been deposed, and we prefer to take our chance of cholera and the rest, than to be bullied into health'. But when Palmerston became Prime Minister a few months afterwards Chadwick's influence made itself felt within a few days in Palmerston's scheme to send the Sanitary Commission to the East. Palmerston wrote to his War Minister instructing him to send Chadwick's most trusted experts to sort out the problems in Nightingale's hospital. His letter shows that Palmerston was extremely well-informed about a new kind of problem there, one that was to receive no mention at all in the House of Commons'

[39]

Sebastopol Report. Palmerston wrote to his Minister of War after Nightingale had been in the East for three months:

> It is clear that, quite independently of the medical treatment of the sick and wounded, there is an urgent necessity for improved sanitary arrangements in our hospitals at Constantinople, Scutari, and elsewhere. Proper ventilation has been neglected, and various other sanitary arrangements have been either not thought of, or not carried into effect.
>
> There are two very able and active men who have been connected with the Board of Health and whom I have much employed about sanitary matters – Dr Sutherland and Dr Grainger. I wish very much that you would send them out at once to Constantinople, and one afterwards to Scutari and Balaclava and the Camp, not to interfere at all with the medical treatment of the sick and wounded, but with full powers to carry into immediate effect such sanitary improvements and arrangements in regard to the hospital buildings and to the Camp as their experience may suggest. I am convinced that this will save a great many lives.[22]

This letter shows extraordinary prescience on Palmerston's part, even if he did not appear to know that Scutari was a suburb of Constantinople. Florence Nightingale never found out about this letter otherwise she would not have given so much credit to Lord Shaftesbury, the great Victorian philanthropist, for the Sanitary Commission. Shaftesbury, Lord Palmerston's son-in-law, did propose a Commission but not until three days after Palmerston sent the above instructions to Lord Panmure. Shaftesbury submitted to Palmerston a different proposed list of sanitary experts to form the Commission including John Simon, the anti-Chadwick Health Officer of the City of London. By the time the Commission was ready to sail, however, John Simon had been replaced by one of Chadwick's engineers.

It seems likely that Chadwick himself proposed the names of his commissioners to Lord Palmerston and persuaded the Prime

Minister to drop John Simon, but Chadwick could not stop his rival's rapid rise to power. John Simon was a well-connected surgeon and pathologist of conservative political views; by the end of the war he was the Medical Officer to the new Board of Health and soon became the country's virtual public health dictator. His high-tech medical and scientific theories of public health were in complete opposition to Chadwick's theory that sanitary science was 'a subsidiary department of engineering'.

The Sanitary Commission which arrived at Scutari on 6 March, 1855, four months after Nightingale herself had arrived there, was a Chadwick commission but without the leader whose name had become a political liability to any government. The members of the Commission, Robert Rawlinson, John Sutherland, and Hector Gavin, had all worked for Chadwick at the General Board of Health. Rawlinson was an engineer, Sutherland and Gavin were doctors who had converted to Chadwick's anti-medical approach. Chadwick proposed Sutherland for the 1855 medical officership of health that John Simon won. Hector Gavin had opposed Simon as a candidate for Medical Officer to the City of London Corporation in 1848, and had been torn to pieces by the selection committee in a public session when they found that he was an associate of Chadwick and had dared in the past to criticise the Corporation's sewers.

Hector Gavin had already written extensively on health matters and would certainly have become one of the great figures of Victorian sanitary reform. He was accidentally shot dead after only six weeks in the East, at the age of thirty-nine. It happened when he was handing a revolver to his brother William, a veterinary surgeon in the 17th Lancers. Witnesses denied having seen in whose hand the revolver discharged accidentally. Hector Gavin lingered for some hours after immediately pronouncing himself mortally wounded. His inconsolable brother William, according to their father's account, died in camp of cholera eighteen days later. The records indicate that there was no cholera in the camp at that time.

Robert Rawlinson, who was to become one of Britain's most eminent engineers, had to go home after he visited the front and was struck a glancing blow by one of the endless showers of Russian cannon balls that bounced through the British lines. This left Dr Sutherland, a rather colourless individual with a short attention span, to sort out the mess with the aid of a number of grandly-named Inspectors of Nuisances whom he had brought from Liverpool. They were exactly what was needed.

At home, Lord Panmure had been concerned about the sanitary state of Florence Nightingale's hospital even before he received Palmerston's letter instructing him to send out sanitary experts. The day before receiving that letter he had written to the officer commanding on the Bosphorus, Brigadier-General Lord William Paulet. It was a rebuke similar to the one that he sent to Lord Raglan, complaining about the filthy state of the Scutari buildings. Panmure followed this up, even before the Sanitary Commission arrived, with a further allegation that the hospital was overcrowded.[23]

When Dr Sutherland and his Inspectors of Nuisances arrived at Scutari, their inspections were soon gratified. They sent home to Lord Panmure a 'Report by Mr James Wilson, Inspector of Nuisances at Scutari Hospitals', which observed that 'The water-closet attached to Lord William Paulet's quarters being in an offensive state, I cleansed it myself, and applied peat charcoal.'[24] Paulet was replaced and sent to the front.

There is something peculiarly Victorian about a functionary with a grandiose title actually cleaning out a general's toilet with his own hands and proudly submitting a written report to the Cabinet describing the accomplishment. Sutherland and his colleagues buried the dead animals that littered the site, paved and drained the yard outside the buildings, cleaned out the aqueduct and built a system to flush water through the sewers that ran under the building. They painted the internal walls with disinfectant and made openings in the roof of the building at strategic places to ensure ventilation. They pestered a reluctant commandant until he ordered the medical staff to reduce the double line of beds in each corridor to one, and made the orderlies empty the rubbish bins and urine containers daily.

Nightingale immediately recognised that the Sanitary Commission was doing something useful instead of just writing reports as previous official visitors had done. Her own reforms had mainly been in disentangling hospital supplies from a mass of red tape. Her sanitary exertions had focused on the personal cleanliness of the patients; she had tried to wash and de-louse them and give them clean clothes. The nearest she got to environmental improvements had been an attempt to clean the floors. She had ordered quantities of mops, scrubbing brushes, and bottles of disinfectant. But the wooden floors of the wards were so rotten that they were hard to clean, and the broken and porous tiled floors in the corridors were hard to get at because of the densely-packed straw mattresses on which the soldiers lay. In any case, cleaning the floors had no impact on the gases that leaked through them from the blocked sewers in the foundations.

Having tidied up Scutari, the Sanitary Commission packed up and headed for the front, leaving someone behind to 'inspect nuisances'. (Older readers may remember with nostalgia the Victorian signs that used to adorn many a dim alley in London's back streets: *Any person committing a nuisance against this wall will be prosecuted.*) After the Sanitary Commissioners left, spring came to the Bosphorus. The nightingales sang in the old Turkish cemetery behind the hospital, and the Judas-trees put out their myriad pink flowers. The death rate in the hospitals seemed to abate and the number of sick sent down from the front declined as the Russian winter passed and the supplies to keep the soldiers healthy began to arrive in the camp. A steam tug appeared at Scutari from England, easing the task of getting sick soldiers ashore from the transports. The number of convalescent soldiers in Scutari began to increase, and Florence Nightingale began to interest herself in their welfare.

Her belief in the common soldier's innate perfectibility was an intellectual position developed during her education by her father. She wrote to the Dean of Hereford asking him to send out (and bill her father for) emphatically *not* bibles, but paper, pens, and ink, encyclopaedias, and diagrams of natural history and the stratification of the earth, for lectures. As for the officers, they should study trigonometry.[25] Like so many others at that time, she came to see the army as a proving ground for social theories, in her case theories about the perfectibility of mankind.

Lord William Paulet, the Officer Commanding at Scutari, accused Nightingale of 'spoiling those brutes' – pointing contemptuously to the soldiers who were carried back insensible from the Greek drinking dens and frequently died without regaining consciousness. Lord Panmure had requested Paulet to use his considerable powers to put a stop to such waste of life. Paulet limited himself to preventing the sale of spirits in the hospital itself.[26] Nightingale's plan was to give the soldiers some other way to spend their time and their pay. Taken in isolation her letters may give the impression that laundries, kitchens, money order offices, reading rooms, and lectures would never have appeared if she had not organised them. However, independent evidence that her role was very important comes from Lord Panmure's comments on her initiative to reduce drunkenness.

Nightingale wrote to Queen Victoria that drunkenness in the army would be reduced if it were made easier for soldiers to send home their pay. When her letter was read to Palmerston's Cabinet, all present complimented it except Panmure who said it showed that Nightingale 'knew nothing of the British soldier'. His comment leaked out of the Cabinet as he may have intended it to. Despite his apparent hostility to the idea Panmure ordered that post offices be set up to civilianise the remittance of pay by the soldiers and bypass the army's unreliable channels. This proved successful: the amount of money sent home exceeded all expectations. When the Commander-in-Chief in the Crimea complained about civilian interference, Panmure sympathised with him and blamed it all on agitation by Nightingale: 'The great cry now, and Miss Nightingale inflames it, is that the men have no means to remit their money home,' Panmure wrote to the Commander-in-Chief. 'This is not true. The soldier may remit his money through the Paymaster, with no trouble at all. We have now offered the Post Office to them, but I am sure it will do no good. The soldier is not a remitting animal.'

Panmure's last sentence has gone down in history as an example of reactionary prejudice, but it must be remembered that at this time he often pretended to share the prejudices of the generals. In every other instance Panmure showed his enduring belief that civilian institutions like the Post Office would always be more efficient and inspire more confidence than their military equivalents. A contemporary critic of Lord Panmure confirms this, claiming that 'civilianisation' was his only objective in army reform.[27] But whether he was sincere or just putting on a front, Panmure's comments show the effectiveness of Nightingale's high-level interference.

Nightingale was also impressed by the work of the second civilian-led commission that Panmure sent to Scutari and the Crimea at the same time as the Sanitary Commission. This was the McNeill-Tulloch Commission into the supply arrangements of the army, whose findings would later provoke a political crisis at home in which Florence Nightingale would become entangled. Sir John McNeill, the leader of the Supplies Commission was one of Palmerston's most trusted friends. He had helped Palmerston, while the latter was Home Secretary in the previous Government, to try prevent the war by convincing Russia that England would fight to stop further Russian expansion.

Sir John McNeill's work as minister plenipotentiary in the court of the Shah of Persia had made him an expert on Eastern politics and on Russian foreign policy. He was the author of a startlingly original anti-Russian publication which was first published anonymously in 1836 at Palmerston's instigation and was rushed out in several new editions in the months before the Crimean War broke out. The pamphlet's originality lay in its use of statistics to demonstrate Russia's insatiable appetite for world domination. It showed how, between 1689 and 1825, the Russian Empire's population had grown from fifteen million to fifty eight million as a result of conquest of territories previously belonging to Sweden, Turkey, Poland, Persia, and Tartary. The Russian frontier had advanced 700 miles towards Berlin, 500 towards Constantinople, 600 towards Stockholm, and 1000 towards Teheran, always by the same insidious creeping forward that Russia was now, in 1854, practising in the Black Sea region.

McNeill concluded the 1854 edition of his book with a plea for a full-scale invasion of Russia, endorsed by a supposed message from the recently-deceased Duke of Wellington: 'Let us hope that our tardiness to accept the combat is but an indication that we foresee its magnitude; and that the two great Western Powers warned as it were by a mighty voice from the tomb against a little war are prepared, if negotiation has failed, at once to put forth all their strength – to hit hard – and to strike home'. Lord Palmerston must have welcomed the inclusion of this noisy piece of sabre-rattling in McNeill's book because he believed that England's feeble reaction had encouraged previous Russian expansion. Kingsley Martin, in his analysis of the wild propaganda that circulated before the war broke out, does not mention McNeill's book and its call for the invasion of Russia. He does deal with the mad theories of McNeill's former colleague David Urquhart, a fanatic whose anti-Russian rantings (published with strangely similar titles to McNeill's book) made McNeill's analysis look moderate and scholarly by comparison. McNeill and Palmerston must have hoped that McNeill's book would help prevent a war. It counterbalanced Urquhart's fanaticism, showing the Russians that England had a genuine grievance and that a negotiated solution was possible. Barred from his natural role of Foreign Secretary by order of Queen Victoria, Palmerston may have been using more covert methods to try to influence foreign policy.

In addition to his literary and diplomatic talents McNeill was qualified as a doctor of medicine. He was also unusually well suited for the job of reporting on the supply arrangements of an army besieging Sebastopol, because he was probably one of the very few men available who had previous experience of a siege. In 1838, he had accompanied the Persian army and its Russian advisers to observe their attack on Herat in Afghanistan. He had reported on the inadequacy of the supply arrangements of the besiegers, and his prediction that the siege of Herat would fail was proved right.[28] McNeill's final qualification was that he was a Poor Law Commissioner in his native Scotland, where he was credited with averting a famine when the potato crop failed – although the number of people affected in Scotland was much smaller than in Ireland.

[46]

McNeill's fellow-Commissioner, Colonel Alexander Tulloch, was a desk colonel who had made a name for himself in India through his hobby of compiling statistics and extracting useful information from them. He showed great ingenuity in collecting sickness and mortality data for the troops on foreign stations. He was probably doing this in order to prove some dietary theories of his own, but he noticed from his statistics that there was a remarkable tendency for military pensioners to live to extreme old age. On investigation he was able to show that relatives of deceased soldiers were concealing their deaths so as to continue to draw the pension. Not content with helping to save the Government money by exposing this trick Tulloch also exposed a number of frauds that the East India Company were practising on the common soldiers by depriving them of their pay and forcing them to buy goods at extortionate prices. His other hobby besides statistics seems to have been baking; he was a believer in the healthy properties of good fresh bread and had set up his own ovens for the troops in Burma.

Tulloch was younger than McNeill and probably more eager to prove himself when they went on their mission to investigate supply difficulties in the Crimea. He was more in favour of exposing incompetence than McNeill, who preferred a less confrontational policy. This caused some friction between the two of them and Nightingale felt obliged to take sides, preferring McNeill. She agreed with McNeill that Tulloch was too intolerant of other peoples' ideas. Nevertheless, she recognised and admired Tulloch's genuine interest in the troops' welfare – no sooner had he arrived in the Crimea than he was up to his elbows in flour, baking bread for the soldiers who had been living up to then on salt meat and hard biscuit. She described him with a word that was probably one of the highest compliments in her vocabulary: 'Tulloch was, in one sense, a kind of Deliverer, and McNeill is a far better man.'[29] It was a common literary device of Nightingale's to describe someone using both an extravagant compliment and a slight put-down incongruously in the same sentence, to catch the readers attention and demonstrate her even-handedness and independence.

[47]

It is easy to see why McNeill fascinated Nightingale, so much so that she rated him even higher than a 'Deliverer'. He was the same age as her father, but while William Nightingale had spent his life in the library John McNeill had been a doctor, spy, diplomat, Persian scholar, author, and saviour of the Scottish crofters. In Persia, as political agent, he had been a leading player in the 'Great Game' that pitted Britain against Russia in a struggle for influence over the states that controlled the overland routes to India. He knew the inside story of many of his friend Palmerston's controversial manoeuvres and he must have held Florence spellbound with his tales.

Shortly after McNeill and the other Commissioners left Scutari for the Crimean front, the Commander-in-Chief Lord Raglan announced his intention of keeping the sick and wounded in the Crimea as much as possible. This reduced the workload at Scutari. Beds and other basic necessities had by now arrived and Nightingale's administrative duties there became more manageable. Nightingale then decided to go to the Crimea for the first time and assess the situation in the hospitals close to the front. For the remaining twelve months of the war the extent of her authority in the Crimea was to remain a source of contention and much of her energy was devoted to defending it against opposition from rebellious nurses and jealous doctors. It would not be until the closing days of the war that the Government would issue a General Order confirming that she was in charge of the nurses in the Crimea and rebuking those who had questioned her authority. Meanwhile, the question grew in importance as fewer patients came to the Bosphorus and more were hospitalised in the Crimea, and Nightingale made several trips from Scutari to the front to try to establish her authority.

When she went to the Crimea for the first time in May 1855, there were eight female nursing staff already there in the party that had left with Mrs Davis as described earlier. In April, the War Office had appointed Nightingale 'Almoner of the free gifts in all the British hospitals in the Crimea war zone'[30] and this gave her an official capacity in which to visit the hospitals there even if her authority as

Superintendent of Nurses was still disputed. She set sail for Balaclava in the Crimea on 5 May, 'having been at Scutari this day six months and, in sympathy with God, fulfilling the purpose I came into this world for'.[31]

According to the rebellious Mrs Davis, during this visit to Balaclava Nightingale arranged a meeting with Dr John Hall, Principal Medical Officer in the Crimea. Hall, who was already notorious for instructing surgeons not to use anaesthetics during amputations, was Nightingale's nominal superior and the two had clashed repeatedly over the extent of her responsibilities. Nightingale presented Hall and his colleagues with a scheme for introducing a new system of hospital management in the Crimea but they refused to accept it. Nevertheless, according to Mrs Davis, Nightingale succeeded after all in introducing her new system in the Crimea one month later. Mrs Davis for one did not like it because it interfered with her liberal use of hospital supplies – it seems to have been designed to ensure that appropriate supplies were issued with minimal paperwork, and no doubt Sir John McNeill had a hand in its design. Dr John Hall understandably grew even more hostile towards Nightingale.

Lord Raglan, the Commander in Chief in the Crimea, visited Nightingale when she was in hospital herself at Balaclava recovering from illness. Nightingale wrote to her father proudly that she had upheld the honour of the family like a son: 'Lord Raglan asked me if my father liked me coming out to the East. I said with pride that my father is not as other men are. He thinks that daughters should serve their country as well as sons. He brought me up to think so; he has no sons, and therefore he has sacrificed me to my country, and told me to come home with my shield or upon it. He thinks that God sent women, as well as men, into the world to be something more than "happy", "attentive" and "amusing". My father's religious and social ethics make us strive to be the pioneers of the human race, and let "happiness" and "amusement" take care of themselves.'[32]

She had to visit the Crimea again four months later. It was after the hospital at Kulali, five miles from Scutari, closed down in

October 1855. The nurses there were Irish sisters headed by one of Nightingale's rivals: they had been in the second party sent out by Sidney Herbert for which Nightingale had refused to accept responsibility. Now her opponent Dr John Hall invited them to take up residence in the Crimea, and to preserve her authority Nightingale had to accompany them there. This visit led to further wrangling between Nightingale and Hall and between nurses aligned with each camp. Things developed to such a state that Lord Panmure asked his confidential aide-de-camp, Colonel John Henry Lefroy, to investigate Nightingale's quarrels with the Hall faction.

John Henry Lefroy was another gifted individual who was to become Nightingale's lifetime friend. Lefroy was to push her towards her fateful decision to fight for reform after the war, a decision that she eventually took as a result of a direct appeal from Lord Palmerston. As a reward for his many discreet services, Lefroy was later granted his wish to be allowed to set up an army educational corps to improve the common soldier. He seems to have been one of the many advanced thinkers who associated themselves with the army because it allowed them to experiment with their social theories. His interests were wide-ranging: he had spent many months in the wilderness of northern Canada, carrying out important studies of the earth's magnetic field, but his main passion apart from running schools for soldiers was cataloguing obsolete cannons.

Not surprisingly in view of his interest in educating the common soldier, Lefroy and Nightingale got on very well at their first meeting and Lefroy reported to Lord Panmure that she was in the right and Hall was in the wrong. He convinced the Cabinet to clarify and extend Nightingale's responsibilities. But when Nightingale asked Sidney Herbert to make her disputes the subject of a Parliamentary enquiry, the Cabinet decided to give her some advice on public relations. Sidney Herbert, who had originally sent Nightingale to the East, was no longer in the Cabinet but Nightingale continued to use him as her intermediary with the Government. The Government in turn used Herbert as their intermediary with Nightingale, as her 'handler'. It may have been at the Cabinet's suggestion that Herbert

wrote her a masterly letter early in 1856 telling her that she had everything to lose and nothing to gain by airing her quarrels in public.

Herbert told her that it would not be in her interest to present to
Parliament her strongly-worded denunciations of her rivals. 'The
reader seeing the vehemence of your language would at once say
"This is written under great irritation and I must take its statements
with suspicion," and he chooses for himself what to put aside as the
result of anger and perhaps puts aside just what you most rely on in
your statement.' He advised her to calm down and not attribute base
motives to her rivals in her dispatches, in case they should become
public. He compared the 'irritation and vehemence' of her written
reports with the'sobriety of tone' and calm marshalling of facts in
McNeill and Tulloch's report on the supply blunders of the army,
which had just been published in London. Herbert told her that
McNeill and Tulloch had reported only objective facts, leaving the
reader to imagine to himself what base motives must lie behind
them: 'The public like to have something left to their own imaginations and are much pleased with their own sagacity when they have
found out what was too obvious to be missed. It is always wise too
in a public document to *understate* your case. If on examination your
case proves stronger than you stated it to be, you reap the whole
advantage. If however, any part, however slight, is shaken, the credit
of the whole is shaken with it.'[33]

Sidney Herbert was never a very accomplished letter-writer, and
it seems possible that his highly-polished letter was drawn up by or
on behalf of someone in the Cabinet and delivered through Herbert
in his capacity as Nightingale's 'handler'. Nevertheless, the letter
infuriated Nightingale. She fired back a response accusing Herbert
of lazing beside the fire, dismissing McNeill's report as irrelevant,
and accusing the Principal Medical Officer in the Crimea of deliberately withholding rations to starve her.[34] She also had to defend
herself against other criticism, including allegations that her hospital was unhealthy. There must have been speculation in London that
conditions at Scutari were partly responsible for the high death rate
there during the first winter of the war, because she wrote to

Panmure denying this possibility in August 1855. She blames the men's deaths on disease brought on by starvation and overwork in the trenches: 'The physically deteriorating effect of the Scutari air has been much discussed, but it may be doubted. The men sent down to Scutari in the winter died because they were not sent down till half dead – the men sent down now live and recover because they are sent in time'.[35]

She was proud of her record at Scutari, and scornful of her detractors, as she showed when asking her sister Parthenope to lobby the Government for a monument to honour the Scutari dead: 'Five thousand and odd brave hearts sleep here. We have endured in brave Grecian silence. We have folded our mantles about our faces and died in silence without complaining. And for myself, I have done my duty. I have identified my fate with that of the heroic dead, and whatever lies these officials, these sordid exploiters of human misery, spread about us, there is a right and a God to fight for and our fight has been worth fighting. I do not complain. It has been a great cause.'[36] All Britain was proud of her, too. Her illness at Balaclava had caused consternation in the newspapers at home, and the news of her recovery had led to national rejoicing. The public was impressed when after her convalescence at Scutari she decided not to return home but to remain at her post. Sidney Herbert decided to exploit the national wave of enthusiasm and sympathy to launch a national appeal for funds to support her – and his – scheme to improve the standard of female nursing. Herbert and the other politicians were pleased to be able to point to one good thing that had come out of a war that was otherwise a catalogue of disasters.

Before the war, Nightingale had resigned from her first hospital position so that she could seek another where she could train nurses. While she was in the East, a doctor whom she knew had written to her to suggest that she help him to establish a school for nurses in one of London's teaching hospitals. Herbert set up a committee to raise money for the project. The exact wording of the committee's resolution for raising money is important because of the obligation that it placed on Florence Nightingale 'on her return to England, to establish a permanent institution for the training of nurses and to arrange for their proper instruction and *employment in hospitals*.[37] These words were to torment her later. At a public meeting in London at the end of November 1855, Herbert launched a national appeal for subscriptions to the 'Nightingale Fund'. The meeting was packed to suffocation and delirious in its praise of the faraway heroine. Herbert read out to the adoring crowd a letter from a soldier who had been in Nightingale's crowded hospital: 'What a comfort it was to see her pass. She would speak to one and nod and smile to many more, but she could not do it to all, you know. We lay there by hundreds; but we would kiss her shadow as it fell, and lay our heads on the pillow again, content'.[38]

The appeal for subscriptions brought in a sum worth several million pounds in today's money, to fund the training of hospital nurses. Queen Victoria sent Nightingale an inscribed diamond brooch and an invitation to meet her when she returned to England. The soldier's letter which launched the Nightingale Fund also inspired a poem by Longfellow which immortalised the Nightingale legend:

> *Lo! In that hour of misery*
> *A lady with a lamp I see*
> *Pass through the glimmering gloom,*
> *And flit from room to room.*
> *And slow, as in a dream of bliss,*
> *The speechless sufferer turns to kiss*
> *Her shadow, as it falls.*

Nightingale's mother and sister were ecstatic with pride after the public meeting in London. Her mother wrote: 'It is very late, my child, but I cannot go to bed without telling you that your meeting has been a glorious one'. Her father was more reserved but could not conceal his 'joy at the meeting which has honoured Flo with its absolute finding of "Well done". I am not easily satisfied but all people seem to agree that there was *there* nothing wanting.'[39]

After the bitter disagreements over her desire to take up nursing the approval of her family was far more important to Nightingale than public fame. 'If my name and having done what I could for God and mankind has given you pleasure that is real pleasure to me' she wrote in reply to her mother's description of Herbert's public meeting. 'My reputation has not been a boon to me in my work – but if you have been pleased, that is enough. I shall love my name now. Life is sweet after all.'[40] She was now famous, and the evidence of her success was visible. Under her management, and after the expenditure of millions of pounds, the British army in the East was in fine health. In five months during the first winter of the war, 10,000 soldiers had died of sickness, but in the same five months during the second winter, only 500 men died out of an army that was now swollen to twice the size. The improvement was not only due to a milder winter, for during that second winter the death rate in the French army before Sebastopol increased by sixty per cent.[41]

In the Spring of 1856, the War Office issued a General Order to the army, specifying once and for all that Nightingale's authority extended to all the hospitals, those in the Crimea as well as those on the Bosphorus. She immediately set sail for the Crimea and took possession of Balaclava General Hospital, where Dr John Hall the previous October had installed a party of nurses who preferred to be independent of Nightingale. The rival nurses now resigned and went home rather than work under her draconian discipline.

The war officially ended on 30 March 1856 when the Treaty of Paris was signed. Britain and her allies had surrounded the Crimean peninsula, forcing the Russians to evacuate Sebastopol, in the previous September. The British had achieved what they wanted from the invasion, and they blew up the Russian dockyards with great ceremony. It is not clear whether it made a great deal of difference to history.

Nightingale stayed on in the Crimea until every soldier had left. She began to have time to read the newspapers from England, and followed with interest the debates in Parliament, where the post-mortem on the war had already begun. She had no idea that she would become involved in the investigation into the mistreatment of the common soldier during the conflict, although the Cabinet was already planning to exploit her popularity in their plan to bring the Army High Command under democratic control.

4

Post-mortem

THE TWO CIVILIAN-LED commissions that Palmerston's Government sent to the Crimea immediately upon taking office in February 1855 reported at different times. The report of Dr Sutherland's Sanitary Commission was not published until twelve months after the war had ended. The other commission, that of Sir John McNeill and Colonel Tulloch into the army's supply failings, delivered its reports while the war was still going on. Panmure presented McNeill and Tulloch's critical report to Parliament at the beginning of 1856, nearly a year after they had started their investigation. It showed how the incompetence or inaction of identified senior officers had caused the deaths of thousands of common soldiers (the report was silent on exactly how many) through overwork, inadequate food and shelter, and scurvy. All of these could have been prevented by the use of supplies that were either already in the army's stores or available in the near vicinity. The Crimean peninsula, as part of Russia, was enemy territory but it was surrounded by Turkish provinces allied with Britain and plentifully stocked with the necessary supplies. They were distant only a few hours from the British camps by steamship, of which the army had large numbers at its disposal.

Queen Victoria was furious that Panmure had presented McNeill and Tulloch's criticism to Parliament for debate in public, but her anger didn't seem to worry Panmure. He wrote to the new Commander-in-Chief of the army in Russia – an old family friend – on 15 February 1856: 'We are about to be involved in a serious difficulty by the ferment made by the report of Sir J. McNeill and Colonel Tulloch. The four officers blamed especially in it for the disasters of 1854–55 are indignant. High personages [presumably a code phrase for Queen Victoria and her husband] are fearful lest this opportunity be seized to get the administration of the Army placed under the control of Parliament! The officers mean to put in written defences against the report, and I shall lay them before Parliament. It is a pretty mess, but I have fought through worse, and hope to get over this without any serious change, or injury to the Queen's authority, which I desire to see upheld.'[1]

Queen Victoria, exploiting her position as nominal head of the army, often required the Minister of War to attend her in person. Panmure was devious in his dealings with her, inventing excuses for disobeying her instructions or implementing them to the letter if he foresaw consequences that she had not anticipated which were favourable to the Government's policies. On one or two occasions, he deliberately misled her. One such occasion occurred on the day after Panmure wrote so complacently to the Commander-in-Chief in Russia, when the Queen sent an angry letter to Palmerston complaining that Panmure had instructed McNeill and Tulloch to investigate the army on behalf of Parliament. She believed that this was an attempt by her ministers to increase the involvement of the House of Commons in army affairs: 'A civil Commission is sent out by the Government to inquire into the conduct of the officers in command in the Crimea,' wrote the Queen. 'It is quite evident that if matters are left so, and military officers of the Queen's Army are to be judged by a Committee of the House of Commons, the Command of the Army is at once transferred from the Crown to that Assembly.

'This result is quite inevitable if the Government appear as accusers, as they do by the report of their Commission, and then submit the accusations for Parliament to deal with without taking any steps of their own.'[2]

We may wonder why Palmerston did not simply reply to this by telling the Queen politely to mind her own business. Palmerston knew that phrases like 'the Queen's Army', 'the Crown', and 'the Royal Prerogative' now simply represented the additional power that ministers had to act independently of Parliament when they judged it necessary. There was no actual power vested in the Queen, though ministers had to keep her informed and she might try to persuade them. The Queen herself, misdirected by the late Duke of Wellington, did not appear to understand these constitutional arrangements. Victoria was presumably correct in her fear that if the Government did not act on the McNeill-Tulloch report, but instead passed it to the House of Commons, it would be destroying the Crown Prerogative (whether that belonged to her or to the Cabinet). The Cabinet presumably thought that it had the right to transfer command of the army from the Crown to the House of Commons if the Government so chose. Palmerston wanted Parliament to debate any matter that required it to spend large amounts of money. In the past, Parliament had been very parsimonious with the army because it did not have enough control over it, and this must have interfered with Palmerston's ambitious defence plans.

Palmerston and the Cabinet did not simply tell the Queen that they had decided to make their Crimean enquiries a Parliamentary affair and that was that. They may have thought that if they revealed their intentions too clearly she might oppose them openly. This could make her extremely unpopular, and damage her value to the Government as a national figurehead. Victoria herself was claiming that the Duke of Wellington had told her to ensure that the House of Commons never controlled the army.[3] Arguing with the Queen did not enhance a Cabinet Minister's quality of life. Lord Palmerston and Lord Panmure therefore pretended to agree with her. Panmure replied to the Queen denying her accusation that he had sent a civil commission to investigate the army, saying that he had only told McNeill and Tulloch to investigate the Commissariat, a civilian department which supplied the army. The War Minister chose his words carefully: 'Lord Panmure presents his humble duty to Your Majesty, and has the honour to inform Your Majesty that at the Cabinet yesterday Your Majesty's letter to Lord Palmerston was read.

'The Commission of which Sir J. McNeill and Colonel Tulloch were members was sent out in February 1855 – their instructions bear date 19th of that month – to inquire into matters purely connected with Commissariat supplies to the Army.'[4]

In specifying the date of the instructions as 19 February, Panmure was deliberately concealing from Queen Victoria the existence of supplementary instructions dated three days later – 22 February – in which he had given McNeill and Tulloch additional powers to investigate why supplies issued to the army by the Commissariat had not reached the soldiers. Any problems discovered here would reflect on officers of the Queen's Army, and not on Commissariat civilians. Panmure must have known that the Queen would discover his deception, and sooner rather than later. Both sets of instructions were printed at the front of McNeill and Tulloch's published report, although the much shorter 'secret' instructions were printed high up on the back of a page where they could easily be overlooked. The result of their temporary concealment was that the criticised army officers unwisely based their defence on the argument that McNeill and Tulloch had exceeded their authority.

The fact that Panmure felt it necessary to use the same deception with both the Queen and the army officers over the scope of his enquiries confirms that, in his mind at least, the Queen and the Army High Command were united in opposition to his plans. Palmerston and Panmure were using the McNeill-Tulloch Commission to bring the army's supply arrangements under the control of the House of Commons, against the wishes of the Queen and her generals. Soon, Panmure would use Florence Nightingale to do the same thing for the army's medical arrangements.

The significance of Panmure's deliberate deception of the Queen and the army has never been remarked by Nightingale's biographers who have accepted without question Nightingale's description of

Panmure as a lazy but bullyable opponent of reform who was under the thumb of the Army High Command. These biographers may have been misled by Panmure's new low-profile strategy which contrasted with his initial approach on taking office soon after his brother's untimely death in camp. Then, he had fired off blistering letters of rebuke to commanding officers far and wide. These letters (which Florence Nightingale of course knew nothing about) caused the Army High Command to claim that he had far exceeded his authority as a civilian servant of Her Majesty. After that, no doubt at Palmerston's insistence, Panmure pretended to have been put in his place, playing his cards closer to his chest.

The Queen, not surprisingly, disliked Panmure's plan to ask the criticised army officers to submit their defence to Parliament, which he described in his letter to the Commander-in-Chief, quoted above. She suggested to Palmerston that the McNeill-Tulloch report should be investigated by an army Board of Generals instead. She must have mistakenly believed that this would keep Parliament out of the affair.

Panmure was the source of the Queen's problems. He had signed the instructions for the investigating team and he had unnecessarily given their report to Parliament. Victoria was in residence nearby at Buckingham Palace and had him at her beck and call, so there are few letters between her and her War Minister at this time. When they did communicate in writing it was usually a sign that they were having a confrontation, as with the Queen's irate letter to Palmerston quoted above. Victoria must have hauled her War Minister over the coals for not having at least censored the 'inconvenient passages' in the McNeill-Tulloch report before presenting it to Parliament. There could be no other possible reason for his putting in writing to her an explanation of why he had not done so, respectfully as ever avoiding the use of the intimate 'I': 'Lord Panmure read the report with a view to strike out inconvenient passages, but he found that he could not do so successfully unless he struck out or altered the evidence also, a step which Lord Panmure could not take, and of which Your Majesty would justly have expressed your condemnation.'[5]

Nightingale's biographers have all taken this paragraph at face value and used it to prove that Panmure *wanted* to censor the revelations in the McNeill-Tulloch report. They have not explained why he included it in a long letter to the Queen which was full of deceptions and flimsy excuses for having let the House of Commons see the report against her wishes in the first place. The Queen was being quite reasonable in expecting Panmure to strike out some of the 'inconvenient passages' if he really had to present the report to Parliament, because the war was still in progress. Panmure's excuse that he could not censor the report because it would alter the evidence is one of the flimsiest ever made.

Victoria must have suspected a note of irony in Panmure's reference to her high ethical standards. But it was not irony so much as outright hypocrisy, because without telling her he *had* struck out the most inconvenient part of the evidence – a table of sickness and mortality that Tulloch had ingeniously compiled and which was to give Florence Nightingale so much grief later. Panmure suppressed it out of a fear that its publication would make it even more difficult for the War Office to get new recruits or contract foreign mercenaries. The Queen would have been very glad to hear that he had suppressed it, but Panmure could not tell her because it would weaken his excuse for not having censored the other parts that she didn't like. His letter to Queen Victoria continued by wholeheartedly endorsing her proposed army Board of Generals to hear the officers' explanations for the destruction of the army. The Queen may have thought that such a court would come down hard on McNeill and Tulloch for exceeding their instructions. She also, apparently, believed that the Board's enquiry would be held in secret. This suggestion led to an uproar in Parliament and the Government had to declare that the proceedings would be open after all. The Queen let Panmure know that she was 'disappointed and annoyed' by this decision, but Panmure pointed out to her that it was her fault. In arguing for a Board of Generals she had cited an 1808 precedent where a Board had been used, and in that case the proceedings had been open. Palmerston and Panmure may have been more aware of this detail

than the Queen when they encouraged her to follow the 1808 precedent. Lord Palmerston, amazingly, had already been in the
Government all those years before as a Navy Minister. Queen
Victoria would have had to get up very early in the morning to out-
smart Lord Palmerston.

With the proceedings of the army's enquiry being made public,
Parliament would be able to criticise its findings if they proved to be
a whitewash of the army. It might have been better for Queen
Victoria if she and the Army High Command had simply ignored the
critical McNeill-Tulloch report. Peace was breaking out in Russia and
the army would emerge with some credit: the public had no way of
knowing whether the defects exposed had now been corrected.
When the Cabinet suggested to the Queen some names of generals
to sit on her Board of Generals, she wrote to Panmure rejecting Sir
George De Lacy Evans on the sole grounds that he had served in the
Crimea and might therefore be prejudiced. She did not mention his
activities as a radical MP. Panmure did not resist, and replaced him as
instructed.

The Government conspicuously tried to prevent discussion of the
McNeill-Tulloch report in Parliament. When forced in the House of
Lords to say whether the Government had commissioned it or not,
Panmure reluctantly accepted responsibility for the report while
giving the impression that he didn't believe its findings. He pointed
out that the army was now in magnificent shape compared to how it
was before McNeill and Tulloch made their investigation. In saying
this, he set himself up beautifully for a riposte. In the House of
Commons Sir George De Lacy Evans scornfully attacked Panmure's
statement in a fine and well-prepared speech. Was it not true, he
wanted to know, that the recent improvements to which Panmure
referred were due to one thing and one thing only – the changes
implemented by the two experts whom Lord Panmure was now
trying to discredit? De Lacy Evans, a hero of Waterloo, who had
been rejected by Queen Victoria for her enquiry into the McNeill-
Tulloch report because he had actually served in Russia and therefore might be prejudiced, had been allowed his revenge.

McNeill and Tulloch were surprised and offended by the Government's refusal to publicly back their report. It was McNeill who first noticed that something was wrong. He told Panmure that Colonel Tulloch (who was acting as McNeill's assistant) had done exceptionally well during their mission, and asked Panmure to ensure that Tulloch was promoted. Panmure rejected the request with a brusqueness that startled McNeill. McNeill had been at University with Panmure. He was also one of Lord Palmerston's oldest friends, and he thought that he had the Government's confidence. The Prime Minister, cornered in a House of Commons debate, was forced to give his verdict on the work of McNeill and Tulloch. To everybody's surprise Palmerston praised them to the skies. This annoyed McNeill even more when he read the account of the debate in the newspapers. He wrote to an acquaintance in the Cabinet demanding to know why Palmerston's War Minister had given a completely different impression in public. Palmerston's praise had made McNeill think that Panmure, the Minister of War, was out of step with the Government and was supporting the Queen and her generals against Palmerston. McNeill decided to boycott the army's Board of Enquiry into his report.

The Board of Enquiry sat in the Royal Hospital at Chelsea. An old disabled soldier once accosted the kind-hearted Nell Gwynne, mistress of King Charles II, and told her such a heartrending tale of hardship that she persuaded the king to found this retirement home for soldiers. It was a stately palace in thirty-six acres of parkland in what is now the heart of London. Sir Christopher Wren designed the building to combine economy of construction with monumental style, using high-quality brickwork with stone trimmings. In the Great Hall, a portrait of Charles II on horseback has looked down on the proceedings of many a court-martial. It was here, in the heart of London's most military borough, that the Board of Generals met in April 1856 to enquire into the very damaging statements made by McNeill and Tulloch about the conduct of certain senior army officers in the Crimea. The generals summoned both McNeill and

[63]

Tulloch to take part in the enquiry, but Sir John wisely refused. Tulloch, burning with indignation and concerned to show his obedience to military discipline, went alone.

The enquiry quickly uncovered Lord Panmure's little deception of pretending that he had only asked McNeill and Tulloch to investigate the civilian Commissariat. Lord Lucan, one of the army officers who had been criticised, refused to answer a question from Colonel Tulloch on the grounds that it lay beyond the scope of the enquiry, having nothing to do with the Commissariat. Lord Lucan claimed: 'Having read the instructions most carefully and repeatedly, I have no hesitation in saying that I believe the object of those instructions was to confine your enquiry to the Commissariat supplies, and that you very much exceeded your duties when you went beyond it.' Colonel Tulloch responded by reading out the 'secret' instructions to Lucan in front of the Board, showing that Panmure had instructed them to enquire into non-Commissariat stores.[6] Until then Lucan seemed to be genuinely ignorant of the second instructions published unobtrusively on the back of the first ones. He may not have had time to read the report properly because he was distracted by a quantity of other litigation that he was engaged in arising out of the disastrous charge of the Light Brigade. Probably McNeill and Tulloch had shown the army officers in the Crimea only the first set of instructions, so as to give the impression that they were not investigating the army itself. Certainly the officers seemed surprisingly willing to sign written statements then, which some of them now tried to modify.

Too late, at Chelsea Lucan discovered that Panmure had tricked them into giving evidence in the Crimea, and had now tricked them again into holding a public enquiry at home. Lucan could not tell the Board the truth in response to Tulloch's reading out of the additional instructions, because he would have had to say: 'But we only gave our evidence on the understanding that it would be used against those civilians in the Commissariat!' He realised that Panmure – that meddling civilian who understood nothing of military affairs – had led the army into an ambush. It must have suddenly dawned on Lucan that the apparently chastened and low profile approach that Panmure had adopted since the row over his rebukes to senior officers was all a pose. That was why Lucan, who found it hard to control his temper at the best of times, suddenly launched into a wild explanation to the Board of Generals of a new theory that Lord Panmure himself had written the so-called McNeill-Tulloch report. The allegation may well have been very nearly the truth – the report only amplified the original criticisms in Panmure's written rebuke to the Commander-in-Chief. But Lord Lucan presented his arguments rather incoherently, and Panmure had put up such a convincing show of hostility to McNeill and Tulloch in public that nobody seems to have believed Lucan's conspiracy theory. Lucan may further have weakened the credibility of his argument by introducing in the middle of it a sarcastic remark about Panmure's gout – a painful affliction that was reputed to be a sign of overindulgence – along with a startling witticism on the subject of scurvy: 'His lordship [Panmure] is said to have had the gout, a complaint from which the military branch of the army may be said to be exempt. Scurvy from bad living, and scurvy treatment, are more their lot and infliction.'[7]

It is highly unlikely that any officers in the Crimea suffered from scurvy: being exclusively of wealthy private means, they were able to ride or send their servants to Balaclava to buy supplies from the many profiteering speculators who set up shop there, including the fruit and vegetables which would prevent scurvy. Many officers had hampers from Fortnum's delivered by private contractors to their huts.[8] But the common soldiers in the trenches and tents round about suffered from the horrible symptoms of scurvy while cases of lime juice lay unused in the army's stores nearby. Lord Lucan's witticism must have had them hooting with mirth in the London clubs, but Queen Victoria was probably not amused. With enemies like this, Panmure may have reasoned, McNeill and Tulloch did not need him for a friend.

After several weeks of hostile cross-examination Colonel Tulloch's health broke down and he had to withdraw from the enquiry. The Board discovered some minor errors in Tulloch's calculations, and this produced a combination of gastric disorder and mental confusion in the embattled Colonel that delighted Lucan and his cronies.

If Panmure thought that the enquiry could trap the Board of Generals into approving the McNeill-Tulloch findings, he was wrong. As foreseen by McNeill and many others, the report of the Board found the army officers innocent of all the accusations, and put the blame on civilians in the Treasury at home instead (at that time the Commissariat was under the control of the Treasury). This conclusion was not surprising: Lord Hardinge, the home Commander-in-Chief and therefore the military superior of the Board's members, had already publicly denounced the McNeill-Tulloch report in the House of Lords, and it would have been hard for any of the Board to disagree with him.[9]

The Board's report, which was a humiliating rebuff to Sir John McNeill and Colonel Tulloch, was presented to Parliament just before the end of the session, in the summer of 1856. Shortly afterwards Queen Victoria even persuaded the Cabinet to appoint her reactionary and anti-reform cousin, the Duke of Cambridge, to be Commander-in-Chief of the army in place of Lord Hardinge. Lord Hardinge, in one of those unusual medical phenomena that are a feature of this story, had been in the midst of explaining the findings of the Board of Generals to Queen Victoria at Aldershot when he was cut down by a fatal stroke. When Florence Nightingale arrived back in England one month later, the whole affair seemed to be over and the reformers defeated.

She had not seemed to be in a hurry to get home. After a subdued embarkation in the ravaged corner of Russia where the war had petered out many months before, Nightingale went ashore at Marseilles and made her way across France incognito, arriving in England on 6 August 1856. Perhaps she hung back because she was nervous about rejoining the world. In the two years since she had left home she had seen Constantinople ravaged by earthquake and fire, had held thousands of dying men in her arms, and had beaten the most powerful army in the world in a battle over the rights of common soldiers whether sick or healthy. What would she have in common with the people at home?

Postponing the reunion with her family, she first went to the Bermondsey Convent of the Sisters of Mercy, where some of her wartime nursing companions had returned to work among London's destitute. They didn't have the problem of fitting back into family life because they had left it for good years ago. Founded by Catharine McAuley, an Irish orphan girl who inherited a fortune, the convent's mission was to minister to the sick poor in the filthiest slums. Being among them in England allowed Nightingale to feel that the *real* world still existed – the world of squalor and death and cruelty. The Bermondsey Sisters had been among her most loyal supporters in the hospitals in the Crimea and Turkey; she must have enjoyed a good gossip with them about the intrigues in the army and medical services in the East since the Sisters had come home three months earlier.

There was a more practical reason for her visit: the Sisters of Mercy had kept meticulous accounts and Nightingale needed these to help straighten out her own complicated financial situation arising from her expenditure of public money in the East. She spent three weeks working on her accounts, first at the convent and then at the family home in Derbyshire, before turning to the question of her future career. She could now begin to openly plan a future in nursing administration. In this, she had the satisfaction of having won a great victory over her mother and sister. Public opinion, which before had been indisputably on their side, was now on hers: nursing had become a useful and respectable activity for women. She no longer had to ask her family's permission to follow her vocation.

She had no idea how she was going to make use of the fund that the public had subscribed in her name during the war for the training of nurses. She was now rather less interested in training nurses in a large teaching hospital than she had been before the war. She was more interested in hospital management: 'If I had a plan it would be simply to take the poorest and least organised hospital in London and putting myself there see what I could do – not touching the

[67]

Fund for years until experience had shown how the Fund might best be available.'

Nightingale described a slightly different plan when writing to her military friends, perhaps because she wanted to keep open as many options as possible. She told them that she wanted to work in army hospitals. Her letters reveal that she recognised the danger that this avenue might be closed if she allowed herself to be dragged into the controversy that still surrounded the loss of Britain's victorious army. She was convinced that the incompetence and heartlessness of the Army High Command had resulted in the deaths of thousands of common soldiers in the camps and hospitals during the winter of 1854. Two years had gone by since then and nobody had been reprimanded. On the contrary, the four officers most to blame had been promoted – even (or so it had been alleged in the House of Commons) after the Government had in its hands the proof of their incompetence.

The results of this incompetence had been visible in the stream of soldiers who were shipped to her hospital near Constantinople dying from extreme malnutrition, exposure, and exhaustion. The men who had amazed the world with their courage at the Alma and at Balaclava had arrived scarcely alive, many having died in transit and many more dying soon after arriving at the hospital. Over 16,000 British soldiers had died of sickness, while fewer than 2600 were killed in battle and 1800 died of wounds. The hair-raising reports of treatment of the sick and wounded published in the newspapers had led to the fall of the Government that had sent Nightingale to the East, but the Army High Command seemed to have emerged from the fuss unscathed. The public now seemed to have lost interest in the accusations of her friends McNeill and Tulloch that senior officers had made no attempt to obtain additional supplies to feed and clothe the army, and had allowed the supplies already at their disposal to remain in store nearby while the troops died for lack of them.

Since the McNeill-Tulloch investigation, there had been a change in the political climate, and demand for army reform had decreased. Public dissatisfaction at the time of the disaster had forced a change of Government, and death had replaced the Commander-in-Chief in the Crimea. The war was now over and the outcome appeared to be a success for Britain and its allies. The Government appeared ready to let sleeping dogs lie.

After the war's end, Nightingale was reluctant to make any public pronouncements at all. The use of female nurses in war was still controversial and she thought that if the women made themselves too visible it would play into the hands of those who were opposed to the idea. She wrote:

> Now the war has ended and we return to England, the less we say about the last two years the better since not only we are the last appointed, the fewest, and the lowest in official rank of the Queen's war servants, but we are the first women who have been suffered in the war service. To return either sounding our own trumpet or, viler still, attacking the system under which, and because of which we worked, can only at once degrade ourselves, and justify, *pro tanto*, the common opinion that the vanity, the gossip and the insubordination of women (which none more despise than those who trade upon them) make them unfit and mischievous in the service, however materially useful they may be in it. Hospital nursing, to be anything other than a nuisance, must remain to the end of time a very humble as well as a very laborious drudgery. But, done aright for God and man, it is a noble work. Let us, please God our consciences bear us witness that we have tried to do our duty, hold fast our integrity nor let our hearts reproach us as long as we live.

She was only reluctantly willing to co-operate through the conventional channels with any official enquiry: 'I ought to show to the War Office that I am at hand to answer any questions.'[10] Nightingale wrote this while she was still in the Crimea, just before the Generals' enquiry into the McNeill-Tulloch report had dismissed its criticisms of the army and exonerated the accused officers. This outcome surprised and shocked Nightingale, who passionately agreed with McNeill's report and had been following the enquiry from afar The failure of McNeill's attempt to expose the cruel treatment of the common soldier must have heightened her sense of injustice, but it made her even less willing to give her opinion on army defects, even in confidence to her official superiors. She feared that she might share the fate of McNeill and Tulloch, whose considerable reputations appeared to have been destroyed by Lord Panmure's despicable failure to support them after he had published their report.

She thought that she would be safer working for reform quietly behind the scenes. But within a few weeks, she had changed her mind again: she *would* campaign for reform, not only privately but also in public, before returning to nursing. As well as ensuring that she would never work in a hospital again, this fateful decision was to involve Nightingale in the continuing political crisis of which she was completely unaware. The squabble between the Army High Command and the Cabinet for control of the Queen's Army was now nearing its climax.

Nightingale was first encouraged to enter the reform camp by War Minister Panmure's secretive aide-de-camp, Colonel John Henry Lefroy, who had been sent out to the Crimea to investigate Nightingale's quarrels with army officials. There is no reason to think that Nightingale ever realised that Lefroy was working directly for Panmure as his aide-de-camp. She regarded Lefroy as an ally of hers against Panmure and the War Office. In late August 1856, when she had been home for a month, Nightingale wrote to him to ask him whether she should respond to the War Office's request for her suggestions for improvement. Lefroy replied that she should go much further and demand that Panmure himself authorise a public 'commission to enquire into the existing regulations for hospital administration'. She would then be able to publicly give evidence to this commission on the army's brutal and incompetent treatment of sick and wounded soldiers. She had never thought of this approach before Lefroy suggested it. Lefroy told her that such a public enquiry would be much more effective than giving her comments to the War

[70]

Office in private as suggested by the civil servants there. He also told her that she was morally obliged to speak out, as the only person possessing the necessary information.

Lefroy made a few disrespectful remarks to Nightingale about his boss Lord Panmure, which must have pleased her. But Lefroy would have been unwise to give her any advice without Panmure's knowledge. Like other reforming War Ministers of the era, Panmure was opposed by his own War Office bureaucrats, and the scheme that Lefroy planted in Nightingale's mind would enable Panmure to outflank these civil servants.

Just six weeks after her return, Florence Nightingale went to see the Queen and the Prince Consort in Scotland with the avowed intention of seeking the Queen's support for the proposed 'Commission on Hospital Administration.' Her letters at the time show that she found the Prince particularly sympathetic, although she was 'somewhat alarmed at his predilection for the Horse Guards' – meaning that she found that the Prince was on the side of the Army High Command. She had no way of knowing in advance that Victoria and Albert at this time would have been horrified at the thought of another public commission investigating army blunders. She knew nothing of the disagreement between Monarch and Cabinet, and did not realise that the Royal couple's deep interest in her story was due to their belief that if the health of the army had been neglected it was a matter for the Queen's Ministers to put right in private. Nightingale thought it was Panmure and his fellow-aristocrats in the army who had 'herded together' to use the Board of Generals to bury the McNeill-Tulloch report two months previously. She was also worried that even if she obtained an official enquiry it would fail because army witnesses would be afraid to speak out.[11] She therefore planned to suggest to the Queen that she make a confidential report to Her Majesty, bypassing Panmure.

When she talked this over with the Queen, Nightingale's interest in making a confidential report to Her Majesty evaporated. She also concluded that the Queen would not be of much use in persuading Panmure to initiate the public enquiry. Perhaps Victoria was a little

[71]

too open with Nightingale about her anger that Panmure had given the McNeill-Tulloch report to Parliament, because Nightingale's assessment of Panmure seems to have moved up a notch at this time, from obstructive to merely evasive.

Lord Palmerston, the Prime Minister, then sent Nightingale a message asking her to make him a confidential report on the war and begging her to stay at Balmoral until Panmure arrived so that she could try to convince the War Minister of the necessity for army reform.[12] The message reinforced the general impression that Lord Panmure was caving in to pressure from the Army High Command, and coming from the politician and friend whom her father most admired Palmerston's appeal must have finally convinced her that it was her duty to fight for reform. In early October 1856 Nightingale met Panmure with the Queen at Balmoral and then alone nearby. Panmure agreed 'in principle' to appoint a royal commission along the lines that Nightingale wanted. Panmure arranged to meet her privately in London the following month to discuss details of the proposed royal commission.

Nightingale moved into the Burlington Hotel, in Mayfair, early in November to begin work on the confidential report officially requested by Panmure, which she hoped would also form the evidence to be submitted to the royal commission. Two weeks later, Panmure called on her there. They discussed her proposed list of experts to sit on the commission, and she was surprised and pleased that she persuaded Panmure to accept so many reformers. He obligingly struck out the name of a War Office official who had opposed Nightingale in the Crimea, and she thought that he must be unaware of the reformist views of Dr Balfour, one of her preferred candidates whom Panmure accepted. It would be surprising if Panmure didn't know that Balfour had bravely stood in for Tulloch when the latter broke down at his inquisition before the Board of Generals, though Nightingale might not have known this because she had still been in the Crimea at the time. Panmure also surprised Nightingale by agreeing extremely wide-ranging terms of reference for her enquiry. Most unexpected of all, Panmure suddenly seemed to have turned against Sir James Clark, Queen Victoria's personal physician and confidant, who was probably present in the discussions at Balmoral. Nightingale thought it essential to have Clark on the commission 'to have Her on our side – as she has done us mischief *in re* Tulloch'. This remark of Nightingale's is the only hard evidence that survives indicating that she believed that Queen Victoria was opposing reform. Most of Nightingale's biographers quote from this important manuscript but omit her criticism of the Queen. Cook, writing in 1913, removed the comment about the Queen's 'mischief', and Woodham-Smith copied Cook's quotation as is shown by her use of Cook's punctuation.

Nightingale also had the impudence to ask Panmure to give a knighthood to Colonel Tulloch, joint author of the officially discredited report criticising the army. By her account, Panmure refused to help with this unless Nightingale persuaded Tulloch to accept some sort of agreement the terms of which were evidently too insulting for Nightingale to consider or even to record in her written account of the interview. Even Nightingale's most fervent admirers would concede that she was sometimes manipulative in her pursuit of the most altruistic objectives. In her account of her interview with Panmure she almost seems to gloat on her ability to outmanoeuvre him. His insulting remarks about her friend Tulloch, his stubborn disagreement on almost every issue, his claim – guaranteed to infuriate her – that 'you can prove anything with statistics' all encouraged Nightingale to believe that with her political supporters she was trouncing a difficult opponent.

Panmure's real feelings – stemming from a personal knowledge of the failings of the Army High Command after his brother's needless death from cholera – would have been too personal for him to discuss openly. But whatever he really felt, without a major political upheaval there was not the remotest chance that he could deliver on his promise to appoint a royal commission in the face of the Queen's and the Duke of Cambridge's certain opposition, least of all with the wide-ranging scope and the slate of reform-minded commissioners that he had promised Nightingale. As the weeks went by, Nightingale became convinced that Panmure was doing nothing to carry out his promises to her, out of fear of the military lobby in the House of Lords. His shelving of the McNeill-Tulloch report had convinced her that he was opposed to army reform. She began to write her confidential report, determined to publish it if necessary.

When she was in Scotland visiting the Queen she also called on Sir John McNeill for whom she had formed such a great admiration in the Crimea. McNeill apparently thought that Nightingale would have a greater impact on public opinion than he and Tulloch, and so he helped her to introduce into her confidential report many of his own findings on the army's mistreatment of its men. Nightingale also contacted Colonel Tulloch to seek his assistance. Colonel Tulloch was still not well; his ordeal before the Board of Generals had broken him physically and mentally. He was now writing a book in which he planned to expose the untruths in the report of the Board of Generals. One remarkable feature of Tulloch's book was soon to prove extremely important to Nightingale. This was the table of sickness and mortality that the Colonel had compiled in the East on his own initiative, which Lord Panmure had suppressed because of its potential impact on morale while the war was still continuing. Now that the war was over, Tulloch published it in his book for the first time in January 1857. He may have showed it to Nightingale a month or so before; she wrote to McNeill in December 1856 criticising the book for being too vehement.[13]

The last member of what we might call the Nightingale team was Colonel Tulloch's friend Dr William Farr. Nothing could be less descriptive of the spirit of this extraordinary man than his dour Victorian title: Superintendent of the Statistical Department of the Registrar-General's Office. The broad scope of Farr's genius owed much to his varied background and early career. His parents were illiterate, being a servant and a labourer in the household of a retired horse-drawn cab driver from Bath named Price who had saved a modest cash sum from his labours. Price recognised an unusual talent in their son and apprenticed him to an apothecary. When Farr was 21, Price died and left him £500. Farr used the hoarded cab fares to travel to Paris and study a most unusual subject in the Paris Medical School: hygiene. He set up in practice in London but found that his humble background was a handicap and his favourite science of hygiene was considered a threat by the medical establishment. No medical school would allow him to teach the subject in England. He became a medical journalist instead, advocating reform of the medical profession. He published articles promoting the use of medical statistics to advance public health, and when the General Register Office was set up he was taken onto the staff.

For the first time births, marriages, and deaths were systematically recorded, and from the very start Farr was responsible for writing the explanations to accompany the summarised statistics produced in the Office. He built an international reputation both for his skill with numbers and his ability to extract inspirational conclusions from them, for the quality of his 'Biometers' or Life Tables showing the deaths per thousand at each age group, and for the insight he provided into how the 'life force' of the population might be prolonged through public health measures. His vision was of a future world where nearly everyone lived to maximum life span, not through advances in curative medicine but through prevention of the diseases which, he believed, weakened the survivors at the same time as causing many premature deaths. 'If the secret roots of death were once pointed out by authentic observation,' Farr wrote, in his habitual lyrical style, 'the human frame might be prolonged to its full ripeness, until it fell as gently as a plant upon the earth'.[14]

Colonel Tulloch introduced Nightingale to Farr about three months after her return, when she had agreed the terms of the proposed royal commission with Panmure but disillusion had not yet set in at the ensuing delay. Farr had helped Tulloch in his appearances before the Board of Generals, presenting himself as an expert witness to help Tulloch demonstrate statistically that Lucan had allowed his cavalry horses to starve.[15] The Board had ignored Farr. In November, with the help of her team – Tulloch, McNeill, and Farr – Nightingale began work on the confidential report that she had proposed to Panmure at Palmerston's suggestion and which she wanted to publish if Panmure did not act. Her confidential report covered not only hospital management but also the cruel treatment of the men that had led to their hospitalisation. Surviving early drafts of the preface to this report show that she supported the conclusions of McNeill and Tulloch, which were that a combination of overwork with inadequate food, clothing, and shelter had killed almost an entire army.

Every expert who had experience of the war seemed to have a different theory about which of the factors had been the most important in causing the men's illness and death, and each tried to find statistical evidence to suit his own theory. Some of them believed that fatigue was the key factor, and tried to correlate regimental death rates with time spent on trench duty. On the other hand Tulloch, who had some pet theories of nutrition in which good fresh bread played a leading role, was convinced that only he knew what had destroyed the army in the Crimea. 'The real disease was starvation,' he wrote.[16] Like Colonel Tulloch, Nightingale still believed that the men had not been shipped off to her hospital until they were already dying. Colonel Tulloch, who was convinced that the sickness had originated in neglect of the Tulloch dietary principles, thought that the Scutari climate might possibly have changed or increased the disease, but Nightingale thought that Scutari was healthy. We have already seen that she had written to Panmure saying that earlier hospitalisation at Scutari could have saved the men: 'The men sent down to Scutari in the winter died because they were not sent down till half dead – the men sent down now live and recover because they are sent in time.'

This letter to Lord Panmure – the first of two crucial letters that her earlier biographers overlooked – is now the only known record that Nightingale ever held the opinion that her patients during the first winter of the war were already beyond recovery when they entered her hospital. It therefore advances an argument that she passionately opposed one year after the end of the war. The unique letter was archived in a group of papers – Lord Panmure's – to which Nightingale had no access later in her life and it may be the sole survivor of many letters on the subject. It is a notable fact that few, if any, of her other surviving wartime letters touch on the question of why so many men were dying in her hospital, a question which she must presumably have discussed in her correspondence. Not being aware of any discussion on this subject all her biographers to date have assumed that her later opinion – that hospital hygiene was to blame – was the one that she held from the start.

When Nightingale asked Dr Farr to investigate the mortality statistics of the war to see whether he could prove that the diagnosis of McNeill and Tulloch was correct, Farr may have immediately concluded that there were other factors at work. He had been studying mortality statistics for many years and he was a believer in the existence of diseases that spread through both the atmosphere and the water supply. He had coined the term 'zymotic' to describe such diseases which he believed were propagated by some chemical product of putrefaction carried by air or water. This explained why the diseases were more easily caught in more crowded environments. He was using what were at that time relatively advanced notions of chemistry to explain why defensive sanitary measures worked – they removed the offending chemicals from the environment. In Nightingale's vocabulary the term 'zymotic' soon came to mean preventable.

Farr's theory was an improvement over the narrow 'contagionist' theory that required direct physical contact for fatal disease to spread. It was an even greater improvement over explanations that attributed disease to overwork, starvation, lack of exercise, a 'broken constitution', or even being out of doors at night. These widely-held theories of disease offered much less insight into how the spread of disease could be halted (except that, in the 'contagionist' theory, isolation and quarantine seemed to be called for – but these measures were not very practical and were also bad for trade). Farr's idea that you could 'catch' fatal diseases not from objects directly but from a contaminated environment, was new and unproven. As far as can be seen, Florence Nightingale was not yet very familiar with it. Only in the case of cholera she had, just before the war, expressed an opinion that it depended on the environment.[17] Like many medical experts she appeared to believe that malnutrition or overwork was the cause of most diseases, and that poor living conditions during childhood could weaken the ability to resist them.

Because of Farr's advanced views on the spread of disease he had supported Edwin Chadwick's attempts to invest public money in cleaning up the cities. Chadwick had been partly responsible for getting Farr his job in the Registry Office back in 1837.

Farr approached Nightingale's Crimean mortality problem with his own prejudice: he believed that armies were a laboratory in which one could prove the relative uselessness of doctors. He had been very impressed at the Paris Medical School years before by studies of the sickness and mortality of armies that showed that different hygiene practices, not medical treatments, accounted for all known differences in army mortality. The chip that he had on his shoulder as a result of his failed medical career had also led him to try to demonstrate that hospitals themselves could spread disease. His investigation had foundered on the poor hospital statistics which made it impossible to tell whether the 'worst' hospitals had a higher death rate because they were accepting a worse class of patients than the others. Nightingale's Crimean challenge seemed to offer Farr the opportunity to prove his theories. In November 1856, a letter from Nightingale reveals the first traces of Farr's influence on her thought. She uses Farr's favourite mortality measure of 'deaths per 1000 living' for the first time to compare the state of the main hospital at Scutari in January 1855 and January 1856. Before, she used to rank the various hospitals in the war zone for merit judged on purely organisational criteria.

Her letter shows that in November 1856 she was still planning a confidential report that focused on the starvation and exposure that had provoked her stream of dying patients. For example, she still pounds the drum for improvements in army supplies: 'The points in my Confidential Report will try to show: 1) how the Army must be taught to "do for" themselves – kill their own cattle, bake their own bread, hut, drain, shoe-make, &c, &c.' She enumerates a total of sixteen points, only two of which refer to sanitary questions and even then she defines this term far more broadly than the cleanliness with which it is nowadays almost synonymous: 'A Sanitary Officer, to advise upon encampment, diet, clothing, hutting, and sick transport.' For the first time she attributes some of the reduction in the death rate at Scutari to the labours of the civilian Sanitary Commission sent out by Panmure at the same time as McNeill and Tulloch, showing a much greater respect for this Commission than ever before. But she still only gives it credit for reducing the already low incidence of cholera at Scutari. Most of the reduction in mortality, she implies, came from the improved quality of her patients as a result of the work of the Sanitary and Supply Commissions in the Crimean camps rather than in her hospitals.

In the same letter, she indicates that she has been to Farr's General Registry Office at Somerset House, and her revealing note describing her visit still survives:[18]

24 November 1856.
Through the kindness of the Registrar-General, went over with him all his books.

Sir Colin Campbell declared his shame when he compared the Sardinian troops with ours [the Sardinian allies kept detailed records of the cause of soldiers' deaths]. Had our Generals but information enough to feel the shame they ought, when comparing the Civil Registration with theirs!

All that is needed to determine cause of diseases and means of removing them is to be found in the former. All that is needed to leave Her Majesty's Ministers in ignorance as to the state of HM's troops is to be found in the latter.

When one business-like head sets out to accomplish one object, if that object is to make beer we see the results in, say, the Burton Breweries. When one mathematical head sets out to accomplish one object, that of classifying and registering the great statistics and discovering the causes of the various events in a population we see the results in a magnificent organisation, magnificent

[79]

because of its simplicity, economy, and efficiency in the Registrar-General's office.

A weekly published return, such as the Registrar-General's office gives, of disease, might have saved our Army. It did the Sardinian. The Government could hardly, in face of such information, have gone on supplying us with salt meat and biscuit.

The Registrar-General showed me a correspondence between himself and the War Office in February 1855 in which he had urged civil registration of soldiers' deaths and been refused.

In January 1855, losing at the rate of 576 per 1000, corresponding week of January 1856 rate of 17 per 1000. The more I think of these things, the more I feel both the absolute necessity of ripping up our army system and the impossibility (almost) of your gaining evidence to do so.

Sir John Hall is now preparing, with Smith, the army's medical statistics of the war. They say they can account for every man but three. If so, if by the process of exhaustion, they arrive at this — if, by proving a series of negatives they arrive at a positive, and call that Registration when we know there were 4000 unaccounted for and Panmure slurs this over, he will ruin us. I am afraid he means to do so. I expect we shall be beat, but at all events let us have a fair battle. Panmure's Commission is most unfair.

The above note is rich in social commentary. Her comparison between the General Registry Office's efficient mass production of statistics and the Burton Breweries' prodigiously efficient mass-production of beer shows that the methods of the industrial revolution had inspired changes in civil government, and marks the awakening of her desire to transfer these methods also to military affairs. But she still implies that proper Crimean statistics would have proved that men were dying in her hospital because of poor food rations in the Crimea. The appearance of the mortality statistics of the Scutari hospitals in the middle of this note suggests that Farr actually calculated them for her during the course of this visit to Somerset House — the beginning of her new education.

Farr also showed her the letter he had sent from Somerset House to Lord Panmure, requesting that the army record the names of its dead (ironically, as a way of eliminating duplicates from casualty figures and turning them into reliable statistics). Nightingale was to make much use later of the reply from Panmure's chief civil servant at the War Office, who in best bureaucratic style did not refuse the request but merely postponed consideration of it until after the complexities (and deaths) of the current war were over. Exactly how many men had died in the war Nightingale did not know, and even when Colonel Tulloch shared his statistics with her they covered only seven months of the two-year conflict. In her letters written after returning to England she often mentioned various total numbers of dead, but without making clear whether the numbers were supposed to refer to deaths in her Turkish hospitals or in the whole of the war zone. Nightingale was obviously quoting vague estimates from different sources without a clear definition of what was included.

The army did not publish its official statistics until twelve months later. By that time Nightingale had long abandoned the practice of quoting vague numbers; she had appointed herself guardian of the Crimean death figures and treated them as sacred relics never to be exhibited without their full statistical regalia and provenance. The foundations of her statistical analysis were laid in her work with Farr in the winter of 1856/7, when she was also busy writing her confidential report confirming the findings of McNeill and Tulloch.

By early 1857, she was smouldering with fury at Panmure's failure to set up the promised royal commission of enquiry, and was threatening to leak her confidential report to the public. Strangely, Sir John McNeill advised her not to do so. Strangely, because Sir John himself had recently threatened to embark on the course that he was now dissuading Nightingale from taking, and for the same reasons. This very correct public servant, who had continually tried to restrain his assistant Colonel Tulloch from rashly airing his grievances in public, had threatened to go to the public himself. He had written to the Cabinet: 'It is possible, however, that the matter may not terminate

[81]

with the Report of the Board of General Officers. Their opinion upon the matters in question may not be accepted by the country as conclusive, and the ultimate tribunal in such cases is public opinion. I should be sorry to be forced to appeal to it, but the Report of the Board may leave me with no alternative.'[19] Following this letter, Palmerston gave McNeill a personal guarantee that he and Tulloch would eventually be vindicated in their criticisms of the army. McNeill had also come to believe that Panmure as well as Palmerston must be on his side, because Panmure had advised Colonel Tulloch not to appear before the Board of Generals.[20] If Panmure had been on the side of the Generals, he would have welcomed Tulloch's conscientious but rash decision which was bound to lead to humiliation for the Colonel.

Now, six months later, Sir John was telling Nightingale to be patient because he must have known that, under a calm surface, the cauldron prepared by Panmure and Palmerston was at last coming to the boil. McNeill himself may have been stoking the fire by implementing his threat with the approval, tacit or otherwise, of the Cabinet. He, or someone else, had been using the Parliamentary recess in the autumn of 1856 to lobby public opinion against the Board of Generals' report. Not through the newspapers, but through personal contacts with influential citizens throughout the country. The Board of Generals' report must have been a best seller, because when Parliament reconvened at the beginning of 1857, every prominent citizen in the country seemed to have formed an opinion on it.

It is possible to defend many of the findings of the Board of Generals if taken in the narrow sense. Rigid army regulations stopped the officers from acting in the best interests of the troops, and a court-martial of the accused officers might have failed to convict them because of this. But the report contained reams of evidence of Lucan's and others' total want of concern at the appalling sufferings of the destitute and loyal troops who surrounded them. This was not what the Board of Generals had intended to enquire into, but it was more than the electorate would tolerate. The electorate now made its views known through a series of ceremonial public addresses to Sir John McNeill and Colonel Tulloch, signed by mayors, aldermen, councillors, magistrates, and other worthies of the largest towns. These addresses thanked McNeill and Tulloch in the most fulsome terms, and castigated Parliament for failing to do the same.

Liverpool was the first, noting in January 1857 that although 'honours have been bestowed upon some of those to whom the sad calamities which occurred were mainly owing, the honest exertion you made to retrieve, in some degree, those disasters, have so far been treated with cold neglect'. Ignored by a supine Parliament, the services of the two Crimean commissioners were nevertheless 'cherished in the affections of a grateful nation'. After Liverpool came Preston, and then a tide of high-flown compliments swept the two commissioners onto the nation's pedestal as the gowns, wigs, and chains of office rose to be counted in the richest towns in the land. Liverpool, Preston, Bath, Edinburgh, Manchester, Birmingham, all declared themselves for McNeill and Tulloch and against the Army High Command. It was impossible, said one municipal address, to decide which was the stronger emotion felt in contemplating both the McNeill-Tulloch report and that of the Board of Generals: was it pride at the first, or shame at the second? And it is equally impossible, seeing these addresses following so closely on one another, to believe that there was not some co-ordination among them.

The House of Commons did its best to ignore the opprobrium heaped on it by the country's civic leaders. According to Florence Nightingale, who by this time had given up hope of reform, the pro-army lobby in Parliament was strong enough to prevent the Government from acting. She thought that Palmerston had missed his chance the previous summer, when he could have called a general election on the issue: 'Eight months ago,' she wrote on 1 March, 'had Lord Palmerston chosen to play a great game and say "I will have Army Reform, and if the House of Commons is against me, let me see if the country is for me", he might have won. Now it is too late. The opportunity is lost and we shall not see another in our lifetime.

[83]

'The Army is strong enough now in the House of Commons to turn out any Ministry as it always has been in the House of Lords ... Had Lord Palmerston been a younger man, this never could have happened. He has not the power to cope with such a multiplicity of subjects alone in the Cabinet, and he sacrifices the great interests of the nation for those of his order, for which at heart he does not care a corporal's button.'[21]

But she was wrong. At the age of seventy three Palmerston was at the peak of his power and the game was not over. He continued to resist the demands of individuals in the House that he publicly honour the two neglected commissioners, and was even dismissive of the value of the McNeill-Tulloch report whereas previously he had praised it. This public about-face did not perturb McNeill, who tried to calm his more ardent supporters by hinting in a letter to one of them that a theatrical performance was in progress: 'There seems to be a general impression among the Members of Parliament that Lord Palmerston spoke under some kind of restraint and difficulty – that there was some unseen influence which he could not over-come.'[22]

In the House of Commons there were many individual members who had no real party allegiance and could not be relied on to support Government policies. Palmerston's party governed with a slender majority and powerful rivals like Disraeli and Gladstone took advantage of every opportunity to try to vote him out of office. They finally succeeded only a few days later, on the issue of policy in China, but by that time the McNeill-Tulloch issue was resolved.

Lord Panmure's response to the town halls' demands for recogni-tion of the services of McNeill and Tulloch was of such astonishing ineptitude that it may have been one of those royal ideas that he decided to implement to the letter for educational purposes. 'Is it not extraordinary' Panmure had once blurted out to his Private Secretary when Prince Albert had just left the room, 'that no person has the courage to tell His Royal Highness the truth?'[23] In response to the calls for public recognition of the two heroes, Panmure wrote to McNeill and Tulloch offering them £1000 each for past services. The offer was couched in terms that showed a total lack of understanding of why such people would put their reputations at risk for the public good. 'This grant is intended, not as a mere pecuniary equivalent for the results of your enquiries, but to convey likewise in the manner which appears to them most proper the recognition by Her Majesty's Government of the zeal and ability with which those enquiries were conducted.'[24] The thought of being governed by people who believed that this was the most proper way to reward this type of public service was enough to make the electorate's collective cheeks burn with shame. Panmure had gone too far. The House of Commons, far from agreeing that the recognition made a debate unnecessary, now united in demanding one. In the debate Palmerston goaded the House to fury by making further disparaging comments about McNeill and Tulloch. It was left to Sidney Herbert to propose the motion that Her Majesty should be asked to confer a more appropriate reward. No more members could speak because shouts for a vote on the motion were so loud, and it was obvious that the Government would be massively defeated if it did not act.

Palmerston, now that the House had finally done its duty and listened to the voice of the people, yielded with a show of displeasure. Within days he gave Tulloch the knighthood that Nightingale had audaciously demanded from Panmure four months before. He made his friend Sir John McNeill a member of the Privy Council, the highest policymaking body in the land, which gave McNeill the title of The Right Honourable. Sir Alexander Tulloch was gratified that Panmure sent for him to give him a personal apology; the War Minister told him that there had been great difficulties that he could not explain.

Palmerston had succeeded in abolishing the Crown prerogative on the question of army supply organisation. He had done so not by overtly delegating responsibility to Parliament (a move that Queen Victoria would have been able to oppose) but rather by allowing the House of Commons to come to the rescue of two heroes of the people, and in so doing to seize unilaterally the powers in question. Palmerston's Government was defeated in a vote in the

House of Commons a few days before this, on a quite different matter. Palmerston had too warmly supported the bellicose and unjustified actions of a British official in China, but despite his defeat in the House popular sentiment was on his side. He decided to ask the Queen for a general election so that he could appeal to the public for endorsement of the foreign policy that his opponents had forced the House to condemn, and the Queen granted his request. Yielding to the popular clamour for recognition of McNeill and Tulloch did not seem to damage his popularity. The country returned his party to power with a hugely increased majority and swept the party of his most troublesome opponents into oblivion. There began a Parliamentary session of such tranquillity that the political diarist Greville was almost in despair: '*June 3rd* [1857]. There is really nothing to write about, but it is evident that the session is going to pass away in a most quiet and uneventful manner. Never had Minister such a peaceful and undisturbed reign as Palmerston's. There is something almost alarming in his prodigious felicity and success. Everything prospers with him. In the House of Commons there is scarcely a semblance of opposition to anything he proposes; a speech or two here and there from Roebuck, or some stray Radical, against some part of the Princess Royal's dowry, but hardly any attempt at division; and when there have been any, the minorities have been so ridiculously small as to show the hopelessness of opposition.'[25]

The period after the April 1857 election, following the triumph of McNeill and Tulloch, was Panmure's last as a Cabinet Minister. Shortly after the election he turned up at the Burlington Hotel bringing Nightingale the thing she most desired, which he would have had great difficulty in giving her before Parliament had established its undisputed authority in the McNeill-Tulloch affair: the agreed instructions for the Royal Commission into the Sanitary Condition of the Army. They were virtually unaltered from her original suggestions, but Nightingale's poor opinion of Panmure was unchanged: 'I know Lord Panmure has some trick in his head, though I don't see exactly what', she wrote.[26]

She usually castigated Panmure particularly severely when he did something right. On a later occasion when he gave her everything she wanted, she said: 'Panmure has granted the Commission with such ample instructions, as you may guess them to be, when I tell you they were written by me. What a fool Panmure must be! Does he not see or does he not care where this will lead him?'[27] Her remarks about him at this time sometimes leave a bad taste, but it must be noted that Panmure appears to have deliberately provoked her, as a fighting-dog's owner might tease it roughly with a stick before turning it on his enemies. He must have learned the trick at the feet of the master, Lord Palmerston, and it certainly worked on Nightingale: 'I have never yet been able to address a letter to Lord Panmure as "The Right Honourable",' she wrote to McNeill when congratulating him on his new title, 'for fear of its creeping out some day as "The Right Dishonourable".[28] The happy ending is that several years later she changed her opinion of Lord Panmure entirely, and gave him his due credit for improving the lot of the common soldier, even though he never allowed her to know just how much he had done to support her. He never explained to her that his procrastination over the Royal Commission had been necessary to unite the country and the House of Commons behind the call for reform, and to save her from the humiliation that her friends McNeill and Tulloch had suffered at the hands of the Army High Command.

Only after Palmerston's general election victory of March 1857 did Panmure dare to send the instructions for Nightingale's Royal Commission to the Queen for signature: 'Lord Panmure presents his humble duty to Her Majesty and has the honour to submit to Your Majesty the draft of a Royal Commission into the Medical Administration of the Army.' He went on to explain to Her Majesty one more time that a Royal Commission was required because of Palmerston's view that Parliament had a right to be informed how its tax funds were being spent, even if ministers and Queen already knew most of the answers: 'Many of the points referred to in this document might be dealt with at once by the hand of authority, subject to Your Majesty's approval, but they entail expense, and the

[87]

opinions of such a Commission will weigh more with the House of Commons than any arguments of a Minister in favour of the increased estimate.' The transfer of responsibility for army medicine to the House of Commons was now assured, because the royal commission would report to Parliament. Should Queen Victoria or the Horse Guards offer any resistance, the House of Commons would rush to the rescue of Florence Nightingale as it had rallied to the other popular heroes McNeill and Tulloch.

It is not clear whether Nightingale was properly able to savour her victory in receiving Panmure's warrant for her long-awaited Royal Commission, because at almost exactly the same time Farr's arguments had forced her into a devastating conclusion. She had finally accepted Farr's view, after much agonising debate, that the McNeill-Tulloch report was completely wrong in its analysis of the reasons for the extraordinarily high mortality among the troops in hospital. Her work with Farr in analysing the differences between the mortality in different areas, and specifically between the front line hospitals in the Crimea and the base hospitals at Scutari, had shown that the epidemic that had killed 18,000 men out of an army intended to number 25,000 had *not* been caused by inadequate food, overwork, or lack of shelter as everyone believed. It had been primarily caused by bad hygiene. The worst affected places had been those where overcrowding had aggravated the effect of poor sanitation. And by far the worst of these, where 5000 men had been killed by bad hygiene in the winter of 1854/5, was Florence Nightingale's own base hospital at Scutari. In the five months before the Sanitary Commission arrived, between November 1854 and March 1855, Nightingale had not been running a hospital. She had been running a death camp.

In those first terrible six months after her arrival, 12,000 patients came to her. They were mostly sick, not wounded, men transferred from primitive regimental hospitals at the front where one in eight would have died. Among those sent to Nightingale's hospital, where medical supplies and skill were relatively plentiful but the men were packed like sardines in an unventilated building on top of defective sewers, instead of one in eight dying it became three in eight.[29] Only a small proportion died on the ships, so that her hospital was easily twice as lethal even without the voyage. And the transfers into her hospital had continued, month after month, while nobody noticed.

The exact process by which Farr convinced Nightingale that bad sanitation was the cause of death can not be reconstructed. She soon afterwards made Farr destroy all her letters to him of this period, telling him that she had not long to live. He replied 'I have always considered Miss Nightingale's letters confidential and have this morning (with great regret) burnt all that I could find.'[30] No letters from Farr to Nightingale on the subject survive in her archives. In the absence of this correspondence Nightingale's biographers, who have tended to rely heavily on her papers, believed that Farr's main influence on Nightingale at this time was in teaching her statistics. But he was extremely well qualified to indoctrinate her in his theories of the importance of hygiene, and her letters to others show that she began to take a much greater interest in hygiene at this time. Farr's job at the General Registry Office was as a statistician, but he used his position as a platform from which to disseminate his public health theories in a series of inspirational papers that he included in the Registrar-General's Annual Returns. He was trying to overcome the shortcomings of Edwin Chadwick, whose packaging of hygiene concepts lacked both scientific justification and emotional appeal. Like Chadwick, Farr was deeply disillusioned with the medical profession, but unlike Chadwick he had been a doctor himself. The historical downgrading of Farr's role in Nightingale's education has made her seem more self-sufficient, but again, it has paradoxically diminished her stature. Her education has appeared shallow, whereas in reality she spent six months being instructed by the leading medical theorist of her time. She must have felt special regard for her teacher by virtue of his being the son of parents whose status in life could not have been lower.

Some fragments allow us to date her final acceptance of the new cause of death around the beginning of May 1857. Before that, an exchange of letters with her father shows that by 20 March, Farr's principles of hygiene had already taken on spiritual significance for her. Her father wrote to her recounting his failure to be selected as a Parliamentary candidate in Palmerston's opportunistic general election. The only reason he had been nominated was because of the magic of his daughter's name, 'for what name was there that could ensure success, like unto the name of Nightingale?' William Nightingale quoted his supporters as asking. But the magic name proved insufficient to sway the selectors, and he sought commiseration from Florence: 'I am given to some sorrowful thoughts and you shall be my comforter. First, to think that of myself I could earn no reputation, that whether physically or mentally incapacitated I've been left behind in the race, and now at the very eleventh hour ... But to return to my text – where am I in my thoughts? I'm with you, and you only. You, my only genius! You might have been my prompter and my supporter in political life. But no! It is clearly written in the book of fate. The outgoing tenant in life must go away to make room for the incoming tenant . . . Shall we have a House of Commons in the next life? Adieu, my child.'[31]

His daughter's magisterial reply is like that of a parent to a child, rather than vice versa:

March 20th '57
   Dearest Pa
   I am sorry that you will not enter the House of Commons in this world. But I am very sure that there is a House of Commons in the next. I hope one upon sounder principles.
   Do you believe that God's word is not 'pray' but 'work'? Do you believe that He stops the fever, in answer not to 'From plague, pestilence and famine, Good Lord, deliver us' but to His word and thought being carried out in a drain, a pipe-tile, a wash-house? Do you believe that mortality, morality, health & education are the results of certain conditions which he has imposed? ever dear Pa
   your loving child
   F.N.[32]

She had obviously drunk deep of Farr's wisdom on hygiene before she wrote this letter, but she had not yet trod her Road to Damascus. During the following six weeks, the full implications of the Crimean experience became clear to her. At the end of March, she visited Sir John McNeill in Edinburgh. In a letter arranging the visit, she appears to be in the process of conversion from the Tulloch view of what had killed her patients (bad food) to the Farr view (bad air). She mentioned 'a system which, in the Crimea, put to death 16,000 men, the finest experiment modern history has seen upon a large scale viz. as to what given number may be put to death at will by the sole agency of bad food and bad air'.[33]

One month later, she was no longer blaming the bad food at all. A copy of an anguished letter from her to McNeill dated 11 May 1857 apparently survived by accident in her sister's archives and shows that her explanation for the wartime mortality had radically changed by then, and that she had perhaps discussed the possible new explanation with McNeill when she visited him at the end of March:

> As you were kind enough to consult me I ought to explain what I said about Scutari, which is a historical instance of sufficient importance to furnish us with much absolute knowledge, no longer within the domain of hypothesis. It is true that the Sanitary arrangements adopted brought the mortality down to 1.8 per cent in the latter year of the war. But in what condition? That of not allowing above 1000 patients in a building 700 feet square, three floors in height. Had this building been differently distributed as to its construction, it might easily have accommodated 3000 patients with good recovery conditions. It is ruinous to build after this fashion. The question is to find a construction which will accommodate the greatest number of Patients upon a given area with the greatest facilities for recovery.
>
> I do not hesitate to say that the causes of the great catastrophe at Scutari were want of ventilation, want of draining, want of cleanliness (too disgusting to detail further), want of Hospital comforts, frightful overcrowding. However good the construction

and ventilation of the corridors, if you fill them with patients, it is the same as building two hospitals back to back. In all our experience, whether of healthy, or of sick men, such a construction generates disease. And our knowledge is now somewhat absolute on these points.

If it is objected that the condition of the men sent down from the Crimea during the first winter was such that they could not have recovered under *any* circumstances, I answer that the Land Transport Corps sent us down men in exactly the same condition the second winter, and that under different circumstances they did recover. Witness our rates of mortality – 1.8 per cent. But again, it was at the expense of limiting a building upwards of 700 ft square to an extravagantly small number of patients.

Our mortality from 'Diseases of the Stomach and Bowels' was at Scutari 23.6 per cent; in Crimea 18.3 per cent.

Why this fatal increase? The condition of the buildings at Scutari is sufficient answer. You will observe that we lost at Scutari nearly 25 per cent more than we did in the Crimea from this cause alone. And the disease was chiefly generated within the building itself. I would furnish the amplest details on this all-important subject to any one interested in it officially as I have already done to Her Majesty.

    & I remain dear Sir John
    ever faithfully yours
    Florence Nightingale[34]

If Nightingale had known about Parthenope's copy of this letter she would certainly have destroyed it, as she must have destroyed the original. This is the second of the two crucial letters that have not been referred to by her previous biographers. The first one was the wartime letter denying that her hospital had contributed to the men's deaths. This second letter written eighteen months later directly contradicts that one, by saying that her patients of the first winter might have recovered and by admitting that 'the Scutari air' *was* to blame for their deaths after all. Nightingale was to spend the next three months trying to persuade the members of the Royal Commission to make her new discovery the centrepiece of their investigation. (She was not an official Commission member, and neither was Farr even though she had tried to get him on.) But according to her 11 May letter to McNeill, her fight to publicise Farr's conclusions had already begun in the most unlikely quarter: the Royal Household: 'I will furnish amplest details . . . as I have already done to Her Majesty'. She can only be talking here about a communication with Her Majesty since the end of March. No trace of correspondence between Nightingale and Queen Victoria's household from this period exists in the Royal Archives, so we do not know how she furnished details to the Queen. But however her plea was made, it seems that it fell on deaf ears. From this time onwards, Nightingale seldom had a polite word to say about Queen Victoria. The following year she referred to herself as 'the greatest sufferer from the Queen's neglect, whose life would in fact have been saved, had she spoken the one word she could and ought to have spoken.'[35]

Farr's calculations showed that there had been a huge variation in the death rates between different hospitals. It caused Nightingale to revise her previous assessment of the relative merits of each one. For example, in June 1856 she had written that the hospital at Balaclava in the Crimea was the worst, and now she found that it had a far better record than any of the hospitals at Scutari. There was also a sudden decline in the death rate overall when Dr Sutherland's Sanitary Commission had begun to clean up the hospitals. These large fluctuations were enough to convince Farr and Nightingale that nearly all the deaths from sickness – over 16,000 men – could have been avoided by better hygiene in the hospitals themselves. If true, this was a triumphant vindication of Farr's theories on the importance of hygiene, which the English medical establishment had rejected when he returned from Paris. The conversion of Nightingale to his beliefs was an important breakthrough for Farr. Her family was on terms of friendship with the political aristocracy – they visited the Prime Minister at his home that Christmas – and this meant that Farr now had a champion who could speak for him in circles from which his own humble background and lowly bureaucratic status excluded him.

Nightingale started to rewrite her confidential report, giving much greater prominence to hospital hygiene than in the version that she had discussed with McNeill in April before she learned of Farr's conclusions. By the end of May she was sending to the printers a new section with the title 'Causes of Disaster at Scutari'. Earlier drafts of the preface still exist and show that before this rewrite it simply reiterated many of the McNeill-Tulloch report's criticisms of the army's supply organisation. The final printed version deals almost exclusively with the sanitation disaster in the hospitals. It refers the reader to an appendix where 'we shall see how much of the mortality was due in the Crimean case also to the frightful state of the General Hospitals at Scutari; how much it depended upon the number which each regiment was unfortunately enabled to send to these pest-houses.' The Appendix is made difficult to find by the fact that Nightingale added it after the main report had been printed, so that its pages bear one of many bewildering sequences of roman numbers that make the report so hard to use.[36] No biography of Nightingale, nor any other publication as far as is known, has ever discussed the contents of this Appendix. Occasionally in the literature there is a reference to Nightingale's introductory statement, but usually with an implicit or explicit statement that the deaths being described happened before Nightingale arrived. The Appendix makes clear that this is not the case.

The Appendix also makes clear who was the source of the data that Farr used to convince Nightingale. It contains an improved version of Tulloch's sickness and mortality table which covered the seven months preceding his visit to the East with Sir John McNeill in the spring of 1855. Tulloch had withheld this table from his official report at Panmure's insistence, but had printed it after the war was over in his rebuttal of the Board of Generals' report. Tulloch's table in the form in which he published it listed several dozen different regiments and gave for each one the number of men hospitalised, the number dying in hospitals in the Crimea, and a separate number of those who died in the Scutari hospitals. When included in the Appendix of Nightingale's confidential report, however, Tulloch's table had acquired an extra column, headed 'Sent to Scutari'. This allows a comparison between the survival rates of patients in the Crimea compared to those in Nightingale's hospital.[37] With this additional information, it is possible to calculate how a soldier's chances of survival were affected by his choice of hospital.

Nightingale probably already knew roughly how many soldiers were sent to Scutari and how many died there and so, when she first saw Tulloch's original table without this extra data in January 1857, she could work out that the death rate was higher at Scutari. This would not necessarily have surprised her very much because she would have thought it was due to a worse kind of patient being sent there. The troops with the heaviest trench duty, for example, might have been sent to Scutari while those from positions more to the rear might well have been sent to different general hospitals nearby. By showing results separately for each of several dozen regiments, however, Tulloch's improved table showed clearly that regiments sharing the same kind of hardship, whether trench duty of difficulties in provisioning, had very different death rates and the rate increased when the regiment sent a higher proportion of sick to Nightingale's hospital.[38] Obviously some regimental medical officers preferred to send all their sick to other hospitals, for example at Balaclava. The choice of hospital was therefore independent of the patient's previous history.

The randomisation of choice of hospital was a godsend to Farr. It overcame the problem that had prevented him from proving his theory that bigger London hospitals had higher death rates. Like many of Nightingale's associates, he had found the army a perfect laboratory for proving his social theories. He did not have access to the statistical tools we have now, so his conclusions remain unproven. It is not known whether he was justified in concluding that sanitation was the main factor influencing survival – but his conclusion had a dramatic effect on Florence Nightingale, who believed it. We will see later why Florence Nightingale did not have statistics during the war that would have enabled her to pinpoint the causes of mortality and take action to redirect patients to safe hospitals. In fact, she *did* have a very small comparison to reflect on while she was still in the East. She found out the number of medical officers who died in the Crimea and at Scutari, and showed that life was more dangerous for them at Scutari than at the front. She used this information during the war to contest claims that medical officers at the front should get the lion's share of medals. A senior medical officer named Mouat (sometimes spelled Mowat) in the Crimea had offended her by saying that his colleagues at Nightingale's hospitals at Scutari were able to 'enjoy themselves in four-poster beds'. Mouat claimed that medical officers like him in the Crimea ran more risks and should therefore get more medals than those who worked with Nightingale. She refuted his claim by pointing out that a higher proportion of doctors had died of sickness at Scutari, apparently without realising that her patients also must therefore be worse off than they would be in the Crimea.

The medal-hungry Dr Mouat got his wish. He was very belatedly awarded the Victoria Cross – the nation's highest award for bravery on the battlefield – for his actions during the war. Military historians are still baffled by official accounts of his bravery and by the fact that it took the authorities an extraordinarily long time to recognise it. According to Nightingale, Mouat claimed after the war that he knew who was to blame for the bad hygiene in her hospitals, and she desperately wanted him to reveal it. But the truth never came out, because when he appeared before her Royal Commission as a witness Mouat remained inexplicably silent on the subject. It was immediately after this that it was decided that his actions four years earlier merited the Victoria Cross.

5

Cover-up

THE ROYAL COMMISSION into the Health of the Army sat from May to July 1857 in London, taking written and verbal evidence from a wide range of military and civilian experts, most of whom had spent time in the Crimea. Nightingale spent most of these three months trying to make the Commission focus on the only subject that now interested her: sanitation in army buildings. Other subjects which she had fought successfully to include in the scope of the Commission's enquiry, like army food rations, hospital supplies, and the training of doctors, seemed to her irrelevant now that with Farr's help she had identified 'the true causes of our disaster in the East.' After her discovery, she altered the draft of her confidential report to focus on building sanitation. She tried to submit this report to the Commission as her evidence, so that it would be published instead of remaining a confidential report to Lord Panmure. In it, she used the higher mortality in her own hospital to show that hygiene was far more important than medical care or hospital organisation.

The Commission's President, Sidney Herbert, was reluctant to publish these revelations that were bound to trigger off a new round of recriminations between politicians and officials, not to mention reopening the controversy surrounding his government's dismissal of the sanitary reformer Edwin Chadwick just when he was most needed. Herbert had good reason for trying to stop the Commission becoming yet another denunciation of official incompetence, because the blunders had occurred while he was responsible for the hospitals. He was also defensive about his former Government's policies, making excuses for the failings of Lord Raglan, their army commander in the Crimea before the Royal Commission as he had done before the House of Commons' Sebastopol Committee. Nightingale put pressure on Herbert as a friend, appealing to his sense of justice. They had now known each other well for ten years, having been drawn together by their common interest in good works. It was Herbert, of course, who as a Cabinet Minister had the idea of sending Nightingale to the East with a party of nurses.

At first she wanted Herbert to assign blame for the disaster to the medical staff whose incompetence in failing to see why the men were dying had made her an accessory to manslaughter. Her desire to identify the guilty doctors who had misled her was new. When she first returned to England she often said that the system was to blame rather than individuals, and that if she reported on the hospitals of the East she would avoid 'all personal assaults upon individual Doctors whose conduct is only the result, to themselves, of the System under which they live.' But that was before she discovered the true cause of the disaster and her involvement in it. Now she wanted to identify the guilty parties. Her first choice as the person to blame for the disaster at Scutari was Sir John Hall, the Principal Medical Officer with the army in the East. Although she and Sir John Hall had clashed repeatedly during the war, she had always coupled her criticisms of him with fair-minded compliments on his ability. Now, preparing the Commissioners for Hall's appearance as a witness, such even-handedness was gone: 'I would only recall to your memory, the long series of proofs of his incredible apathy – beginning with the fatal letter approving of Scutari, October '54,' she wrote.[1]

This allegation – still a subject of dispute – that Hall had given written approval of the Scutari buildings in October 1854, was not Nightingale's only charge against him. As the winter set in and the camps and hospitals of the static army became fouled with corpses and excrement, Hall and his staff did nothing about it, or so she claimed. Hall, in response maintained that he and his staff had recommended the cleaning of the camps to their superiors who had ignored their advice. According to Hall the civilian Sanitary Commission sent out by the new Palmerston Government only succeeded because they had power to act independently of the army, which he did not. Nightingale demanded that Herbert cross-examine the doctors to see whether they had complained about the sanitation and if so to whom:

'I have thought a good deal of what you told me yesterday [she wrote to Herbert] and my conclusion is to make you a confidential Report great as is my objection to that system. If I were you I would say to Dr Mouat and Co. that you must have documentary evidence of what they state. Their object is (not to give this but) that you should make a general statement in the House of Commons. I know as a fact that none of these men knew what the others were doing. Therefore Mouat's statement can only be taken for himself. Nor would I take it even for himself without *documentary evidence*. But if Sir John Hall and Dr Mouat can prove that they did during the winter 54/55 make all the sanitary recommendations subsequently made by the Sanitary Commission – you will have done immense good by bringing this out more even than by the other. For you will have fixed the responsibility in the right quarter for the operative causes which occasioned the loss of an army. You will have proved that if the Medical Officers had the knowledge they had not the power.

'I trust that you will not let it drop. For I look upon the sanitary question as even more essential to the life of our army if possible than that of supplies. I look upon what you told me yesterday as the most important thing I have heard. Remember that the Duke of Wellington destroyed the army of Massena at Torres Vedras by no other means than this. The Russians lost 60,000 men before we

[99]

left Bulgaria by no other means and Napoleon 288,000 men . . . I know that Mouat as Principal Medical Officer of Balaclava is very much annoyed that Sutherland has not been able to mention him as having originated sanitary improvements there although he has mentioned men of very inferior rank: Matthew, Jephson, and Taylor, the best of them all of the Land Transport Corps. Please observe that *none* of these have been promoted or decorated. [Mouat had already been awarded a CB and Hall a knighthood.] You could not do me a greater service by which I mean our men than by bringing out such attacks and contradictions as will necessitate a clear explanation of all the conclusions we wish to see drawn.'[2]

This note, only a rough draft of which survives, shows that Herbert had been reluctant to cross-examine the senior army doctors for the public record about their claim that they had recommended sanitary improvements. Nightingale wanted him to do so because, if the cross-examination showed that they *did* make recommendations as they claimed, it would clearly place the blame on those to whom they made them. Nightingale knew that at least one doctor had warned the authorities at home that conditions in her hospital at Scutari were dangerous. This was Lord Raglan's personal physician Dr Henry Mapleton, who had been so frightened by the state of the sewers at Scutari in October 1854 that he had recommended to the authorities at home that the sick be sent straight to England. Herbert's Commission called Mapleton as a witness, but from the questions they asked you would not have known that Mapleton had ever thought about the subject, much less made one of the most radical and sensible suggestions of the war. His proposed repatriation of the sick would have made an ideal use of Brunel's new steamship *Great Britain*, already in service as a troop carrier.

During the cross-examination of Hall and Mouat, both the Commission and the witnesses stayed away from the subject of whether these doctors had approved the sanitation in hospital buildings. Herbert asked Hall whether he had complained to the now dead

Commander-in-Chief, Lord Raglan about the unhealthy choice of campsites and about the inadequate rations. These were tactical matters that Raglan was responsible for, not the Government far away in London. Hall replied that he had done so, and Herbert asked him to hand in documentary evidence, as Nightingale had suggested. But nobody asked Hall whether he had approved the defective hospitals at Scutari. When Herbert called Mouat, Hall's subordinate, as a witness neither Herbert nor Mouat raised the question of whether Mouat had complained about sanitation during the Crimean War. Herbert gave Mouat the opportunity to raise the subject, by asking Mouat whether he had ever complained about army sanitation. In reply Mouat gave numerous examples of his tussles with the army over barracks hygiene in India and Ireland, but never mentioned the Crimea. Herbert did not ask him about the Crimea directly as Nightingale had insisted that he should.

These witnesses did not therefore repeat their private allegations in front of the Royal Commission where they would have appeared in the published evidence. The case of Mouat, who according to Nightingale had asked Herbert to state in Parliament that the doctors had made sanitary recommendations in the Crimea, is particularly striking. He declined to repeat this claim in public, and Herbert did not try to force him to publicly repeat it or withdraw it. If Mouat did have the documentary evidence that Nightingale insisted that he should be made to produce, it has never seen the light of day. Nightingale did not have a high opinion of Mouat, judging from the bad character reference she gave him later when he was being considered for promotion: 'Mouat was the typical clever fellow, the unscrupulous blackguard, the unmitigated rogue. I believe I need hardly say that, in all this, I am referring exclusively to his conduct to his men, as *Inspecting* [i.e. Senior] Medical Officer. I do not refer at all to his medical practice, on which it is not my business to give an opinion.'[3]

Nightingale may have been alluding to the fact that Mouat helped to enforce Sir John Hall's instructions to the army surgeons not to use their supplies of chloroform to anaesthetise soldiers while amputating their limbs. Chloroform had achieved respectability in the previous year, when Queen Victoria used it while giving birth. Hall, however, wrote 'Dr Hall takes this opportunity of cautioning Medical Officers against the use of chloroform in the severe shock of gunshot wounds, as he thinks few will survive if it is used. However barbarous it may appear, the smart of the knife is a powerful stimulant, and it is much better to hear a man bawl lustily, than to see him sink silently into his grave.' Mouat was the most senior Medical Officer to support Hall's instruction against chloroform, and dismissed the widespread criticism of it as unfair to Hall. Nightingale helped the surgeons at Scutari to ignore the order.[4]

Nightingale's bad reference did not stop Mouat from rising to the top of the Army Medical Department, covered with honours of which the most prestigious was the Victoria Cross. It was given to him for bravery at the extraordinary action known to history as the Charge of the Light Brigade, when a lightly armed and unsupported body of English cavalry charged over a mile of open ground at several strong and well-prepared batteries of Russian artillery. History records that one of the heroes of the Charge was Surgeon James Mouat, whom Nightingale called 'the unscrupulous blackguard, the unmitigated rogue' and who kept quiet at the Royal Commission about his previous claim that Sidney Herbert's Government failed to heed the doctors' hygiene warnings. The problem for Mouat's reputation is that later military historians do not see how he could have earned the VC during the Charge. He was supposed to have bravely treated a wounded officer on the battlefield, and drawn his sword to defend himself from Cossacks while doing so. But the wounded officer concerned had made his way back up the valley and fallen out of range of the Russian guns and under the noses of the English heavy cavalry. Military historians do not understand how Mouat could have been under fire nor how he could have been attacked by Cossacks. Historians have also been puzzled by the timing of Mouat's award, four years after the battle and after two other medical officers had received the Victoria Cross for more recent acts of bravery.[5] The award came shortly after Herbert published Mouat's evidence to the Royal Commission on the Health of the Army, in which Mouat did not publicly repeat his allegations that reflected badly on Herbert's Government. The problem of explaining the belated award of a VC to Mouat is, according to one military historian who was unaware of his role in Nightingale's Royal Commission, 'an interesting puzzle that will probably never be resolved.'[6]

Mouat, unmitigated rogue or not, may well have complained about the sanitation. But to Nightingale the question very quickly became irrelevant. Half way through the Commission's proceedings, she became convinced that army doctors had no official training or responsibility in such matters and therefore could not be blamed for her disaster. She altered her confidential report to show that doctors could never be properly trained to approve the sanitary state of buildings, and that other experts would be necessary for this. We know of this change through her correspondence with Lord Grey, a former Secretary at War who had himself conducted a Royal Commission into the Administration of the Army twenty years before, to whom she sent an early draft of her confidential report for comments.

Lord Grey sent back a long review of her first draft in which he rejected her idea of removing the responsibility for preventive medicine from the Army Medical Department.[7] Nightingale took account of his criticism by modifying her recommendations to demand only separate responsibility for building sanitation, and she tried to educate Sidney Herbert and the Commission on this new distinction: 'Dear Mr Herbert,' she wrote on 1 July, . . . I have had a long letter from Lord Grey on Army Hygiene matters which I want to show you. He is wrong in some matters. And the distinction between personal hygiene and that of buildings is not seen by him, nor indeed by your Commission. These will require two separate organisations being quite distinct in themselves.' The note probably did not improve Herbert's or the Commission's understanding of the distinction she was trying to draw. The mistake she made was to use the word hygiene in two contexts, making the distinction between personal hygiene and that of buildings appear to be only a question of object not one of technique. Elsewhere, she defined 'personal hygiene' to mean 'clothing, diet, duties, positions etc. of troops', and this was very different from her new concept of building hygiene. She would have done better to use a different term for the cleanliness of buildings, but unfortunately the English language did not yet allow such a distinction. 'Hygiene,' 'sanitary,' and 'sanitation' referred simply to health preservation at that time. In his 1842 report on the 'Sanitary Condition of the Labouring Population,' Edwin Chadwick had investigated all aspects of health, and his proposed 'sanitary reforms' involved introducing the concept of cleanliness into what was previously known as 'sanitary science'. The almost complete reversal of the meaning of this term over the period 1857–1880 can cause confusion over how much was public knowledge at any specific date. But in 1857, when Nightingale's Royal Commission was in progress, Chadwick's proposals were completely out of favour.

Nightingale wrote to Lord Grey replying to his criticism of her draft and explaining why she still thought that building hygiene should not be the responsibility of army doctors. She practised her arguments by writing herself a little parable in which she imagined calling upon the Royal physician to oversee the installation of sewers in Mayfair, where she was writing these words during a particularly putrid summer: 'Memorandum on Lord Grey's letter. The difficulty is with barracks, garrisons, existing hospitals etc. A very intelligent and highly educated Officer of Health alone can deal with these. Instances might be multiplied to illustrate this: 1. New Burlington St is not drained. It would require £20,000 to drain it. Would you ask your doctor, Sir James Clark [the Queen's physician, who also attended the Nightingale family], the head of Doctors in matters of personal hygiene, about this?'

She then applied the lesson of this parable to Scutari: '2. Scutari hospitals. The most hideous sanitary evils were festering in these – evils which, every time the number of patients was *doubled*, raised the mortality per cent more than twice i.e. from three and a half to ten per cent. For six months nothing at all was done [she is talking about the first six months of her superintendence]. Yet these hospitals were seen by all and reported upon by most of the Senior Medical Officers out in the East. These hospitals had within their walls at various times, the best informed men on sanitary [i.e. health] subjects in the Army and every one of them missed the evils and failed to suggest the remedies.

'More than this, they were reported on as splendid buildings, convenient for the reception of the Sick and Wounded and this, when the mortality at Scutari was 200 per cent per annum and at Koulali 300 per cent per annum!'[8]

Her choice of Sir James Clark in this imaginary anecdote, as an example òf a doctor who was not well qualified to rule on sanitation, proved very apt. Four years later, Prince Albert, Queen Victoria's husband, fell ill from typhoid fever caught from the terrible drains in Windsor Castle. Sir James Clark, in attendance, agreed with the Queen that her beloved Prince Consort's symptoms were due to overwork and worry over the bad behaviour of their son with an actress. Four years earlier, Sir James Clark had been a member of Nightingale's Royal Commission, but he nevertheless allowed the Prince Consort to remain in the fatal chambers at Windsor, where he passed away as peacefully as a common soldier in the Scutari hospital.

Lord Grey, as a seasoned politician, reacted to Nightingale's revelations by casting the blame for her new Crimean catastrophe on his party political rivals, saying that it had been the fault of Lord Raglan, the Commander-in-Chief in the Crimea and that he, Grey, had publicly opposed Lord Raglan's appointment. Nightingale herself was not immune to a similar temptation to blame her rivals, as her hasty initial condemnation of her old enemy Hall shows. But within a few weeks her discussion with Lord Grey had convinced her that Hall was not the main suspect in the case. As her understanding of the limitations of medical training and responsibility improved, she was able to identify another one. If doctors were *not* qualified to judge the sanitation of buildings, then who had ordered them to do so? If, despite their lack of formal training, they *had* alerted their superiors to the sanitary defects, then which was the superior who had the power to act and had failed to act? Either way, whether the doctors had complained about the sanitation or not, the trail must lead in the same direction. It led to the Cabinet Minister who had been responsible for the choice of the Scutari building as a hospital, or who had delegated this choice to an unqualified soldier and doctor (Lord Raglan and Dr John Hall). The trail led to a man whose sincerity and dedication to duty were recognised by all; a man who was admired by his colleagues of all political parties and was widely tipped as a future Prime Minister of England. He had been a member of the Cabinet at the time that the Scutari hospital was opened. He had volunteered to take temporary responsibility for the hospitals out of a personal interest in the subject, to help his colleague the Minister of War. He was, Nightingale now concluded, personally responsible for the loss of an army in those same lethal hospitals. He was her intimate friend Sidney Herbert, who was now the President of her Royal Commission.

By our standards it was not his fault. But Nightingale was a harsh judge, and part of her outrage was due to her discovery that England was being ruled by people who were not familiar with modern science and who made no attempt to consult those who were. Herbert was a perfect example of this type of politician. To him, good intentions and a social conscience were the essential qualifications for a role in government. Herbert's biographer Lord Stanmore was a privileged observer as well as an equally ingenuous participant in the system of aristocratic rule that brought Sidney Herbert into Government, and his memoir of Herbert is all the more revealing because of its author's uncritical acceptance of the system. The biographer himself was a part of this system; he was the son of Lord Aberdeen whose Government had resigned in the face of Parliamentary criticism of its handling of the war. Herbert had been a Minister in Aberdeen's Government, and his biographer Lord Stanmore was at the time both an MP and his father's Parliamentary secretary.

From other evidence as well as from Lord Stanmore's account, Sidney Herbert appears to have been unworldly, to put it mildly. Take this example of Herbert's examination of the Director-General of the Army Medical Department on the first day of the Royal Commission's sittings:

> *Director-General:* I wish to keep up the competitive examination [for medical officers] though I fear it will not be practicable, as eight candidates have withdrawn since the questions put at a late examination were published.
> *Herbert:* Why?
> *D-G:* I suppose they thought that they were too severe.
> *Herbert:* They could not be too severe if they knew what they were?
> *D-G:* But they did not. I do not put forward the questions that are to be asked at forthcoming examinations.[9]

It takes a high degree of unworldliness to presume, as Herbert seemed to do, that the Department would use exactly the same questions year after year in a competitive examination as if it were a driving test. According to Lord Stanmore's account, Herbert's own experience of competitive examinations while at Oxford University had been limited: 'Sidney Herbert had originally intended to take honours, and had read for them; but he was induced, as his University course drew on, to desist from their pursuit, and took an ordinary degree in 1832. His health was at no time of his life strong, and it proved unequal to the strain imposed on it by severe study.'[10]

Herbert was the second son of Lord Pembroke. His older brother, Lord Herbert, had contracted an unwise marriage with a Sicilian lady and lived abroad. Sidney became wealthy himself as a result of a bequest of large estates in Shropshire and Ireland. He made a financial arrangement with his absent brother under which Sidney became the master of the ancestral home at Wilton, one of the finest in England. As a young man Sidney Herbert was renowned for his charming manners and his physical grace. It was for these qualities, in addition to his aristocratic birth, that he was regarded as a potential ruler of the nation even while he was still at Oxford. Stanmore quotes from 'a periodical of the day' which interviewed Herbert in his rooms at Oriel College and, with a sarcasm so polished that it seems to have been lost on Lord Stanmore, recorded how little the future ruler was aware of modern approaches to government: 'Sidney Herbert's features and complexion are almost of feminine delicacy, and he is tall and slender almost to fragility . . . We ask of his studies, as one who almost of necessity must bear a part, more or less influential, in the public affairs of this great commercial country. He points to Herodotus, to the Nichomachean ethics, and smilingly to Mr Newman's earliest sermons, and to a new edition of Wordsworth. Adam Smith and James Watt, trade, colonies, and commerce, have no place in that room.'[11]

When Herbert first became a Cabinet Minister at the age of thirty five, the political diarist Greville was dismissive: 'Sidney Herbert and Lord Lincoln come into the Cabinet . . . Sidney Herbert is a smart young fellow, but I remember no instance of two men who had distinguished themselves so little in Parliament being made Cabinet Ministers.'[12] Three years later, Greville was even more dismissive: 'Lincoln has turned out worth a dozen Sidney Herberts.' This was the man whom everybody agreed would one day be Prime Minister of England. His suitability for this post lay in his ability to fit into any of the coalitions which were common at that time, because he had no enemies and no preconceived ideas or ideology other than a social conscience. A well known contemporary description of him has been widely misunderstood in this context. 'He was just the man to rule England. Birth, wealth, grace, tact, and not too much principle'. Some have interpreted the last words to mean 'unprincipled', but this is almost the exact opposite of what the speaker intended. The comment was a genuine compliment, reflecting on Herbert's open-mindedness. Nobody who knew him could possibly have called him unprincipled. He had no enemies, it may be true, but there were those who were envious. The man had too much. In addition to 'birth, wealth, grace, tact' there was one of the most magnificent stately homes in England and a ravishingly beautiful wife who was besotted with him. And what had he ever done to deserve any of it?

There is some of this envy, surely, in the comment made by an acquaintance of Herbert when Herbert's health began visibly to fail: 'How can a man like you get so ill? If I could lead your life I would live 1000 years, and never have a headache.'[13] This was a remark of awful cruelty, because Herbert's protracted and fatal illness must have manifested itself within days of Nightingale telling him that she now held him personally responsible for the death of 16,000 men. Within a very short time she would find another whom she held even more responsible, but that could not absolve Herbert. The spark of life within him had died, though he worked on like an automaton for four more years.

Nightingale's obsession with tracking down those responsible for losing the first army sent to the East in 1854 was a product of the times as much as a personal crusade. Armies had been lost before, usually from the same causes, but the social and economic cost of such a calamity had recently escalated as a result of changes in society which the military authorities had not noticed. Nightingale, in the confidential report she was writing for the Cabinet, exhumed the old reports from the Peninsular War and showed that troops who were billeted indoors in comfort died in great numbers while those who shivered beneath the stars usually lived. There had been no attempt at the time to find out why.

What had changed was that by 1854 the army was no longer made up of 'the scum of the earth, enlisted for drink' as the Duke of Wellington is reputed to have said with memorable objectivity fifty years before. At the time Wellington made that remark, men enlisted for at least twenty years, and the army was a dumping ground for those who had no hope of gainful employment. By the 1850s such people had become rarer, and a new form of enlistment – Limited Service Enlistment – made the army an attractive opportunity for young men temporarily at a loose end and wishing to see a bit of the world. The politician responsible for the Limited Service Act was Lord Panmure, the man who later sent civilians to the East to investigate the army. It was an earlier step in his plan to integrate the army into civilian life, contrary to the philosophy of the Duke of

Wellington. The main opponent of the Limited Service Act in Parliament had been none other than Sidney Herbert.

The men who died in their thousands on the floors of the eastern hospitals were therefore a loss to the economy of Victorian England in a way that earlier generations of soldiers had not been. One of Nightingale's nurses described a typical one of them: 'Charles was a lad pretty well educated, the son of a Berwickshire farmer who died before his children were settled in life or provided for. He went to London to seek employment; failing to find it he wrote home saying that rather than hang about idle, or return to be a burden on his mother, he would enlist as a private.' He died at Scutari in February 1855. Such men were part of the mobile labour force of the new industrial economy, and the country felt the loss even more sharply than the sum of individual bereavements. It was this communal loss that Nightingale tried to represent when she spoke of 'my 18,000 children.'[14]

The author's great-grandfather was one of that generation of footloose and careless youths from whom the Crimean army was drawn. Driven from his Devon home by poverty at the age of nineteen, he 'took salt water for it' – went to sea – instead of joining the army like so many others. At the beginning of 1855 he was digging for gold in Australia while the corpses were piling up at Scutari. After detouring through India and China he settled in a new country as a farmer, and died leaving enough property to fund his grandson's return to London to qualify as a surgeon. Had he gone to London instead of Plymouth, there is a good chance he would have ended up dead on the floor of a hospital in Turkey.

Nightingale wanted the country to know why so many young men had died. She wanted the country to know that they had been guinea-pigs in one of the most perfect imaginable experiments, the results of which proved that Farr, Chadwick, and the 'sanitarians', as they later became known, were right. The reason for early mortality in all walks of life was defective building cleanliness. Her confidential report to War Minister Panmure, nearing completion, analysed the results of the dreadful experiment at Scutari. She wanted Sidney

Herbert to accept this report as her written evidence before the Royal Commission, and print it in full in the Commission's public report.

Her confidential report was being privately printed for submission to the Government during July 1857 as the Royal Commission heard its final witnesses. Nightingale was overwhelmed by stress and paperwork, and had acquired a rather unusual part-time secretary: Arthur Clough, her cousin's husband, a young man whose early brilliance had led disappointingly to a number of complicated poems and a clerical job in the Civil Service. Clough was in the Lake District during July, exchanging proofs of her confidential report with Nightingale and her printers. On 14 July his letter to her contained the advice: 'if you want to present it [your confidential report] in time for the Commissioners to get it from Lord Panmure, it must be thus, I think.'[15] The only reason she needed Lord Panmure to release her report must have been that she wanted the Commission to publish it. The report, entitled 'Notes on Matters affecting the Health, Efficiency, and Hospital Administration of the British Army, Founded Chiefly on the Experience of the late War,' was a confidential report to the War Minister, and Lord Panmure would have to release it to the Commission.

None of Nightingale's biographers mentions this letter of Clough's, which is not in the Nightingale papers and which supports the view that she wanted the Government to publish her confidential report and reveal the gruesome secret of Scutari. Some of her biographers erroneously state that her evidence as published and her confidential report are identical. This is the case with Professor Smith, who uses this claim to justify his conclusion that she *defeated* Herbert's attempts to suppress her confidential report.[16] Others say that her published evidence is a summary of her confidential report, but they do not say that the most controversial part is omitted – the data which shows that sending patients to Scutari was to send them to their deaths. Woodham-Smith maintains that Nightingale *pretended* that her report to the Government remained confidential, as a way of creating more interest in it.[17] But Woodham-Smith's theory fails to explain why Nightingale took action to stop a scheme to publish it in America, or why she refused members of the public who wrote to her printers asking to buy a copy. Since she herself was obviously eager to see the report widely diffused, the only reason for her acting to limit public circulation in this way must have been that she could not betray the Government she served by allowing her confidential report to become completely public.

Herbert did not want to publish her data on the higher mortality at Scutari. He thought that if hospital cleanliness was the key lesson to be learned, she should limit her evidence to the subject of future hospital construction. For safety's sake, he wanted her to submit written answers to agreed written questions. She wrote a letter rejecting this proposal, and this letter has never been published in full, apparently because it has defied explanation: 'Dear Mr Herbert, I have really tried to write questions for my own examination as you directed and I cannot. I feel thus:

1. I am quite as well aware as you can be that it is inexpedient and even unprincipled to go back into past delinquencies.

2. What is more, I feel for you who were victimised by a System, which you could not possibly understand, till you saw its results.

3. But it would be equally untrue and unconscientious for me to give evidence upon an indifferent matter like that of hospital construction and leave untouched the great matters which will affect the mortality of our sick (and have affected them) far more than any architectural plan could do.'

These opening paragraphs show that she considered Sidney Herbert's ignorance of the 'system' to be a mitigating factor but not a sufficient reason for her to keep silent. Nightingale wrote an almost identical letter to her close confidant McNeill in which she referred to the unnamed accused person as 'he', showing that she was referring to Herbert himself and not his Government collectively. Woodham-Smith omitted the second, accusatory, paragraph when printing the letter to McNeill, while Cope printed it but claimed that the paragraph refers to Dr Hall. The letter sent to Herbert shows that she cannot be referring to Hall. All previous biographers believe that Nightingale was justly, if vindictively, blaming Hall throughout her

Royal Commission, probably because Hall's brutality on the chloroform issue made him such a convenient villain. They have not
analysed her exchange with Lord Grey which shows that she decided
that Hall, villain or not, was innocent because doctors should never
be asked to judge the cleanliness of buildings. The inescapable
conclusion was that the new suspect was the Minister who allowed
Hall to do so – Sidney Herbert. She went on to explain to Herbert
why she could not remain quiet: 'People, Government, and
Sovereign all think that these matters have been remedied while I
think that nothing has been done. It would be treachery to the
memory of my dead if I were to allow myself to be examined on a
mere scheme of hospital construction. My only object in proposing
to give in my Report (in my Examination) was that nobody would
read it or if any did, he might take or leave what he liked.'

The meaning of the last sentence above appears to be that unless
the Royal Commission printed her previously confidential report as
public evidence, the Government would be free to ignore the inconvenient parts of it. Finally, she threatened to boycott the
Commission if he refused to let her tell the whole truth: 'The only
question is: what can be done to prevent a recurrence of the evils
from which we have suffered? And I ought not to consent to be
examined on anything less – though I would much rather not be
examined at all.'[18]

The Royal Commission did not print her confidential report as
evidence in their public report. Of course, they could not have done
so unless and until the War Minister agreed to remove its confidential
status. Perhaps Lord Panmure had originally intended to do so;
perhaps the Cabinet had requested it as a hedge against failure to
secure a royal commission. But it seems unlikely that Panmure could
have foreseen that Nightingale would turn her confidential report
into such a deadly missile. He must have been awe-struck at the sight
of the missile heading towards its chosen target – his long-time political rival Sidney Herbert and the previous Government in which
Herbert had served. Nightingale's report completely vindicated,
though she did not yet realise it, the policies of Panmure the War

Minister whom she still despised. It showed that the up-to-date civilian expertise that Panmure was so keen to introduce in the army might easily have prevented the disaster. Her report was never published, though twelve months later she sent copies of it to a number of distinguished people, each time with a covering letter containing strict instructions not to let anyone else see it or even to leave it lying around. After the deaths of the recipients, these copies found their way into specialised libraries and created the false impression that it had been published after all.

Herbert may have argued that suppression of Nightingale's account of the disaster at Scutari was necessary to protect the new public enthusiasm for nursing which accompanied the adulation of Nightingale in the press, in ballads, pictures, memoirs, poetry, and works of fiction. With such a reputation working for her, he would have argued, there was no limit to the amount of good that Nightingale could do in opening up the nursing profession. To expose the futility of her work at Scutari would not only cause unnecessary pain to the families of those who had died, but also destroy both Nightingale's reputation and the new freedom of educated women to seek respectable employment.

Nightingale now seemed to care precisely nothing for the survival of hospital nursing as a profession. Scutari had convinced her that nursing improvements were an irrelevance. Facilitating female careers in nursing was a sub-optimisation that addressed the wrong part of the problem. Her most fiery and popular book *Notes on Nursing*, written soon afterwards, was in fact propaganda directed *against* doctors, hospitals, and hospital nursing. Her reputation as the merciful angel of Scutari and as the founder of secular hospital nursing was no longer an embarrassment to her, it was a devilishly cruel and macabre joke at her expense. The Nightingale Fund, which she held in trust for training hospital nurses, had become a monster that terrified her. She tried unsuccessfully to resign from the Fund and then turned her back on its Nightingale Training School, behaviour that has puzzled previous biographers who are unaware of the reasons for her 1857 change of heart.

[114]

The quarrel between Herbert and Nightingale over the suppression of the evidence was to have devastating results for both of them. Witnessing Nightingale's anguish may also have been too much for her secretary Arthur Clough, whose health went into rapid and fatal decline shortly afterwards. Clough was not a worshipper of Nightingale, but there must have been a strange affinity between them judging from his frequent use of intense water imagery in his poems. Running water is the bloodstream of any sanitary system, and Nightingale's later work on India revolved around securing water supplies. One of Clough's more simple and pessimistic poems, summarising his disillusion with the intellectual pursuits that were his whole life, even seemed to equate futile intellectual effort with defective plumbing, through its image of 'broken cisterns':

> *Away, haunt not thou me,*
> *Thou vain philosophy!*
> *Unto thy broken cisterns wherefore go,*
> *When from the secret treasure-depths below,*
> *Wisdom at once, and Power,*
> *Are welling, bubbling forth, unseen, incessantly?*
> *Why labour at the dull mechanic oar,*
> *When the fresh breeze is blowing.*
> *And the strong current flowing,*
> *Right onward to the Eternal Shore?*[19]

An intimate exposure to Nightingale's problems in the summer of 1857 would certainly have weakened Clough's already enfeebled will to row his boat against the current.

Sidney Herbert must have made a compromise with Nightingale because eventually she agreed to give evidence to the Royal Commission that avoided blaming him or his former Government. It was not simply that Nightingale took pity on her old friend, because the tone of their letters thereafter show that their former intimacy did not survive. It seems that Herbert must have promised that he would devote his political reputation to her objectives if she agreed to limit her public evidence. She referred to some kind of obligation in a letter to Sir John McNeill a few months later: 'Sidney Herbert is the most sensitive of men on the subject of his personal obligations, this gives me a hold over him.'

The Royal Commission entirely suppressed Farr's comparative analysis of hospitals and Nightingale's conclusions. In the Commission's final report there was only one mention of the excess deaths at Scutari compared to other hospitals. That was in a quite irrelevant written response to a question asking Nightingale how she would organise a general hospital. Quoting a statement from Sir John Hall that among 442 patients treated at Balaclava hospital the death rate was twelve per month, she wrote: 'If these men had been sent to Scutari, there would have died not twelve but 189'. Herbert reviewed her written evidence before allowing it into the report; either he missed this or thought that the estimate was so outlandish that nobody would understand it. In any case, being a comparison between a single pair of hospitals in a single month it was not as convincing as the full table of regimental comparisons that Nightingale had wanted to include in the written evidence.

Nor did the Army's official *Medical and Surgical History of the British Army*, published in the following year, support Nightingale's allegation of higher mortality at Scutari. The numbers of patients sent by each regiment to Scutari, which convinced Tulloch and Nightingale that her hospitals at Scutari had a higher death rate, have never appeared in any published document and have not, as far as is known, been preserved in any official archive. If Nightingale had not given copies of her confidential report to individuals whom she could trust to preserve it for posterity, we would not know about the secret of Scutari.

Instead of analysing the medical errors of the Crimean War, the Royal Commission's final report dwelt more on the continuing high mortality among soldiers in barracks in peacetime. This was in line with Herbert's plan to focus more on opportunities for future improvement than on the mistakes of the past. It was known that mortality among soldiers in peacetime was higher than among civil-

Florence's sister Parthenope with their mother

Florence's sister Parthenope with their father

Florence Nightingale

Florence Nightingale in old age

Surgeon James Mouat VC, CB

Amy Hughes, author of *Practical Hints on District Nursing*

John Henry Lefroy, Lord Panmure's troubleshooter

Mary Seacole, Crimean nurse and hotelkeeper

Lord Panmure

Colonel Tulloch, Supplies Commissioner

Dr William Farr

Sir John McNeill, Supplies Commissioner

Sidney Herbert

Lord Palmerston

Sir John Simon, the national Superintendent of Health

Elizabeth Davis, the Crimean nurse

ians; there was no agreement on how to account for it. Various explanations were possible including immoral behaviour, alcohol, smoking, and idleness. It was only when they discovered the real cause of the huge mortality at Scutari that Farr and Nightingale could argue convincingly that the same cause – bad sanitation in the crowded barracks – accounted for the high peacetime mortality.

The Commissioners' report affirmed that bad sanitation was causing unnecessary deaths in barracks in peacetime. But it did not quote the results of the Scutari 'experiment' to justify this conclusion, even though it was the strongest possible evidence. Instead, the Commission relied on the less convincing evidence that most of the deaths in peacetime were due to respiratory diseases. The Commissioners discussed the mortality at Nightingale's hospital at Scutari not by comparing it to that at other hospitals, but by comparing it 'before and after' sanitary improvements were made, using the difference to push for similar improvements in barracks.

Herbert did agree to include in the report a diagram that Nightingale had produced with Dr Farr's help to illustrate the high mortality at Scutari. This diagram was carefully constructed to convey only the main 'before and after sanitary improvements' message. It consists of two polygons, one swollen with preventable deaths covering the first year of the war, and the other much smaller covering the period after the Sanitary Commission did its work. This diagram, which she referred to as the 'bat's wing' from its shape, revealed nothing about the relative mortality in different hospitals. It also avoided using a left-to-right time series approach that would have emphasised that the disaster began *after* Nightingale's arrival. Farr obviously knew the truth; he sent several variations of the diagrams to Herbert with the comment: 'Miss Nightingale kindly promises to place these diagrams in your hands. They throw a terrible light on the seat of her labours – which surpasses all I had imagined. I suspect that a Defoe could scarcely bring it home to our minds.'[20] Afterwards he enjoyed a long professional relationship with Nightingale during which both of them were perpetually in hot water with the medical establishment for their criticism of hospitals. Farr's finest hour came when he managed to coax his most advanced life table – the English Life Table No. 3 – out of one of the very few working machines ever to be built using the principles of Thomas Babbage's Difference Engine. He thus became the first person to calculate and print a table of numbers with a computer, to meet demand from the life insurance industry.

Farr later may have had reason to regret that Nightingale's confidential report was suppressed, and specifically that an attempt to publish it in America was thwarted. 'Had the conclusions which Florence Nightingale reached been heeded in the Civil War in America, hundreds of thousands of lives might have been saved,' wrote one expert many years later when referring to the confidential report.[21] One of Farr's sons, Frederick, ran away to America and joined the Union army in the Civil War. He fought at Gettysburg but then wrote to his father asking for his help in getting out. Not being particularly well-connected, Farr tried to enlist the help of medical colleagues in America, to no avail. The boy died in the closing days of the war of fever caught in an army hospital.[22]

The events immediately following the censoring of Nightingale's evidence to the Royal Commission are not well documented. The archive material is much sparser and does not allow us to follow her evolving thought as it does during her gradual discovery of the causes of Crimean mortality. The nature of the compromise she reached with Herbert can only be guessed at in the light of subsequent events. For example, she may have agreed never to allow her findings to be published, but in terms that did not prevent her from privately circulating it after a period of twelve months had elapsed. Just as she initially blamed Hall and then moved on to blame Herbert when the limits of Hall's responsibility became apparent to her, so she may have decided that the trail did not stop at Herbert. Without any written evidence all that can be said is that much of what came later can be explained by her discovery of another guilty party. It may even be that Herbert defended himself by casting blame on this other person. It might not have been very chivalrous, but he might with some justification have told Nightingale that he had done what was necessary to ensure the success of his hospital plan.

Herbert had, after all, selected an expert to implement his ill-thought-out vision of a general hospital remote from the battlefields. A person who was to be present on the spot, equipped with a regional intelligence network covering all the hospitals in the war zone, and who reported directly to the Minister of War in London. A person who was one of the world's recognised experts in hospital management, not just an impractical philanthropist. In charge, trained for the job, and equipped with unprecedented powers, there was one person who could have made the whole Scutari experiment a success. It was this person, she seems to have concluded, whose shortcomings had caused the loss of an army. This person, of course, was Florence Nightingale.

Nightingale was an objective analyst, and if she blamed herself it was probably because she found logical reasons to do so, although she may have exaggerated their importance. There are a number of reasons why she might have blamed herself for the epidemic at Scutari that began around the same time that she arrived. It reached its peak in January 1855, two months later, when over 1000 men were dying each month from diseases which, she later claimed, they contracted in her hospital. In the single month of January, more than ten per cent of the entire army died of disease, most of them in front of Nightingale's eyes.

It is unlikely that she would have blamed herself for not knowing that clean air was necessary to health. Few people held this belief at the time, and she had little experience of such things before the war. There is no evidence of a mania for environmental cleanliness before she met Farr. Much later in life she reflected on Pastor Fleidner's institution at Kaiserwerth where she had her first experience of hospital work in 1851, and referred to the hygiene there with hindsight as 'horrible'. A review of Nightingale's letters home from Scutari in January and February 1855 when the epidemic was at its peak shows that her endless and justified complaints and requests for action included no comment on any need for improvements in ventilation or drainage. But there was no reason why she should associate these matters with the symptoms that she observed; neither did she have any training or experience that would cause her to question the doctors' claim that the men were already dying when they entered the hospital. (This, incidentally, is still the army doctors' claim, reasserted as recently as 1974.)

With hindsight her expansion of her Barrack Hospital must have seemed to her ill advised. She persuaded some of the medical officers to join her in a plan to renovate some disused parts of the building, and when the construction ran into funding difficulties she paid for it herself. This increased the number of patients exposed to the hospital's defects, just in time to raise the epidemic to its peak, and she could never be sure if the end result had been to increase the mortality. She could have made the workmen drill holes in the roof instead, as Sutherland later did, but here again she should logically feel regret rather than guilt.

She had also put pressure on Lord Raglan to send more patients to Scutari instead of leaving them in primitive hospitals at the front where, as she later found out, more of them would have lived. She applied this pressure by opposing his requests for nurses to be sent to the other general hospitals. When she was overruled and the nurses did go, she called it 'a mistake' and refused to supervise them, as we have seen in the account by Mrs Davis. This was a part of her plan to centralise the hospitals and the nursing service, and reflected her desire to bring more patients under her undeniably superior standard of nursing care. But it was a sub-optimisation, because her superior nursing could not make up for the worse state of her hospital. When Raglan decided in May 1855 to stop sending patients to her, she was upset. Analysing this objectively after the war, it is unlikely that she would consider it to be a major contributor to the disaster because her protests did not, after all, stop the nurses from deserting to the hospitals nearer the front. Part of her reason for not co-operating with hospitals at the front was that her authority in those hospitals was not clearly defined, and she naturally preferred not to have any confrontation that she was not assured of winning.

During the war she needed to know that she had official support in whatever she did. In later life she made almost a fetish of demonstrating that she could assert her authority with no official support or status whatsoever.

Her wartime failure to exploit the energy and drive of the maverick nurses who did desert to the front – some of them immoral, intemperate, and even possibly insane – as part of a distributed system of hospital control was one of the missed opportunities during the war. It was another lesson that she was to put to great use later. The most obvious use that she could have made of the nurses in the outposts during the war was in the collection of information, for example mortality statistics that after a few weeks would have revealed why and where the men were dying. Her later obsession with mortality statistics shows that this omission must have tormented her, but she never tried to hide the evidence of her blunder. In several documents that she preserved (including the notes of her first visit to Farr's General Registry Office quoted earlier)[23] she bemoans the absence of army mortality statistics when in fact they existed all the time! As she found out later, Colonel Tulloch collected a comprehensive set of them covering the months when the tragedy was occurring under her nose, and it was these statistics that later allowed Farr to diagnose the cause.

Colonel Tulloch got his statistics from the army in the field simply by asking. He admits that he had no authority to ask for such information, as he was supposed to be investigating the supplies, but he was a seasoned sleuth and realised that he could exploit the desire of one part of the organisation to expose the inadequacies of another part. The doctors were claiming that the army was creating too much work for them by treating the soldiers too harshly, and they were prepared to give him what they thought was evidence of this: 'At a very early stage of our enquiry,' wrote Tulloch, 'we saw the necessity, before venturing on any report as to the suffering of the troops from the non-distribution of the supplies, that the extent of the sickness and the mortality during the previous winter should be carefully examined. It is true we had no authority for this extension

[121]

of our enquiries, but it appeared absolutely requisite to test the allegations against the army officers by numerical evidence. The medical officers supplied the information readily, as affording one of the best evidences of their unparalleled exertions, and of the difficulties they had to contend with.'[24]

These medical statistics had been regularly kept at regimental level since before Nightingale's arrival, and if she had used the same method of enquiry she could have discovered them in time to act immediately.

Worse, Tulloch makes it clear that it was the failure of Nightingale's Scutari hospital to send mortality statistics to Nightingale's nominal superior in the Crimea that prevented the authorities at that end from discovering that they were shipping men off to almost certain death. 'It is one of the most serious considerations connected with the history of this period,' Tulloch wrote, 'that the loss by disease was at first much underestimated. For several months, no accurate or complete returns appear to have been received from Scutari, to show what had become of the invalids sent there. It was only by degrees that the small proportion who returned, of those who had left the Crimea sick, awakened a suspicion of the fatal character of the diseases, and of the extent to which the constitution of the troops had suffered by the hardships and privations they had undergone. Had it even been surmised by the principal medical and military authorities that the loss in that army averaged about a battalion every week by disease alone, measures would have been adopted to check it.'[25]

Tulloch meant by this that if the staff at Scutari had informed their superiors in the Crimea of the death rate at Scutari, the authorities would have stopped the flow of patients one way or another. Tulloch did not suspect that the hospitals themselves were fatal, but that made his criticism even more pointed. He published this criticism in January 1857 when Nightingale was just starting her statistical analysis, and he had no intention of pointing the finger at Nightingale. As nursing superintendent, it may not have been Nightingale's job to inform her superiors in the Crimea of the death rate. But then, neither does it seem to have been anyone else's job, and Nightingale was probably the only person in the hospital who didn't believe in this excuse for inaction. She *did* have the necessary statistical skills, because she had insisted on studying mathematics against the wishes of her family. Even before the war she had admired the work of the statistician Quetelet, and on her own initiative she had collected data from different hospitals throughout Europe. This one omission of hers would probably have been enough to convince her that she was partly to blame for the disaster, although there may have been other reasons that we do not know. Even without such reasons, she must have suffered extreme anguish when she had to admit that her patients had died from causes that she had been denying for two years. Her father had made her a proud woman, and now the scale of her humiliation was grotesque.

Lord Raglan, the well-meaning but incompetent Commander-in-Chief, died in the Crimea a few days after a failed attempt to capture Sebastopol that cost many lives and never stood a chance of success. Medical men nowadays attribute his death to cholera, but Florence Nightingale was convinced that he died of depression resulting from this last failure, aggravated by his refusal to openly show his feelings. 'I could never return to England now' he is reputed to have said, 'They would stone me to death.'[26] After 1857 Florence Nightingale's shame appears to have been far greater than Raglan's. If shame caused his death then she only survived because she was young and strong, while Raglan was a frail old man of 67 who could not hope to live long enough to redeem himself.

The shame of facing her family would have been the worst for her, particularly her father and sister. Her mother was less important. Totally ignorant of what was going on, Fanny Nightingale had watched awe-struck as grandees like the Duke of Newcastle called at the Burlington Hotel to see her daughter. 'These men seem to make her opinions their law,' she wrote to Florence's father,[27] unaware of how many great political reputations lay in the palm of her daughter's hand when she was obsessively tracking down those responsible for the martyrdom of the common soldier. It is not clear whether

[123]

her mother ever found out the truth about Florence's humiliation by the findings of her own Royal Commission. But her father and sister were another matter. Parthe had crowed to the world during and after the war how holy and dedicated her sister was, but only a year before the war she derided Florence's nursing ambitions: 'I believe she has little or none of what is called charity or philanthropy,' wrote Parthe about Florence to a mutual friend. 'She is ambitious – very – and would like to regenerate the world with a grand *coup de main* or some fine institution, which is a very different thing. Here she has a circle of admirers who cry up everything she does or says as gospel. It is the intellectual part which interests her, not the manual. When she nursed me everything which intellect and kind intention could do was done but she was a shocking nurse. Whereas her influence on people's minds and her curiosity in getting into varieties of minds is insatiable, after she has got inside they generally cease to have any interest for her.'[28]

And now the sister who could write those terrible words was breathing down Florence's neck and learning her innermost secrets, despite Florence's desperate attempts to keep her away from London. Parthe had copied out the anguished letter that Florence had written to McNeill when she had first discovered what had really killed her patients. Parthe must have understood the implications of her sister's discovery. Did Parthe tell their father? He must have found out, one way or another. How could Florence bear to face him? The man who had raised her with infinite care to be something in the world, to compensate for his lack of wordly success. The man who was happy to live in her shadow, who had written to her so openly of his attempt to exploit her fame to get himself elected to Parliament. That good man who had called her, with innocent and transparent pride, 'you, my only genius.'

All her life she had been trying to prove that her mother and sister were wrong; that she could create a secular female nursing profession. All her life she had been trying to impress her father, to reward him for the support he had given her against them. She had written to her parents in her hour of triumph announcing that she had suc-

[124]

ceeded: 'If my name and having done what I could for God and mankind has given you pleasure that is real pleasure to me. I shall love my name now. Life is sweet after all' And, to her sister: 'I have done my duty. I have identified my fate with that of the heroic dead. It has been a great cause.'

It was a proud young woman who had written these words. It would be hard to find a more severe case of *hubris*. But however great was her sin of pride, no human heart could possibly have dreamed up the dreadful punishment that she now had to suffer: a crushing burden of shame that seemed to be designed with exquisite cruelty for her alone. She collapsed mentally and physically around the 20 August, 1857, three weeks after giving her evidence to the Royal Commission in its closing days. There is a gap in the surviving family papers at this time, and no details survive of the scenes that must have taken place at the Burlington Hotel. Whatever happened there seems to have permanently frightened Parthe back into her wits. It is not hard to imagine what kind of outburst Florence may have unleashed against her sister in her agony. We must be grateful that the gap in the records prevents us from intruding on these scenes.

Usually the subject of a biography dies at the end of the book, but it is easier to make sense of Florence Nightingale by imagining that the woman we have been reading about died here, aged thirty-seven. A large part of her did die in the Burlington Hotel on that quiet August day, just after the Royal Commission had ended its frantic three months of activity, Parliament had gone into recess, and the politicians had deserted London for their country estates.

There have been many problems trying to reconcile her statements and actions before and after her breakdown, usually leading to charges of 'inconsistency' against her. One of these so-called inconsistencies of the early post-Royal Commission period is her withering remark about doctors, made to Sidney Herbert in 1859: 'As for doctors civil and military there must be something in the smell of medicine which renders absolute administrative incapacity. And it must be something very strong for they all have an opportunity to develop administrative capacity, almost more than in any other profession.'[29] If she had so little confidence in doctors, it has been said, why did she appoint four of them to positions on the Council of the Nightingale Fund in 1856? The answer is that she put them on the Council *before* she found out, during the Royal Commission, that doctors have feet of clay.

When she first went to Scutari she had gone to extreme lengths to submit, at least in appearance, to the medical staff. She threatened her nurses with instant dismissal if they attended to a patient before being ordered to do so by the doctors. After 1857, there was a complete reversal of this: she insisted that army nurses must report not to the medical officers but direct to the Minister of War.[30] For her this was non-negotiable. She had discovered that the doctors were a part of the problem. These 'inconsistencies' show that trying to use a biographical portrait of Nightingale up to 1857 as a guide to her later life is like trying to find your way around London using a 200-year old map. All the major inconsistencies in her life occur on either side of the August 1857 divide.

After that date, Nightingale seems to have suffered very badly from repressed feelings of guilt. This guilt was worse than the 'survivor syndrome' which diminishes the feelings of self-worth of someone who survives a major tragedy. It must have come from the feeling that her negligence and arrogance had contributed to the loss of the army, possibly compounded by a realisation that she had at first refused to admit to the truth and had then unwisely agreed to a cover-up, thus betraying three times 'her murdered men.'

Although she destroyed many documents from this period it is not likely that they would have contained any expression of guilt. She probably could not put her feelings into words, at least in the first decade or so. A failure to articulate such feelings would give them a tremendous power as a driving force in her life. What can't be talked about can only be – and must be – acted upon. Assuaging her guilt through action became an obsession.

Many different explanations for her collapse after the Royal Commission have been advanced over the years, and Nightingale's own explanation for it is itself revealing. She believed that the trigger for her breakdown was her family. Her mother and sister were persecuting her, following her to London, lodging in the same hotel, and pretending to help her with the Royal Commission while in fact obstructing her work. They had always obstructed her, had never loved her, and now they were trying to claim credit for making her famous. If they had only left her alone during the Royal Commission she 'could have waded through'. 'What have my mother and sister ever done for me? They like my glory, they like my pretty things. Is there anything else they like in me?' Most significant of all, it was her sister's ungrateful and spiteful behaviour that had caused 'the disease which is now bringing me to my grave'.[31]

Any thirty-seven year old woman who has been running a vast nursing empire, has seen thousands of men die unnecessarily in front of her eyes and has become a national heroine would find it difficult to convince an impartial observer that the attitudes of her mother and sister, however neurotic, were sufficient to ruin her health and happiness. She was placing the entire blame for her situation on people whose only crime was their genetic closeness to her. They had created her, or were near-copies of her. Such irrational hatred of those who are genetically closest appears to be consistent with repressed self-loathing.

This diagnosis that Nightingale suffered from repressed guilt explains some of her later behaviour. Her later writings are consistent with it. First, she had a habit of omitting all references to the Crimean War whenever she – rarely – praised her own achievements. Second, she punished herself with what was virtually a sentence of life imprisonment beginning in the weeks after the end of the Royal Commission. 'Last month,' she wrote in September 1861, 'makes four years that I have been imprisoned by sickness.' Third, she further developed her religious beliefs to excuse the errors of philanthropists, holding that a well-intentioned mistake will always be turned to the benefit of mankind. And finally, as we shall see when we look at her working methods, she adopted a completely new leadership style, characterised by one over-riding feature: if she had used the same approach at Scutari, the disaster would never have happened. She was like a general who loses a battle and, realising with hindsight how he could have won it, spends the rest of his life trying to find an enemy with whom to fight the same battle over again to achieve the correct result.

On 21 August, Florence fled from London to the spa town of Malvern. On the 25 August she wrote a short note from Malvern to her family saying she was glad to be alone. When Dr Sutherland wrote to her telling her not to work too hard, a letter flew back bizarrely accusing him of being in league with her sister Parthe. Somehow she got control of herself again. The mental turmoil subsided as she began work at Malvern on the sequel to the Royal Commission – designing a number of committees with executive powers to reform army administration. Her condition stabilised.

The secret remedy was undoubtedly her father's teachings. As she had said to Lord Raglan: 'My father's religious and social ethics make us strive to be the pioneers of the human race.' In particular, she formed the protective notion that what had happened to her was not a catastrophe but rather the first small step in God's grand plan for her. 'Mankind creating mankind' is a system of philosophy that forgives and even requires all mistakes. Her use of this mental construction to convert her disaster into a consolation and a strength is an impressive testimony to the power of human thought. In her analysis, God could not have been wrong to send an ignorant woman to Scutari. Sooner or later, someone with a sense of duty to Him would have to make the mistake if repetitions were to be stopped. It was not very hard for an imaginative young woman to come to this mystical conclusion, because there was something unearthly about the scale and design of her personal disaster that made it look like the result of a heavenly plan.

Everything had conspired to prevent her from avoiding the tragedy, and to maximise its impact upon her. She had been so *close* to recognising the epidemic for what it was. Only weeks before going to Scutari she had noted in a letter to her sister the new evidence that environmental factors were responsible for disease, and had castigated the Church of England for its futile prayers for deliverance from the cholera epidemic that was then terrorising London: 'You [the Church of England, with which Parthe was more aligned than Florence] pray against "plague, pestilence, and famine", when God has been saying more loudly every day this week that those who live ten feet above a pestilential river will die, and those who live forty feet above will live.'

Her notion that cholera was associated with sewage was not yet widely accepted, even though Dr John Snow proved it just two weeks after she wrote those words by taking the handle off the contaminated Broad Street water pump and stopping the Soho cholera epidemic dead in its tracks. It may seem strange that the woman who held such relatively advanced views could have failed to see three months later that the poisonous gases from the blocked sewers, trapped inside the unventilated Barrack Hospital, were killing her patients by the thousand. But her experience in the London cholera epidemic was of no use to her, because not many of the patients at Scutari died with the unmistakable and dreadful symptoms of cholera.

Destiny also took unfair advantage of her at Scutari by sending her patients with symptoms ghastly enough to distract attention from anything they caught after arriving in her hospital. Many of them were starved and frost-bitten, so that it seemed a miracle that they were alive at all. Their limbs were blackened and mortified; some had lost their hands and feet to frost-bite and their bones protruded from their disintegrating extremities. Long-untended wounds were infested with maggots. It was easy to believe the doctors' view that they were already beyond recovery.

These sufferers whom she failed to rescue were the 'common soldier', an object of veneration to her when she was at Scutari and central to many philanthropists' ideas of social improvement. She was continually in trouble for spending too much time on this brute and not enough on the officers. One of the most hostile senior officers complained to the Commander-in-Chief that she habitually neglected her 'equals or superiors': 'Whatever philanthropy she may have on a great scale, she does not appear to be amiable in ordinary intercourse with her equals or superiors. She likes to *govern* and bestows all her tenderness upon those who *depend* upon her. For instance, she will not give a thought upon any *officer* who may be in the most wretched state.'[32]

'Bestows all her tenderness on those who *depend* on her' seems to have been a serious criticism in those days. In fact, her philosophy made her dependent on *them*, the common soldiers. Now she found that her fate had made her betray them over and over again. But it was even more symbolic than that. For these were not just *any* common soldiers. The men whom fate sent to her hospitals that winter in the last extremities of suffering were the very same men whose bravery and patriotism had astonished the world during the victories of the war's earliest months. They had overwhelmed an impregnable fortress at the Alma, terrifying the Russian defenders with their unflinching acceptance of death and mutilation. They had risen from the grass at Balaclava in what was to become famous as the 'Thin Red Line', and showed that British soldiers were the only infantry in the world who would not yield under pressure when fighting in line rather than in a square. Their line had, incredibly, stopped a Russian heavy cavalry charge without breaking. For maximum effect, these heroic common soldiers had to be consigned to brutal and incompetent officers so that they could be reduced to living wreckage in the trenches and then sent to young Florence Nightingale in a pest-house, to teach her God's laws of hygiene.

No, you wouldn't have to be a religious fanatic to suspect that there had been some intelligence at work here, an intelligence which wanted to make use of Florence Nightingale. Whatever faults she may have had, there could not be a God who could create this much evil just to punish her for a little bit of arrogance. Therefore it must be for a different purpose. And her friend Sidney Herbert, who had made as many mistakes as she had, must also have been part of God's design. Without him, she would not have been sent there to be taught what she had to learn. 'Your mistakes', as he had remarked to her sister a few weeks before leaving for the war, 'are part of God's plan.'

This could have been what she came to believe at Malvern, during her solitary breakdown. This could be how she managed to hide her feelings of guilt from herself. The education that her father had given her was as strong and at the same time as finely wrought as one of those elaborate Victorian steam engines. The image that seems to fit her temporary breakdown best is that of a safety valve that, under the pressure of an unexpected load which prevents the piston moving, opens to release a rush of steam. Then it is as if she ruthlessly slams a steel wedge into the valve. From then on, we can only cringe and wait for the possible explosion as the engine strains silently against the load. Then, bearing testimony to her father's amazing workmanship as an educator, the machinery begins to move.

She refused to allow anyone to come to Malvern to visit her but her father went anyway and forced his way into her room. They had a secret conversation. He was so shaken that he refused to talk about it with anyone. Years later, when her mother insisted that her father explain what happened that week in Malvern, he reluctantly provided a few details. Then he described the scene in her room, which was on the top floor of the house used by a well-known hydropathic doctor, where Florence sat alone, staring out of the window: 'There was a sort of solemn isolation from an outward world,' wrote her father, whose prose style was usually quite down-to-earth. 'There was a room where in the high region of storm and wind she sat alone as it were, looking over the great plain, meditating from her window like one of her own Prophets looking towards Jerusalem. It was a scene fit for the most contemplative of human minds – it was *above* the earth. Its like will not form part of human thought again.' In his account to her mother he recorded only one sentence spoken by Florence to him on that occasion: 'If I had health,' she said quietly 'I should be seeing what was going on in hospitals.'[33] Florence was on the mend.

6

Vengeance

Much of the population of England in the 1850s lived in conditions reminiscent of the Scutari Barrack Hospital in its worst days, and in some districts fewer than half of the children survived their fifth year. The urban poor in particular, lived surrounded by filth on a scale probably unmatched anywhere in the world. The cities, their population swollen by unprecedented commercial success, teemed with horses and other animals and their dungheaps. In 1855 there were twenty six cowsheds in the square mile of the City of London alone, and 266 cows. There were numerous urban workshops making use of every part of an animal's corpse, from the stomach to the skin. Until its repeal in 1851, a tax on windows encouraged the construction of unventilated houses. The towns had few sewers; the well-off had cesspools but many of the poor threw their excrement into ditches or into the street. The viscous remains of human cadavers bulged out of the overloaded church graveyards into the streets and cellars nearby. Piped water supplies were often drawn from the river at the same point the sewage entered it, and the flow was so unreliable that to this day every Englishman keeps a water storage tank in his attic. As late as 1866, a cholera epidemic claimed 18,000 lives in one year.[1]

In the year following Nightingale's breakdown, 1858, London was visited by a man-made calamity known as the Great Stink, when the River Thames proved quite incapable of removing the vast quantity of horrors poured into it. The smell was so bad near the river that railway travellers leaving London Bridge station were seized by attacks of vomiting. These conditions may have had a negative effect on the life expectancy of the general population, but they made a positive contribution to Nightingale's mental health and possibly to her survival. She could distract herself from the contemplation of her defeat at Scutari by throwing herself into the old battles again. Amazingly, the battles at home were the same. First, political interests were preventing further expenditure of public funds on improved sanitation in England, saying that such improvements would not reduce the death rate. Second, the doctors were insisting that the London hospitals should be located where they were convenient for *them*, not for the patients.

These were the first two great issues in civilian public health on which she campaigned after her return, while she was also working for reform of military hygiene. On both of these civilian issues she appeared to suffer defeat. Political influence proved more decisive than rational argument, and Nightingale's political influence in civilian life was not as strong as in the military, where she exerted considerable influence at the War Office through Sidney Herbert. In the civilian public health field she was up against the victorious opponents of Edwin Chadwick. When Parliament retired Chadwick and abolished his Board of Health just a few months before Nightingale went to war, there was an alternative and more politically acceptable national public health leader already waiting in the wings. This was the surgeon and pathologist John Simon, who had risen to prominence in the only piece of England where Chadwick's dictatorial power had never held sway: the City of London.

In 1848, when Chadwick's Board of Health was first established, the City of London had refused to allow its opulent but filthy Square Mile to be incorporated into Chadwick's empire. 'That nasty turtle-eating Corporation' of the City of London, as a contemporary MP described it,[2] had obtained its own Act of Parliament to regulate its sewers independently. To buttress its independence, the City of London Corporation appointed its own salaried Medical Officer, and this was John Simon's first public appointment.

In the City of London appointment and in later ones, Simon easily defeated several other medically qualified candidates who had previously aligned themselves with the Chadwick approach of engineering-led public health. These candidates had publicly criticised the nation's sewage systems and water supplies as dangerous to health, and in so doing had offended vested interests and cut themselves off from the mainstream of their profession as well as spoiling their chances of selection for the City appointment. These medical deserters who had failed to capture the City for Chadwick included both Dr John Sutherland and Dr Hector Gavin, the medical members of the Crimean Sanitary Commission.

Even Dr William Farr, who had convinced Nightingale that 16,000 men had died in her hospitals because of the doctors' ignorance of hygiene, had been a candidate for the 1848 City of London job. Farr withdrew his candidacy early, which was wise in view of the selection committee's contemptuous treatment of Hector Gavin and the fact that Farr, like Gavin, had dared in the past to criticise the Corporation's sewers (cesspools, really) and ally himself with the Chadwick tendency. Farr owed his job at the Registry Office in part to Chadwick, whose most famous contribution to setting up the registry system was the idea of including the cause of death in the returns.

Chadwick's rival John Simon had impeccable political and technical credentials for the City of London appointment. His father was a member of one of the City Livery Companies, and a prominent member of the Committee of the London Stock Exchange. Simon himself was a respected surgeon, and had become a Fellow of the Royal Society at a young age through his research in pathology. He had established a reputation for himself in the City by following the example of William Farr and publishing inspirational and controversial annual reports. When a national Medical Officer of Health was appointed, Simon was the obvious choice.

So after Chadwick's fall his allies saw their official careers blighted. Their one brief resurgence was when Palmerston sent some of them to the Crimea. Not surprisingly, the career doctors attached to the army in the Crimea attacked Sutherland's Sanitary Commission, composed as it was of renegade doctors who had sided with Chadwick. Sutherland's report (unlike that of McNeill and Tulloch into the supplies question) was not published until the war was over, and then with the minimum of publicity. Immediately there broke out a pamphlet war between Sutherland and Sir John Hall, the army's Principal Medical Officer. Hall alleged that the Sanitary Commission had done nothing to reduce the death rate, while Nightingale trumpeted its achievements and Sutherland cautiously claimed partial success. It was the same argument that had raged ten years earlier over Chadwick's schemes. The Crimean experience did not restore the prestige of the Chadwick school; by the time Sutherland's Commission had completed its work, the medical professionals under the leadership of John Simon had seized control of the civilian public health movement and curbed what they perceived to be Chadwick's excesses.

John Simon, during his two decades of leadership of the public health movement, tended to employ medical men on the way up the career ladder of that profession, on a temporary basis, rather than doctors and engineers committed to sanitation of the type favoured by Chadwick. He also spent a significant part of his public funds on medical research and on treatment, and on his own admission regularly blinded his political masters with science to prevent them from controlling him. The low-tech Chadwick school did not prosper during the Simon era. They fitted in as best they could in various underpaid niches of public life, working together loosely in what we might call a sanitary underground.

Simon believed that disease could only be prevented when its causes had been discovered, and he was not convinced that Chadwick had discovered them. The implication of this was that Government should devote resources to medical research rather than prevention. Instead of *compelling* local authorities to clean up the cities, Simon wanted to *persuade* them to do so by using arguments based on superior knowledge obtained through medical research. It would be his highly paid job to acquire and deploy this superior knowledge. His philosophy fitted perfectly with the objectives of medical professionals, and was politically attractive because it did not involve compulsory measures.

Nightingale and the Chadwick school claimed that Simon was pursuing knowledge and 'big science' for its own sake, and that like most medical men Simon was only interested in finding new ways of explaining what the patient had died from. 'What is needed now is not to *know*, but to *do*,' said Nightingale.[3] In 1857 she replaced Chadwick as the spokesperson of the sanitary underground. She had abandoned her loyalty to the doctors and had become, like Dr Sutherland and Dr Farr who had carefully recruited and groomed her for the task, a medical deserter.

Nightingale knew that Chadwick's self-important and intolerant approach had alienated the entire nation and had stalled the compulsory public health movement that Chadwick himself had founded. Chadwick's ideas are now unquestioned, but at the time his opponents were able to attack them on the grounds that they interfered with liberty and commerce. He was also a public relations disaster. He managed to give the impression that his great humanitarian schemes could only work if he was in charge, and he always talked in pounds, shillings, and pence rather than in human terms. With an air of goggle-eyed contempt for their stupidity, he would bore his audiences rigid with theoretical calculations of how his proposed municipal piped water schemes would, by bringing soft water to the cities, save thousands of pounds worth of soap. Only the soap manufacturers would get excited by such calculations, and then in the wrong direction.

Nightingale saw that the way to implement Chadwick's schemes was to remove all trace of the Chadwick approach. A soft, insidious, consensus building was needed, with no authoritarian discipline, no personality cult, and an emphasis on basic human values. To her consternation, the great Edwin Chadwick came to her assistance in publicising the results of her Royal Commission on the health of the army. He insisted on writing an article about army hygiene in an influential magazine. She wrote to Chadwick advising him to leave some things to the reader's own judgement: 'while stating the case and its remedies fully and openly to leave the inferences to us, the readers, as far as possible.' This was the woman who two years before had flung back in Sidney Herbert's teeth the advice he gave her to tone down her despatches, telling her that 'the public like to have something left to their own imaginations and are much pleased with their own sagacity when they have found out what was too obvious to be missed.' She had come a long way since the war. And Nightingale had one further piece of advice for Chadwick when he was drafting his article. She thought that it might be a good idea if the great sanitary leader, twenty years her senior, could for once address his readers 'as if you loved them'.

Her first public clash with Chadwick's rival, the nation's new Medical Officer of Health John Simon, came when Simon publicly supported the claim of his colleague Dr Edward Greenhow that sanitary improvements could not reduce the high mortality from whooping cough, scarlet fever and measles. Nightingale believed that sanitary measures available at the time could prevent many of the deaths from these diseases. She put forward her arguments by publishing repeated attacks on a statement to the contrary that Simon had made in his official 1858 Board of Health report. Both Nightingale's and Simon's biographers have often cited her criticism of Simon's report as evidence that she did not accept the germ theory of disease. A more careful investigation of the controversy does not support this interpretation. Nightingale was quite correct that sanitary measures were effective against the diseases in question, and John Simon was wrong despite the scientific appearance of his arguments. All previous accounts of the quarrel between Simon and Nightingale award victory to Simon. These accounts omit to mention that Simon later altered the records to make it appear that he had never made the statement that she criticised.

Simon and Greenhow's claim first appeared in a June 1858 paper that they submitted to the new Board of Health analysing the causes of death in different districts recorded by the new registration system. Simon maintained in his introduction to the paper that because people died of measles and scarlet fever in every district whether clean or dirty, therefore these diseases are a 'a further – practically speaking, unavoidable – cause of premature death.' Mortality *could* be almost entirely eliminated, they claimed, for those diseases which could be shown to be already entirely absent from some districts, such as cholera, dysentery and typhus which they classed as 'diseases of filth'. Removing the filth would almost eliminate the disease. Simon explained that measles and scarlet fever were, by contrast, diseases in which 'the multiplication of poison takes place exclusively within the human body' rather than depending on the medium outside the body. 'Wherever human beings may cross one another's path, the susceptible person may contract the infection' of whooping cough, measles or scarlet fever.

There was a logical flaw in their argument that, because of this, the high mortality was inevitable. They assumed that if it was inevitable that many people would *catch* the infection (through crossing one another's path) then it was also inevitable that they would *die* from it. In his section of the paper, Simon partially contradicted himself on this point by saying that 'the fatality of these diseases is greatly and evidently proportionate to exterior conditions' such as overcrowding and poor ventilation. But elsewhere in the paper, in describing the mortality as inevitable, Simon ignored this qualification. A clue to his apparent self-contradiction is his use of the word 'science' in the following quotation from the same paper: 'Liability to these infections is a more or less considerable risk which science hitherto cannot avert.'[4] This sums up Simon's view of prevention, which was very different from Nightingale's. His definition of 'preventable' appeared to be that *science* could prevent it. He seemed to believe that overcrowding and poor ventilation were unalterable, but that science would eventually be able to compensate for them.

It was as if Simon dreamed that only scientific discovery would be able to leapfrog over the political obstacles that caused so much trouble when public health officials had tried to improve the dwellings of the poor during the Chadwick era. It was a dream that was to lead to a lifetime's disappointment for John Simon, but it was not an irrational dream, as Pasteur's achievements show. England passed temporary and unpopular laws compelling dog owners to muzzle their pets during the 1880's and 1890's, and succeeded in eliminating rabies in this way. But France did not do so, and used Pasteur's rabies vaccine as an alternative method of control. Simon would have preferred Pasteur's high-tech approach of attacking the disease itself rather than the conditions that produced it. Nightingale, in contrast, believed that public health meant promoting measures that would 'make the public care for its own health'.

Simon's co-author Dr Greenhow, for whom Simon had obtained the post of Lecturer in Public Health at St Thomas's Hospital, used their findings to attack Chadwick's sanitary movement directly. He did so in the pages of *The Builder*, a weekly magazine that represented the commercial and ideological interests of the sanitarians as the *Lancet* did for the doctors. Nightingale wrote for *The Builder*, and she may have contributed a small article which linked the bad drainage in some areas of London to increased mortality from scarlet fever in those areas, and called for sanitary improvements. Dr Greenhow wrote to *The Builder* objecting to the article's description of scarlet fever as a 'preventable disease', and warning against the exaggerated claims of the sanitarians: 'It is so very important that no false expectations of the benefits derivable from sanitary exertions should be raised in the public mind . . . There are, indeed, certain diseases which are not only believed to be preventable, but of which it may be asserted that we can point with considerable confidence to the local conditions by which they are produced. But this does not apply to scarlet fever, the particular disease referred to by your contributor as a preventable disease. No one, so far as I know, has ever been able to trace scarlet fever to any other origin than intercourse, either direct or indirect, with persons already sick with that disease.' The letter concluded that the causes of mortality 'demand much careful investigation, and that, with certain exceptions, such investigation must precede any further progress in the art of preventing disease.'[5] In this he was reiterating Simon's doctrine that 'Disease can only be prevented by those who have knowledge of its causes',[6] and was effectively calling for a halt to sanitary expenditure and a diversion of funds to medical research.

Nightingale's anonymous reply in *The Builder* maintained that scarlet fever epidemics were 'mitigable and preventable; and the lay public, with their present advance of sanitary knowledge, will support this view. The cure for "infection", if there be "infection", is cleanliness and fresh air.'[7] Greenhow replied that he knew of a town where sanitarians had improved the drainage and water supply but scarlet fever had broken out among the children nevertheless. Nightingale's anonymous response was, 'With regard to the appearance of scarlet fever in drained towns, we are not aware that any sanitary reformer ever expected that towns would be put in a good sanitary state solely by drainage and water-supply. These were never considered in any other light than as a basis for improving the dwellings of the working classes. The improvement of the houses in ventilation, lighting, free circulation of air in courts and alleys, diminution of overcrowding &c. have yet to be embodied in Acts of Parliament, or to be carried out by private exertion . . . When these things have been done, and have failed, we shall have time to discuss with Dr Greenhow,' she added in a typically malevolent Nightingale touch, 'the propriety of putting a quarantine on medical men and others coming from infected houses, which is the only logical result of his doctrine.'[8]

To summarise Dr Greenhow's argument: it was that those whom he disdainfully called 'sanitary amateurs' had no 'scientific' proof that better sanitation could reduce scarlet fever mortality, and that since other factors seemed to be involved (i.e. personal contact, but he also claimed family predisposition was a factor), public money should be spent on more research into these factors rather than on more sewers and slum clearance. The scientists had an unshakeable faith that scientific research must in the end yield useful results. The sanitarians had an unshakeable belief that since excretion was the body's way of getting rid of poisons that were an undesirable by-product of the life process, reducing the inhalation or ingestion of the products of excretion must improve health. The argument was over which of these two theories was more deserving of public funds. In the absence of proof, the arguments could go on forever.

Nightingale thought that she *had* proof, in the appendices of her suppressed confidential report. It was at this point, twelve months after her breakdown, that she privately distributed copies of her confidential report 'Notes on Matters affecting the Health of the British Army' which contained unpublished evidence of the public health disaster at Scutari. She sent it to dozens of the leading personalities of the day whom she knew personally. When sending it to medical people, she included a second volume[9] containing a 'Note on Contagion and Infection' in which she attacked Simon's pronouncement of 'inevitable mortality', which was so similar to the fatalistic and self-serving attitude of the doctors at the Scutari hospital. Nightingale claimed that this official pronouncement of the country's chief Medical Officer could be and was being used by the enemies of sanitation to block expenditure on sanitary schemes.

Probably, the need to rebut Simon was the trigger that made her distribute copies of this banned report, which remained confidential to the Government which had never authorised its publication. Apparently she felt she now had the right to distribute it privately as long as she bound the recipients not to pass it on. 'One would have thought,' wrote Nightingale in her 'Note on Contagion' 'that, after the sanitary experience of the last fifteen years, the word "contagion" would have disappeared from our language; but, even in the last document issued by the expiring Board of Health, written by their Medical Officer Mr Simon, and based on erroneous statistical evidence, it is stated that "a further – practically speaking, unavoidable – cause of premature death in every civilised country is the risk of its *current* [meaning 'fast-spreading'] *contagions*". And this refers to whooping-cough, measles, and scarlet fever, the mortality from which we are to presume, is "unavoidable" '.[10]

It seems likely that this 1858 denunciation of Simon and his 'scientific' approach to public health caused ill feeling between Nightingale and the medical profession that persists to this day. Heroic efforts have been made ever since to patch up the quarrel posthumously, so to speak, making use of her earlier service to the medical profession to argue that she shared its goals throughout her life. We now know that Nightingale was right: the mortality from scarlet fever, measles, and whooping cough could, like that from the more obvious 'diseases of filth' be almost eliminated by sanitary measures that were available at the time which she suggested and which Simon and Greenhow opposed.

John Simon reprinted his paper nearly thirty years later and surreptitiously retracted the statement that Nightingale had criticised. Simon and his editor kept the date June 1858 in this reprint, and claimed that 'the revision of the proof sheets by Mr Simon himself has been for the purpose of giving clearer expression to his original meaning and not for the purpose of altering his opinions which were founded upon the existing state of knowledge at the time.' Despite this claim, Simon went much further than merely clarifying his meaning. For example, he deleted some passages in which he had cast doubt on Dr John Snow's then recent discovery of the mechanism by which cholera spread. At the time, he had refused to accept Snow's simple 'unscientific' proof based on observation of the results of different water supplies to different houses. 'We must wait for scientific insight,' Simon had characteristically told his employers in the City of London.[11] In the 1878 reprint Simon also altered his original 1858 statement that the deaths from measles, whooping cough, and scarlet fever are 'practically speaking, unavoidable' to read 'in some degree, unavoidable'. Nightingale would have found it hard to quarrel with this. The reprinted version of Simon's paper is much more common than the original, being in an elegantly produced and widely distributed retrospective collection of his papers rather than in an obscure and cheaply printed government report as it was in 1858.[12]

It is wrong to claim, as many experts have, that this argument between Nightingale and Simon showed that she did not believe in germs or infection. A statement by Nightingale in the same 'Note on Contagion' in which she attacked Simon shows that she recognised infectious substances. She says, 'There are two or three diseases in which there is a specific virus which can be seen, tasted, smelt, and analysed, and which, in certain constitutions, propagates the original disease by inoculation, such as small-pox, cow-pox, and syphilis, but these are not "contagions" in the sense supposed.' She attacked Simon's theory that germs spread whooping-cough, measles, and scarlet fever rapidly through the community by attaching themselves to clothing and other materials, which is how she claimed that the medical authorities defined contagion. She specifically endorsed the concept of infection, which did not pretend to understand the mechanisms of transmission: 'The word "contagion" therefore is altogether objectionable. The word "infection" expresses a fact, without involving a hypothesis.' Her criticism was correct, even though occasionally patients may have been infected by germ-laden objects. Her suggestion that the rapid spread was due to transmission through the air was more accurate. Simon's theory was dangerously wrong because people used it to argue that the reduction of overcrowding would be ineffective.

Although Nightingale was correct, and better living conditions can nearly eliminate what Simon called 'inevitable' mortality, her proposals for acts of Parliament compelling local parish councils to eliminate overcrowding and improve ventilation seemed impractical to many of her contemporaries. Edwin Chadwick's attempt to force local government to improve living standards had antagonised most local politicians and caused his downfall. The desire to avoid this fate may have led Simon to downplay the importance of sanitation and to portray public health as a question of scientific advance.

To understand how Simon's approach may have seemed politically more acceptable in Nightingale's day it is only necessary to look at our own attitude to the health of developing countries, as illustrated by the recent reports of the World Health Organisation. The developing countries, where four fifths of the world's population live, have something in common with the cities of mid-Victorian

England. In those countries, two-thirds of the population still does not have adequate sanitation, and one quarter do not have access to clean water. The possibility that the developing countries might solve their own health problems by improving sanitation would seem remote to most people. The idea that the rich nations might force them to do so – at a relatively modest cost estimated at $68bn[13] – may seem absurd. The principle of national sovereignty is as sacred today as was the autonomy of local parish councils in the 1850's, when to most rich people in England the poor were like foreigners.

Instead of interfering in the sanitation policies of developing countries, rich countries tend to share with them the fruits of scientific research, for example in helping them to treat disease. This attitude leads the World Health Organisation to classify diseases by a method that obscures the sanitary origin of much of the world's death from infectious disease, in a way strangely reminiscent of Simon and Greenhow's paper. The World Health Report of 1996 reveals that infectious disease is the world's major cause of death and accounts for one third of all deaths in the developing world just as it did in 1850's England. Whooping cough and measles, two diseases familiar to the Victorians, still cause many deaths among children. WHO breaks down the mortality figures by 'mode of transmission', and lists whooping cough, measles, and pneumonia as diseases whose 'mode of transmission' is from person to person. But most of the people who die from these diseases, the report makes clear, have already been previously weakened by 'other infections'.

Bacterial pneumonia is the main killer among the WHO list of diseases 'transmitted from person to person.' Many healthy adults have the bacterium responsible – *Streptococcus pneumoniae* – in their throats. Acquiring the germ by person-to-person transmission therefore seems to be a normal part of growing up. Only children who have previously been weakened by other infections fall ill as a result of acquiring it, and some die. The WHO report does not identify the other infections which cause the delayed death of children when they catch the common pneumonia bacterium, but adds the deaths of these weaklings to the total for diseases transmitted from person to person instead of the total for whatever disease caused their fatal weakness.[14] If most of the diseases transmitted from person to person only kill those who have been weakened by another infection, then other infections must bear some of the responsibility for the mortality. The likely culprits – Farr's 'secret roots of death' – must include diarrhoea, transmitted by defective sanitation, which is by far the most common infection of all but which appears to have a low mortality when the figures are arranged according to WHO's classification. The true – delayed – mortality from such diseases, which according to WHO are not transmitted from person to person, cannot be calculated from the WHO statistics and is in fact camouflaged by them. WHO does not try to calculate how many of the eleven million annual deaths listed as being caused by diseases transmitted from person to person – one fifth of all deaths in the world – could be prevented by improved sanitation.

The WHO system of disease classification therefore seems to be aimed at counting the deaths that could be avoided by battling against infections, and in so doing withholds the number of lives that would be saved by improving sanitation and making infections harmless. In its conclusions, the WHO report actually falls victim to the illusion thus created that curative medicine is the only solution. It says:

> WHO has set the target of reducing deaths from acute respiratory infections [largely pneumonia] in children under age 5 by one-third by the year 2000 – equal to more than 1.4 million lives saved per year. But achieving this target is threatened because, as mentioned earlier, the two cheapest and hitherto best antibiotics to treat pneumonia, the leading killer among acute respiratory infections, are now much less effective due to bacterial resistance. This means that either more expensive drugs must be used, or that more children will die from these infections.

The last sentence states categorically and erroneously that drugs alone can prevent these deaths, and implies that improving sanitation or reducing overcrowding can play no role. This error no doubt arises because the political obstacles to sanitary reform are as important today as they were in Nightingale's time. She would attack these obstacles head-on and would still claim today, as she did in 1859, that fatal diseases can only spread where sanitation is defective. 'If disease ever appears to spread,' she wrote during her rebuttal of John Simon's theories, 'no stronger proof of neglect of hygiene could be adduced. And if the practical aspect of the subject were recognised and acted upon, we should hear little more of the spread of disease from person to person.' As usual she chose her words carefully to avoid saying that person-to-person transmission does not happen.

After her attack on John Simon's official doctrine of inevitability in 1858 it did not take Nightingale long to pick another quarrel with him, this time over the location of a new hospital. The charity hospital of St Thomas's, where Simon was senior surgeon, had to move when its site was required for a new railway station. Nightingale had established herself as an expert on hospital design through her articles in *The Builder*, and the authorities of the hospital sought her help in planning the replacement hospital. Nightingale and her sanitarians wanted the new hospital built in the London suburbs, as did some of the resident staff. She was convinced that a hospital in the suburbs surrounded by acres of parkland would be healthier than one in the centre of London, where in any case she maintained that there were already too many hospitals.

John Simon and other non-resident specialists wanted the charity hospital rebuilt on a central London site. They lobbied government officials for a town site and claimed that if the hospital moved to the suburbs then Simon and other 'practitioners of eminence' would not be able to provide emergency cover since their private patients required them to stay in central London close to the town houses of the rich. (Paying patients never went into hospital in those days, even for major surgery; it was far too dangerous.) A letter from Simon and others to *The Times* complained that if the hospital moved to the suburbs 'ultimate responsibility for the patients would fall on resident officers not engaged in private practice, with the result that the standard of skill would degenerate.' The resident doctors, after this amazing insult, mounted a counter-attack with their sanitary allies using statistics that showed that London hospitals killed more of their patients than suburban ones.

Naturally Farr and Nightingale were happy to provide statistical arguments for moving to the suburbs, using comparisons of the mortality of hospitals in London compared to those outside. They infuriated the medical profession by assuming in these comparisons that hospital hygiene was the only factor influencing patient mortality. They assumed that the severity of the disease and the quality of the treatment made no difference to whether a patient lived or died. This was an assumption based on the studies that Farr had seen in Paris into the mortality of armies in the Mediterranean. It was an assumption based on the lesson of Scutari.[15] The darker, more sinister belief lurking in the shadows was the idea that the main beneficiaries of the central London hospitals were the rich patients of society surgeons and physicians like John Simon who were practising their skills on the sick poor in hospital so as to better treat the rich in their safe townhouses. This argument, explosive and demagogic though it is, must be mentioned because it was never far beneath the surface of Nightingale's later popular writings.

When she threw in her lot with those who favoured a country site for St Thomas's, Nightingale seems to have compromised the plan to use the Nightingale Fund to improve career prospects for female hospital nurses. The resident staff at St Thomas's agreed to let her design the new hospital – provided that she allowed the Nightingale Fund to pay for student nurses who would not only study but also provide service under contract to the hospital. Several of the Nightingale Fund Councillors were unhappy about losing control of the nurses, but they may not have understood or sympathised with Nightingale's new priorities.

Apart from her service at Scutari, Florence Nightingale's name is best known for the nurse training school that was eventually established at St Thomas's with the Nightingale Fund's money. Most modern historians agree that Nightingale's early biographers created

a myth by exaggerating the importance of this school, the independence of its nurses, and Nightingale's personal involvement in it.
They have been unable to explain why she took so little interest in a
project that had been so close to her heart before and during the war.
During the war, Nightingale had accepted responsibility for the Fund
which was to bear her name, and had agreed to a board of trustees
and a trust deed aimed at establishing an institute for training hospital nurses. When she returned from the war she postponed a decision
on how to use the money, but after the Royal Commission was over
and she had recovered from her collapse she suddenly appeared to
want nothing more to do with it.

As described earlier, Herbert had launched the Nightingale Fund
by reading aloud at a public meeting a letter from a soldier describing how he and his comrades in the Scutari hospital kissed
Nightingale's shadow as she passed. With this beginning, it would not
be surprising if the new Florence Nightingale now felt oppressed by
the obligations that she had undertaken under the trust deed. Press,
public, and politicians bombarded her with demands that she dedicate the rest of her life to carrying out the original nursing objectives
of the Fund, in a teaching hospital and under the supervision of the
medical profession. It must have seemed to her as if she was being
condemned to repeat her errors at Scutari for the rest of her life.

Sidney Herbert and his wife still wanted to improve the standard
of the hospital nursing profession, and Herbert continually pestered
Nightingale to use the Fund because he felt responsible for persuading the public to give money to it and he was being criticised for
not putting it to good use. Not surprisingly, she tried to resign from
her position with the Fund, but Herbert would not allow it. It may
have been partly in desperation, to ensure that wild horses could not
drag her back to work in a hospital, that she took to her bed. By 1859
she was claiming that her health prevented her from supervising the
use of the Fund. Eventually Herbert began to organise a scheme to
use the money to establish a nurse training school in Kings College
Hospital, and it seems to have been this that spurred Nightingale into
action at St Thomas's. It was to stop Herbert's scheme that she

deployed the Fund as best she could to promote her new objectives by making her alliance with the resident staff at St Thomas's.

For Nightingale, the new hospital was to be a temporary expedient – necessary for the 150 years or so that it would take to upgrade people's homes to make them safer for the care of the sick than any hospital could be. It would be a safer version of the Scutari Barrack Hospital – a general hospital in the clean London suburbs, 'remote from the battlefield' to which patients would be carried from the city by Brunel's new railways which were the perfect replacement for the ghastly hospital ferryboats of the Black Sea.

The hospital did not move to the suburbs, because John Simon defeated Nightingale and the resident staff and managed to get it built on the banks of the Thames opposite the Houses of Parliament where it was convenient for his private practice and his public health career. The Nightingale Fund set up its nurse training school there and Nightingale ignored its activities, claiming to be incapacitated by illness. She did succeed in designing the new buildings, using her favourite scheme of many separate 'pavilions' to improve ventilation. Her buildings still stand, despite the frequent appearance of projects for their replacement. Whatever the sanitary advantages, her pavilion plan proved useful in limiting bomb damage during the Second World War, only a few of the pavilions being badly damaged. The bombs missed Florence Nightingale's archives which were stored in the hospital, but destroyed those of John Simon. Simon would be better known to posterity if he had agreed to the hospital site on forty acres of parkland in Lewisham that Nightingale had favoured.

Nightingale and her sanitarians were also right in arguing that London had too many hospitals, and the findings of the 1992 Tomlinson Inquiry into London's Health Service confirms it. Using maps of London and its hospitals very similar to those in Nightingale's 1863 *Notes on Hospitals*, the Tomlinson report showed that central London has too many hospitals and a poor network of health care delivery outside these hospitals. Nightingale's claim that the new site for St Thomas's would be unhealthy was also proved right by later experience. At Scutari, she seems to have used up her ration of being wrong. It is not enough to be right, of course. Neither does it necessarily diminish the value of Simon's ideas if he was wrong. The interplay of the medical and the sanitary ideas may have been much more useful than either alone. Despite the fact that Simon appeared to be a public health dictator, he was not able to stop the irreversible trend to sanitary reform that Chadwick had initiated and which the world followed.

There was a much more important reason why the outcome of Nightingale's battles with Simon was largely irrelevant. If Nightingale believed (as she did in the late 1850s) that doctors and hospitals were detrimental to people's health, it was pointless to argue with surgeons about hospital location or with physicians about sanitation. By the time the battle for St Thomas's was lost Nightingale had written a best-selling book which flew over the head of the Medical Officer of Health and into the minds of the only people who could keep the population away from the doctors and their hospitals entirely: the housewives and domestic servants of England.

Published in 1860, *Notes on Nursing* sold fifteen thousand copies in its first two months, and has never been out of print in the 140 years since. Many of the early readers must have discovered that their two shillings had bought them something other than what the title and the author's reputation seemed to promise. Many of them must have been hoping for advice on what to expect from a career in hospital nursing, the profession that Nightingale had made so fashionable. Instead they got a radical anti-nursing, anti-medical, anti-hospital propaganda pamphlet. Lytton Strachey, in *Eminent Victorians*, noted the anti-nursing bias of Nightingale's best-seller, calling it 'compendium of the besetting sins of the sisterhood, drawn up with the detailed acrimony, the vindictive relish, of a Swift.'[16] Many a reader must have been bewildered by the first sentence of the book's preface, and turned back to the cover to see whether this was the book that she had intended to buy: 'The following notes are by no means intended as a rule of thought by which nurses can teach themselves to nurse, still less as a manual to teach nurses to nurse.'

What on earth *is* this book then? The answer, 'hints for thought to women who have charge of the health of others', is perplexing. What is such a woman if she is not a nurse? The answer was: she is Everywoman.

Within the first dozen pages the reader learns that professional hospital nurses have been trained to obstruct God's reparative processes and that children's hospitals increase child mortality. The reader – Everywoman – finds herself ridiculed for her own belief that 'nature intended mothers to be accompanied by doctors'. Later, she learns that doctors cannot agree which is their ethical duty: to alleviate the suffering of a patient who has an interesting medical condition, or to let the suffering continue so that they can observe it. Unfortunately, the manuscript drafts of this first edition have disappeared, otherwise we would be able to see why Dr Sutherland was so alarmed by the anti-medical bias of the opening pages that he persuaded Nightingale to tone them down. What we see now is the censored version.

The book was targeted at women in domestic service who might have to care for the sick in their homes. From the 1851 census Nightingale had discovered that nearly two thirds of the nurses in Britain were working in domestic service in private houses. Half of these nurses were nineteen years old or younger. This explains the paternalistic style of the book, which jars to the modern reader. The book also loses much of its effect today because it was written in an era where fatal sickness was a familiar resident in every household. Twenty three in every 1000 of the population were dying every year, mostly from the fevers and infections that cause us no more than minor inconvenience now that the annual death rate is more like nine in 1000. Nightingale wanted her book to keep people out of hospital and to downgrade the role of physicians in the eyes of ordinary people. Doctors, she wrote, do not cure. The human body cures itself, doctors may be called on to perform a kind of 'surgery of functions' analogous to a surgeon's task of removing a bullet from a wound so that the body's reparative processes can act. What this 'surgery of functions' was she never properly explains, and most of the anecdotes about physicians in the book do not reflect to their credit. She has more praise for surgeons – a typical anecdote shows a surgeon opening the windows and a physician then closing them to the detriment of the patients – something that Nightingale claimed actually happened at Scutari.

She dismissed with a few short and equivocal remarks the traditional profession of nursing with which her readers identified her – the application of poultices, administration of medicines, care of bedsores, prevention of bleeding etc. She notes its great value, but then spoils this tribute by saying that few patients die for lack of it. True nursing, she writes, should from now on be defined as 'the proper use of fresh air, light, warmth, cleanliness, quiet, and the proper selection and administration of diet – all at the least expense of vital power to the patient.'[17]

Her book did not accuse the doctors of fraud and conspiracy, but blamed her readers for delegating too much authority to them. She did not attach herself to the strong anti-medical movements of the day. She was in favour of the compulsory smallpox vaccination, for example, whereas the most virulently anti-medical campaigners of the time were anti-vaccinationists who accused the medical profession of the most awful crimes under cover of the compulsory programme that had existed (in theory) since the 1820s. But the book shows signs that Nightingale may have believed in a medical conspiracy even if she preferred not to base her crusade on it. She notes that if her readers follow her advice they will reduce the work of doctors, and adds rather too jauntily that no doctor would object to this. And she claims that some doctors would not interfere if they thought that a patient was being accidentally poisoned by a copper kettle, for fear of losing a mine of information.

It is not possible to say whether *Notes on Nursing* contributed to a reduction in civilian mortality from infectious diseases. But what John Simon had called the 'inevitable' mortality from measles and scarlet fever declined in the years following the book's publication, for reasons that remain a mystery.[18] If her book had this practical effect it could easily make up for Nightingale's apparent failure to impose her theories at high political level because of lack of support from the medical profession.

The medical profession has usually preferred not to criticise Nightingale's ideas directly. This seems to be because of the great public reverence for her, a reverence all the more extraordinary because by the time *Notes on Nursing* was published a large number of influential people knew that her image as the saviour of Scutari was a sham. They knew this from the confidential report on the disaster at Scutari that Nightingale had written and circulated to many of her prominent acquaintances, to obtain as wide a readership as the ban on publication allowed. When Nightingale's attacks did succeed in goading the doctors beyond endurance, they usually retaliated with an attack on some more accessible individual who had collaborated with Nightingale or repeated her ideas. For example, they attacked William Farr after Nightingale used Farr's statistics to argue for the removal of hospitals from central London. Nightingale was also pro-tected at the time by her social connections – in particular by her family's friendship with Lord Palmerston who was extraordinarily popular. Farr's humble background made him particularly vulner-able. But this snobbery can hardly be an explanation for a reluctance to attack Nightingale's sanitary ideas today.

A good example of a recent criticism of Nightingale by proxy appears in the analysis of the Scutari hospitals written by the Director General of the Army Medical Service in his *History of the Army Medical Department*, published as recently as 1974. This modern Director General dismisses outright Nightingale's theories about the causes of the disaster at Scutari, but without mentioning her: 'The historian Fortescue describes the hospitals in these words: "The commonest appliances were wanting, the foul chaos reigned everywhere, breed-ing torture and death." This implication that the bad hospital condi-tions caused their deaths is untrue, and from Miss Terrot's account [Miss Terrot was one of Nightingale's nurses and her moving account is extensively quoted above] it can be seen that many men were dying on admission. It was intestinal ulceration caused in the majority of cases by dysentery or by typhoid which was killing them and no treatment known at that time could have saved them.'[19]

The Director General's last sentence in the quotation above, analysing the medical cause of death, is presumably correct from a medical point of view. From this point of view it is irrelevant that some of the soldiers might have spontaneously recovered if the conditions in the hospital had been better, or even if they had been left outside. His statement that no treatment could have saved them is surely correct if you take it for granted that the author, Lieutenant General Sir Neil Cantlie KCB, KBE, MC, MBChB, FRCS, can only be referring to medical treatment. The Army Medical Department's responsibility, he implies, was limited to administering the latest available medical treatment for whatever medical conditions presented themselves.

But the Director General's analysis of the medical cause of death provides no evidence at all on the effect of hospital conditions. He appears to think that it does, and like many experts he fails to understand the limits of his own expertise. In saying that bad hospital conditions did not cause the patients' deaths, the Director General is expressing an opinion on a separate matter in which he was no more qualified to speak than Nightingale; in fact, by virtue of being a medical specialist, he was probably less qualified. He seems to confirm Nightingale's prediction that doctors could never be trained in hygiene. By quoting the historian Fortescue the Director General avoided criticising Nightingale, whose writings are the source of Fortescue's information.

It is more common for the medical profession to attack Nightingale on its own territory, so to speak, by alleging that she refused to acknowledge the existence of germs.[20] As in the case of her argument with John Simon described above, the evidence for this charge often turns out to be inadequate. In private letters to people with strong views on the subject, like Edwin Chadwick, she often gave the impression that she supported their conservative attitudes towards the new theories of microbial infection. One can expect to find variations in emphasis in these private letters when written to different people, and they tell us more about how Nightingale worked than about what she believed.

It would be much more important if it could be shown that she tried to stop ordinary people from protecting themselves against germ infection. Monica Baly, a nursing educator and former officer of the Royal College of Nursing who has written several books on Nightingale, is one of the few authors who cites an instance of this specific enough to be verified. Dr Baly maintains that Nightingale objected to mothers boiling milk for their children, even fifteen years after Koch had discovered the tubercle bacillus, and that Nightingale also discouraged antiseptic practices. Dr Baly quotes as evidence the fact that Nightingale crossed out the words 'milk for children should be boiled' in correcting the proofs of a popular health care book written by one of her protégées, and on the same proof document made disparaging remarks about antisepsis.[21] Dr Baly's statement that Nightingale tried to encourage mothers to feed raw milk to their children after 1896 is important because cow's milk was often lethal for infants at that time. But it arises from a misunderstanding, as an examination of the evidence shows.

The author of the book that Nightingale is said to have censored was Amy Hughes, a Nightingale disciple who lived well into the twentieth century. Hughes, like many others, preserved the letters that Nightingale had written to her. These letters, which biographers have not consulted, show that the charge against Nightingale is groundless. They contain her suggestions for improving Amy Hughes' book. These suggestions show that Nightingale did not *delete* the sentence about boiling milk; she replaced it by instructions for a better method of sterilisation. The following are the notes that Nightingale sent to Amy Hughes as a suggestion for replacing the crossed out 'milk for children should be boiled': 'Boiling all milk doubtful. So many [children] dislike boiled milk, and many doctors say "only up to the boil". The disagreeable taste is not the only or even the principal objection to boiled milk. If you separate the skim [that forms during boiling] from the milk, you separate a most

[155]

important ingredient. You must then cut up the skim and put it back into the milk. And what a mess that is! Persuade your cook not to boil it but to *stop at the boil*.'[22]

The temperature at which pasteurisation destroys the bacteria in the milk is well below boiling point. Nightingale's proposed correction to Amy Hughes' book did not cast doubt on germ theory, and in fact would increase the use of safe, sterilised milk. In the published version of the book Amy Hughes replaced 'milk for children should be boiled' by Nightingale's advice to heat it to near-boiling.[23] And Nightingale's alleged scathing remarks about antiseptic practices – the use of chemicals or other agents to kill germs? Amy Hughes' collection of letters shows this is also a misunderstanding. What Nightingale told Amy Hughes was that in her book there was 'too much praise of antiseptic. Not much said about *aseptic*'. Far from mocking scientific advance, Nightingale was urging Amy Hughes to alert her readers to the new aseptic techniques designed to exclude germs rather than to allow germs to invade the body and then try to kill them.

In promoting aseptic techniques Nightingale was, in 1896, unusually advanced. Nearly forty years later some surgical operations were still being carried out in London hospitals using the obsolete antiseptic methods, as this description of one of the last practitioners shows: 'It was quite an experience in 1933 to assist [A. J. "Pa" Couzens] to resect the bowel or remove the cartilage from a knee, using an antiseptic technique with considerable skill. Clad in a short-sleeved white coat, with maskless face, and with bare hands, swabs, and instruments constantly bathed in lysoform, he not infrequently smoked a cigarette during the operation.'[24]

Although, as these examples show, Nightingale publicly acknowledged the importance of protection against microbial infection, she opposed the use of public funds for research into germs, saying: 'However ingenious a theory may be the wisest thing is never to expend public money on it.' She rewrote her will to cut out a beneficiary who planned to use the money specifically for medical research. Her explanation for cancelling the bequest was that the intended recipient had 'proposed a small Endowment for Research, which I believe will only end in endowing some bacillus or microbe, and I do not wish that.'[25] Opposing endowed or publicly funded research into germs while supporting protective measures against them may seem like a contradiction, but may be only a sign of cynicism about the role of publicly-funded research. Pasteur's most successful and pioneering work on germs was, of course, funded by the private sector – the brewing industry. It is not surprising that those with a vested interest in publicly-funded research should try to demonstrate that Nightingale's position is an ignorant one. It is Nightingale's fault entirely that people can portray her ideas as contradictory and shallow. It has happened because, as we shall see, she destroyed all traces of the formation of her ideas and the insights that created them in 1857.

Before this, when she was at her most vociferous during and shortly after the war, she had relatively little understanding of medical issues. Her defence of the common soldier's dignity was important and fruitful – her scheme to reduce drunkenness was inspired in its simplicity – but there was little evidence of any medical insight. When she first came back to England in 1856, she was also completely dependent on people like Sir John McNeill and Colonel Lefroy for ideas on the subject of administrative reform. This is shown by her letters imploring McNeill to tell her what subjects to raise in her interview with Queen Victoria. Her output at that time was essentially second hand. Her repetition of the McNeill and Tulloch ideas on the subject of army baking, shoemaking and so on was important – because the authorities were resisting these sensible ideas – but it showed no evidence of original thought. Her criticisms of the plans for the new Netley hospital, which pre-date her conversion to Farr's theory, were given to her by Sutherland.

She destroyed the evidence of her education during the Royal Commission so successfully that her stridency of the years before tends to obscure the low-key and more philosophical approach that came afterwards.

Commentators have often treated her medical and sanitary ideas

as trivial because they do not believe she did enough research to have
a proper theoretical foundation. In this they underestimate the
importance of her development in the year after her return from the
war. For instance, Lytton Strachey in *Eminent Victorians* says that if
Nightingale's experience had been treating yellow fever in Panama
instead of cholera at Scutari she would have spent the rest of her life
maintaining that the only way to deal with disease was by destroying
mosquitoes. A little practical knowledge, he implies, was for her a
dangerous thing. Strachey's error is in supposing that Nightingale
learned anything at all during her experience at Scutari. She learned
nothing there about sanitation. As we have seen, she learned her
lesson afterwards, analysing highly complex data in a room in the
Burlington Hotel under the tutorship of the best medical scholars in
the world. And there, she drained the cup of knowledge to its bitter-
est dregs.

Her theories do not pretend to come from deep technical insight
into the mechanisms of disease but rather from a sense of what
would be most appropriate in designing the higher form of life that
she believed mankind to be. It would not make much difference
whether the detailed design for the human species had come from a
Supreme Being or from a process of evolution – although she preferred to speak about the former. *She* would not have designed the
world so that advances in human health could only be achieved by
training a small number of experts to wage continual war against a
lower form of life such as microbes. She therefore did not see why
God would have designed us that way, even if he had created those
lower forms of life.

Nightingale's refusal to rely exclusively on 'germ theory' in individual diagnosis has also brought her into conflict with the experts.
Medical historians have, for example, directly criticised her for her
'overconfident' diagnoses that the deaths of Sidney Herbert and
Lord Raglan were caused by their emotional problems. She claimed
that Herbert died of regret at not having succeeded in reorganising
the War Office of which he was the chief. And according to her,
Raglan had turned his face to the wall in the Crimea and died of

depression at his failure as Commander-in-Chief, a depression aggravated by his persistence in maintaining a calm outward appearance. It is remarkable that in Raglan's case she diagnosed repressed guilt as a source of ill-health, a diagnosis which must have seemed more farfetched in her time than it is now, and which the present work uses to explain some of her own symptoms. This diagnosis of repressed guilt casts doubt on recent medical speculation that she may have suffered from chronic brucellosis. A paper in the December 1995 edition of the *British Medical Journal* claims that all her symptoms after 1857, which some experts had hitherto thought to have been neurotic or feigned, could have been the result of infection by the bacterium *Brucella melitensis* through dairy products while in the Crimea. Having seen what Nightingale thought about the doctors' love of useless theorising, we can only tremble to think what would be *her* reaction to this medical explanation for her own illness and mental state.

The *BMJ* article implies that *Brucella melitensis* is sufficient to account for Nightingale's state of mind, by citing her feelings of worthlessness and failure as being compatible with the depressive symptoms of the disease. But this diagnosis was made with incomplete information, because the medical expert making it did not know that before her first collapse and the onset of these symptoms Nightingale had suffered a spectacular humiliation in front of all those whom she most respected, when she had to admit that she had been wrong about the cause of death at Scutari. In reality, the theory that she had brucellosis may be true but almost trivial, because the microbe may have flourished abnormally because of her depressed state.

The case of Florence Nightingale's illness shows that the versatility of germ theory as an exclusive explanation with minimal evidence makes it a dangerous monism, a single truth that may obscure others. Medical experts seek no further explanation than that the lost Crimean army simply died of typhoid and dysentery, and that the thirty-seven-year-old Nightingale worked obsessively from her bed for eleven years because she had caught brucellosis from goats' milk. We might call this the germ theory of history; it encourages the belief that nobody was responsible for the Crimean hospital disaster, and implies that Nightingale's reasoning powers were impaired by organic disease.

Nightingale's dependence on logical reasoning rather than technical explanation was a consequence of her Unitarian upbringing. Many of her public health pronouncements also reflect the Unitarian emphasis on 'deeds not creeds'. Her comment disparaging John Simon's call for more research is a good example that has already been quoted: 'What is needed now is not to *know*, but to *do*'. Her strong antipathy to medical dogma, which drove her to reject unproven theory even when she didn't have a better replacement, probably stems from Unitarianism too. John Simon's theories, like the Church of England's creed, acted as a loyalty test which those seeking public funding or patronage had to pass and in doing so had to recognise the superior knowledge and authority of the hierarchy. Unitarians were more worried about the Church of England's abuse of power and its use of the creed as a loyalty test for teachers and other public servants than about the truth *per se* of its doctrine of the Trinity. Nightingale's brand of Unitarianism claimed that ordinary logic and observation were enough to reveal that benevolent forces are at work throughout the universe. From this she could infer that the Supreme Being is infinitely wise and benevolent, and what wiser and more benevolent way to create man than to give him the means to create himself? It is not surprising to learn that the young Charles Darwin was taught by Unitarians. In his *Origin of Species*, published one month before *Notes on Nursing* in 1859, Darwin showed by logic and observation how all living species can create themselves.

Some philosophers regard Darwin's theory of natural selection not as a scientific theory at all, but as a logical truth, which any one of us could have discovered through our normal senses and reasoning power if we could have freed ourselves from superstition. The simple but not obvious logic of natural selection also shows how unlikely it is that killing germs will eliminate fatal epidemics. First, if microbes rely on person-to-person transmission to propagate themselves, it would simply not be very smart of them to kill their hosts, or to put it another way, any strain that did so would soon be displaced by a less harmful strain. If microbes suddenly cause fatal epidemics, therefore, it is an evolutionary step that is not good for either microbe or man. Man is more likely to be responsible than the microbe for this state of affairs, because he can make bigger evolutionary jumps. The most obvious evolutionary jump that could be to blame was man's decision to live together in close confinement, in cities for commercial reasons or in armies for purposes of war. Mankind did not have to know exactly *why* sanitation palliated the evils of urban life. It would be logical to suppose that sanitation would cure some urban evils by creating an environment in buildings more like the uncrowded countryside for which the human frame was designed.

Following this kind of logic, Nightingale initially believed that improved sanitation could make even hospitals healthy, but she soon concluded that there was a better way to solve the problem. Between 1858 and 1860, as her respect for the destructive power of infection in hospitals increased, her proposed response was not more research but rather the complete elimination of hospitals. A century and a half later, when in the advanced economies Hospital Acquired Infection has become one of the leading causes of death, these proposals seem even more sensible than they did at the time.

Her initial attitude to hospital infection is shown in her 1858 'Note on Contagion'. Nightingale stated there that infectious patients did not have to be segregated from others in hospital, 'as long as proper precautions are observed'. Although such patients could infect others, it would only happen if the wards were too crowded and badly ventilated. 'Emanations from the sick' could be fatal or harmless, according to her, depending on the extent to which they are diluted in pure atmospheric air.[26] Her view that infectious patients in hospital could be made harmless to others by adequate ventilation may have been true in principle, while not being very practical. In fact, Nightingale did recommend the segregation of infectious patients, but only (she claimed) to simplify the nursing. She must have realised the shortcomings of her approach, because she soon stopped defending the concept of an ideal hospital and at the same time her interest in improving hospitals diminished. In 1860 she wrote: 'Missionary nurses – these are our aim. Hospitals are an intermediate stage of civilisation. While devoting my life to hospital work I have come to the conclusion that hospitals are not the best place for the poor sick.'[27]

Her vision of an advance to the next stage of civilisation – when hospitals and the dangers they posed could be eliminated – took her to our own time and beyond: 'My view you know is that the ultimate destination of all nursing is the nursing of the sick in their own homes ... I look to the abolition of all hospitals and workhouse infirmaries. But it is no use to talk about the year 2000.'[28] Now, as the year 2000 approaches, infections caught in hospital remain in fourth place in the table of leading causes of death, after heart disease, cancer, and strokes. Nearly four per cent of the UK population will die of hospital acquired infection (HAI). The fact is that in developed countries microbes appear to be almost harmless except when caught in hospital.

Medical experts attribute the high death toll from HAI to the emergence of strains of microbe which live in the hospitals and have become resistant to antibiotics. They attribute the proliferation of these resistant microbes to the previous use of antibiotics in hospitals. To quote a recent (1997) medical report on HAI: 'Greater care must therefore be taken when prescribing antibiotics to ensure that the most appropriate antibiotic is prescribed in terms of type, dose, and duration of therapy. Appropriate investigations to identify the causative pathogen may facilitate this process. Unless such measures are taken the problem of microbial resistance to antibiotics will continue to escalate.'[29]

From this, it appears that the medical experts now claim to have a solution to the public health problem that they have created with their own antibiotic drugs. From now on, they propose to identify the germs with perfect accuracy in each case, and to prepare a tailor-made mixture of antibiotics that kills not only the germ but also every single one of the mutations that might escape to form a resistant strain! Perfect knowledge and accuracy are the goal; until that goal is reached, any failure will simply make the problem of HAI worse, even if it cures the individual patient. This paradoxical consequence arises from the authors' mistaken belief that improvements in medical diagnosis and treatment are the only solution to public health problems.

Nightingale and Farr, in their non-medical approach to public health, did not seek to obtain perfect knowledge of organisms associated with disease but rather to use logic and statistical analysis to identify preventable conditions that affect mortality. William Farr would be ecstatic to be given the statistical tools available nowadays – computer software for multiple regression analysis, for example – and it is remarkable how many opportunities we neglect to uncover his 'secret roots of death'.

One unexploited opportunity is the 16,000 women who die young each year from breast cancer in the UK, deaths that cause terrible suffering to them and their families. Enormous differences in breast cancer mortality exist between countries – with the UK's rate being four times as high as in some other OECD countries. Such a wide variation between countries would shout out 'preventable causes' to William Farr and his colleagues. Nevertheless, when in 1995 the House of Commons Health Committee recommended that the Department of Health should commission a statistical study to identify possible local factors, the Government rejected the recommendation. The reasons for rejection were that research funds were 'finite' and that comparisons are irrelevant. The cost was not estimated.[30] Plenty of money is available for clinical research by medical experts.

It would be interesting to know what Farr and Nightingale would have had to say about this Government decision. Farr might say that we are rejecting the most precious bequest of the dying – their death statistics, which can help to increase the life span of their descendants. Nightingale would probably make it an issue of duty to God. She had come to believe that statistics were the language in which God reveals his laws to mankind and shows us how to serve Him.

Refusing even to look at God's messages, she would probably say, is sacrilegious.

These examples are not designed to show that Farr and Nightingale would necessarily have been able to find the answer to any modern public health problem. They show, rather, how far modern administrations have continued to delegate public health to the medical profession, in opposition to Nightingale's views. We do not seem to be tuned to the Nightingale wavelength any more than was the civilian public health establishment of her day.

She had more success with the military establishment where she had built up a powerful network of supporters. By 1858, her mystical devotion to the army's dead had already produced some strange works of art – her famous statistical diagrams. She had persuaded Herbert to include in the Commission's report an annex containing coloured diagrams of the mortality of the army, so that she could publish it as a separate book which would have the authority of Government by virtue of the statement 'Reprinted from the Report of the Royal Commission' on the title page. She thought that this colourful book would have more impact on the military authorities than hundreds of pages of text, and she had 2000 copies printed on higher-quality paper and with more ornate type than that used in the official report.

One of the more unusual diagrams in this book is a visual poem illustrating the Royal Commission's main conclusion that the mortality of the army in peacetime was too high. She and William Farr showed that the mortality of soldiers in barracks at home in Britain was twice as high as in the civilian districts which surrounded them, despite the fact that army recruits were volunteers who were selected for their good previous state of health. The statistics showed that if the army mortality could be brought down to civilian levels, 1200 soldiers' lives could be saved every year. As she put it, 1200 soldiers were being killed by bad barrack sanitation every year just as if the army were taking 1200 young recruits out onto Salisbury Plain every year and shooting them. This was the conclusion that the Royal Commission under Sidney Herbert wanted to emphasise, to focus on

[164]

continuing evils and opportunities for improvement rather than investigating too closely the cause of past 'delinquencies' in the Crimea.

In her 1857 book of statistical diagrams, Nightingale's visual poem to peacetime mortality consists of four rhyming couplets of horizontal bars, the first bar of each couplet being black and the second, longer, being red. Each pair of bars represents the death rate of English males in one of the four five-year age brackets between twenty and forty years. The black bar represents civilians and the second (nearly twice as long) represents soldiers in peacetime, in their barracks in England. At the end of each black bar is one word: *Englishmen*; at the end of each red bar, two words: *English Soldiers*. The thin rectangular coloured bars are reminiscent of the engraved maps of famous battlefields, where hand-coloured rectangles face off against each other to illustrate the positions of regiments at various stages of the battle. The red bar also brings to mind the famous Thin Red Line of Balaclava, where a two-deep line of red-jacketed British riflemen had risen from where they had been lying on the grass and turned back a horde of grey-clad Russian heavy cavalry bearing down on them and thus saved the port and its vulnerable hospitals and stores behind them. On Nightingale's chart and under her command the Thin Red Line rose again, this time from the grave, to pour its deadly fire into the Army High Command.

Arthur Clough must have helped her to produce these diagrams and it is intriguing to think that this one in particular may be a lost poem by the author of 'Say not the struggle nought availeth'. The chart is headed 'Lines' in ornate script, followed by the businesslike 'Representing the Relative Mortality of the Army at Home and of the English Male Population at Corresponding Ages'. The word 'Lines' recalls the title commonly used in Victorian poems, as in 'Lines on the Death of Bismarck.' There is no logical reason for repeating the pictorial message four times, except for rhythmic and poetic effect. The rhythmic effect is provided by the words at the end of each bar, whose cadence recalls the harsh rattle of a kettledrum, beating alone in a soldier's funeral procession: 'English men, English soldiers, English men, English soldiers, English men . . .'

Nightingale must have spent a large part of her father's fortune in privately printing deluxe editions of this type of material, commemorating the dead and recording the signs by which God was revealing to her the laws of sanitary progress. In 1858, the doctors from the Crimea published an anonymous pamphlet casting doubt on Nightingale's Crimean mortality figures as published in the report of the Royal Commission and accusing her of exaggeration.[31] In reply, she published her anonymous 'Contribution to the Sanitary History of the British Army', a restatement of her statistics and a comparison with the official figures recently released by the Army Medical Department.

Nightingale's last word on Crimean mortality statistics, her *Sanitary History*, was produced in the format of a Government blue book but on such high-quality paper that its diagrams are still fresh and bright today. Instead of the 'bat's wing' diagrams of the earlier publication, which were erroneous as well as ugly, Nightingale drew more visually attractive circles representing the mortality with coloured segments like the petals of a flower. Nightingale showed in the *Sanitary History* that the newly-released official death statistics from the war, if true, proved that she had understated the number of deaths at Scutari. The real purpose of the book was to establish Nightingale as *the* authority on Crimean mortality, and point out the flaws in every other official and unofficial source. She had made herself the guardian of the mortality statistics.

In her obsessive exhibition of these statistical relics in graphical form, Nightingale had become Nemesis, or at least a priestess of the cult of that ancient goddess. Nemesis, in Greek mythology, was the daughter of Night and the grandchild of Chaos. She was the goddess of vengeance, persecutor of those who insulted the relics and the memory of the dead. She was also charged with punishing those mortals who are too proud, visiting them with losses and sufferings so that they may become humble. Few mortals can have been more severely punished by the gods for excessive pride than was Florence Nightingale. Now she was to become an avenger in her turn. She was the only one of her family to be born and to die with the name

Nightingale. Her father's name was Shore; he had changed it when he inherited the Nightingale fortune. His sisters thereafter called him Night. Nemesis, like Florence, was the daughter of Night. The Greek deity Night rode in a chariot drawn by owls and bats. An owl visited and spoke to Florence during the war, it will be remembered, when she was at her most complacent, watching the sun set gloriously over the masts of the British fleet on the evening before the arrival of the Sanitary Commission at her hospital. Florence thought at the time that her talkative nocturnal visitor was the ghost of an owl that she had once kept as a pet.

But Nightingale was to go further than merely guarding the relics. After the suppression of her confidential report in 1857, she received extensive support from the War Office for her scheme to eliminate the excess peacetime mortality in the barracks. War Minister Panmure agreed to let Herbert chair the four sub-commissions that were formed in the wake of the Royal Commission into the Health of the Army. One of these was to make visits of inspection to all the army barracks in the land and authorise the immediate expenditure of money on sanitary improvements where needed. Sidney Herbert himself undertook these barrack inspections in the face of great hostility from the army officers. Herbert's health was failing fast – he was suffering from acute nephritis, quite possibly a delayed consequence of a violent scarlet fever epidemic in the crowded and insanitary dormitories at Harrow, the exclusive boarding school that he had attended as a child.

It is hard to imagine a less congenial task for one of the richest men in England than that of barrack sanitary inspector, even if he had been in good health. But as Nightingale said, she had a hold over Sidney Herbert. She set him the task of eliminating the excess mortality in the barracks, which she and Farr had calculated at 1200 soldiers per year. If this result could be achieved then the lesson of Scutari would have been put to use, proving that 'your mistakes are part of God's plan'. The advantage of soldiers from the statistical point of view was that they were as near as possible interchangeable. In Nightingale's scheme, by reducing barracks mortality to civilian levels, she and Sidney Herbert could each year bring 1200 common soldiers back from the dead.

In mid-1859, after Herbert had spent two years trudging around dingy barracks inspecting drains under the hostile glare of the army dinosaurs, Palmerston became Prime Minister again and appointed him Minister of War. The more obvious choice might have been Palmerston's previous War Minister, Lord Panmure. Sidney Herbert was still blamed by many for the errors of the first winter in the Crimea, which Palmerston and Panmure had corrected after Herbert left office. But Palmerston in 1859 needed to put together a coalition to defeat the existing Tory Government, and he needed to include members of other parties including Gladstone. Sidney Herbert was a protégé of Gladstone and, in addition, mutual admiration between Gladstone and Herbert's rival Panmure was distinctly lacking. Probably Gladstone also thought that his ailing friend Sidney Herbert deserved something better than the drudgery that Nightingale was imposing on him.

Nightingale did not mean to let Herbert off the hook. Now that he was War Minister she wanted him to carry out a complete reorganisation of the War Office. Without this, any army health reforms that Nightingale and Herbert had implemented would not become permanent. The War Office seems to have been lacking an organisation chart – everybody in it gave their opinion on every question and nobody seemed to have authority or accountability for any decision. The nearest thing in modern life would perhaps be the incompetent Town Hall of a scandal-prone inner London borough as portrayed in the most lurid press accounts. The reorganisation of the War Office was obviously not a task for which Herbert was suited. Panmure might not have been much better, although he seems to have had greater skill in outwitting his own civil servants on tactical issues. When Herbert's illness was diagnosed as fatal in early 1861, he tried to persuade Nightingale to agree that he should resign as Minister of War. She talked him out of it. For the next six months he argued with his War Office subordinates over the plans for reorganisation. In June he collapsed and she accepted that he would resign although she claimed that after two years' rest he would be able to resume his task.[32]

At the beginning of August 1861 Sidney Herbert died, aged fifty one, at his magnificent country estate of Wilton. It was four years to the day since his agreement with Nightingale that he would dedicate himself to saving soldiers' lives. At 1200 per year, that would be 4800 lives – the same as the number of soldiers who died in Nightingale's hospital at Scutari. But they had not yet started to pay off the debts of Balaclava General, the hospital ships, and the rest of the 16,000 unnecessary deaths. According to Nightingale, Herbert's dying words were: 'Poor Florence; our joint work unfinished.'

Her harsh treatment of Herbert continued after his death, when his distraught widow wanted to publish an article praising his achievements. Liz Herbert asked Gladstone, who had been Herbert's political mentor and was now Chancellor of the Exchequer, to persuade Nightingale to help with this article. Gladstone sent Nightingale a draft and asked for what he quaintly called 'numbers and other statistics' to support its claims. Gladstone told Nightingale that Liz Herbert believed that her husband would rather be remembered for having saved soldiers lives than for anything else. Nightingale did not have much sympathy for this desire to achieve immortality through personal fame. Herbert, she once said 'Never said "*I* did this"' about something he had achieved. It was the trait she admired most in him and, after the war, went out of her way to emulate.

She wrote to Gladstone that Herbert would much rather the newspapers published his unfinished plan for War Office reorganisation so that it would have some chance of succeeding. As to the successes claimed in Liz's article, such as the Royal Sanitary Commission, Nightingale alleged that most of them were due to another man. Of all people, Nightingale gave the credit to Lord Panmure! This must have been a cruel blow to Gladstone, who would have been held in contempt by Lord Panmure for helping to persuade Lord Aberdeen to start an unnecessary war and then wanting to join the French in suing for an early and humiliating peace.[33] It also sounds hypocritical given that Nightingale could previously never mention Panmure's name without going into paroxysms of spite, because of his supposed cowardly treatment of McNeill and Tulloch and his obstruction of her Royal Commission.

She may have meant her praise of Panmure to insult Gladstone rather than flatter Panmure, but in fact Nightingale did change her opinion of the much-maligned former War Minister. Panmure had recently admonished her in private for her repeated denigration of his work. He reminded her that although barracks mortality was still high, he had reduced it significantly before and during the Crimean War. He also reminded her that it was he, not Herbert, who ordered the Sanitary Commission to go out to the East and end the epidemics in the hospitals. In reality, as we have seen, it was not Panmure but Palmerston who decided to attack the problem by sending the Commissioners. Panmure's initial approach had been to write furious letters to all those in command in the East telling them to clean up the camps and hospitals and distribute the stores in their warehouses. His orders were justified, but this way of conveying them only made him enemies.

Palmerston therefore probably deserved most of the credit that Panmure was claiming from Nightingale, but on the other hand Panmure couldn't tell Nightingale what he had *really* done for her. She could never be allowed to know that he had risked everything by disloyally misleading Queen Victoria so that McNeill, Tulloch, and Nightingale would succeed. It would have earned him Nightingale's undying admiration, but it was hardly the thing that an ex-Minister could reveal. Nightingale did admit to Panmure that he had made important contributions to army health, and then warned some of her supporters to stop criticising his record.[34] She went much further than this when rejecting Gladstone's request for help with Liz Herbert's proposed eulogy of her husband. She told Gladstone that Herbert's lifetime of dedication to the British soldier, as described by Liz, had an unexplained two-year gap in it from March 1855 (when Herbert left the Government) to February 1857, during which time she implied that Herbert had gone fishing. She wrote her own short analysis of Herbert's later achievements as an alternative to the widow's eulogy. In this piece, she gratuitously reminds readers that Herbert had been blamed for the disasters in the Crimea and then describes at length Lord Panmure's role in identifying and remedying them. Panmure had organised the Royal Commission that Herbert had chaired, and in case anyone should say that superiors should not get all the credit she pointed out that Herbert in turn had his own subordinates to do the real work.

She sent this masterpiece to Gladstone saying that she had not been able to think of a way to leave out mention of Lord Panmure without giving Panmure an opportunity to complain. She would be glad if Gladstone could help her to find a way to eliminate Panmure from her article, because 'the name of Panmure is an abomination in my ears'. This was extremely well-crafted irony. Gladstone must have known that she had criticised his enemy Panmure in the past, but even in her most spiteful period she would never have used such language. Gladstone had a rather biblical way of expressing himself.[35] She offered to brief Chancellor of the Exchequer Gladstone on three important areas where Government action would be much appreciated by his late protégé Sidney Herbert, and also hinted that Gladstone himself as a senior Minister at the time was even more responsible than Herbert for the loss of the army in the Crimea. Gladstone wrote back thanking her for her article about Herbert and informing her that the family had decided not to publish anything for the moment. As for the briefing she offered, he did not think he would be able to master the details of such an intricate subject. He gave up acting as an intermediary and returned to his primary tasks of trimming the national budget and proving to his own satisfaction that Homer was a Christian. Nightingale later assessed Gladstone as 'the most unsanitary brute that ever was.'[36]

In public, at least, Nightingale's adulation of her dear departed master Sidney Herbert was unbounded, and it is this contrast that most of her sympathetic biographers have found most difficult to deal with. She appears to have wanted to stop Liz Herbert's eulogy so that she alone could manipulate and ruthlessly exploit Sidney

Herbert's memory in the pursuit of her own objective of reforming the War Office. She had urged Herbert to continue working even when he was dying, and made light of his symptoms. Even though her goals can be portrayed as altruistic, biographers usually try to retain their readers' interest by portraying the subject as more or less human, and this behaviour of Nightingale's has seemed to many to be beyond the pale. Some biographers avoid the problem by omitting most of the details, and others hint at neurosis, bereavement, overwork, or other 'explanations' that in the end are no more helpful than germ theory in shedding light on human behaviour. If we can now attribute Nightingale's breakdown to her belated discovery that she had contributed to the poisoning of thousands of common soldiers, and if the shock of this discovery was compounded by her guilt at having agreed to cover it up, can this explain her subsequent behaviour?

Nightingale is difficult to describe after her breakdown, but this may be only that her shock unlatched a potential that is rarely seen. Some of us may feel like saying a prayer of gratitude that life, with all of its vicissitudes, does not seem likely to place us in the situation in which Florence Nightingale found herself after her discoveries of 1857. Neurosis is not an explanation for Nightingale's behaviour, which was if anything much too rational. Far from being a very complicated person, she may have been one of the simplest to understand. She may have been simply panic-stricken. Death or madness aside, it is not clear that she had any alternative course open to her except to succeed in her work, at whatever cost. Sidney Herbert's obligation to her was the only real asset that she had in this work. Given the circumstances, many ordinary people would have acted exactly as she did.

Whether or not she eventually succeeded in reducing the mortality in the barracks, the numbers involved seem trivial by the scale of later conflicts. During the 1914–18 World War, 6,000,000 soldiers were killed on the Western Front, and more British soldiers died in action on the first day at the Somme than from all causes in the whole of the Crimean War. This prompts the question: of what relevance was Nightingale's supposed concern for the welfare of the troops if only half a century later they could be sacrificed on such a scale? Did her efforts really represent any significant progress? The answer is that the efforts of Nightingale and other reformers were of great importance in what followed, in a way that they could not foresee. It was partly because of her that the Crimean War put an end to the Duke of Wellington's old model of a small volunteer army that was free of civilian interference and civilian methods.

During and just after the Crimean War the British army finally succumbed to the industrial revolution. It was then that the first weapons of industrial mass destruction were mooted. The engineer Brunel lobbied for a government contract to bombard the Russians from a steam-powered submarine that he had designed, and the indefatigable naval hero and inventor Lord Cochrane persuaded the authorities to witness a demonstration of his scheme to overthrow the fortress of Sebastopol by the use of poison gas. Fortunately for the reputations of both men, the schemes were not taken up; in Cochrane's case a change of wind direction during the trial made the authorities uneasy about the safety of their own troops; during the 1914–18 war, of course, the authorities were not so fussy.

These high-tech inventions were not allowed to revolutionise warfare until the administrative reforms were completed that integrated military and civilian affairs. Lord Panmure, in civilianising the army, introduced modern industrial supply arrangements for the Commissariat and limited-service enlistment to tap new sources of manpower. Lord Palmerston put the army under the control of Parliament, facilitating approval of higher defence spending. Nightingale discovered a way to stop large armies dying of disease, something that had never been possible before. And Gladstone, as Chancellor of the Exchequer, forged the final link in the chain which was to make total war possible: he made the income tax permanent, a tax which he called 'an engine of gigantic power for great national purposes.' From then on, warfare enjoyed access to the entire resources of the state: financial, human, and industrial.

As a part of this democratisation of war, the standard of

weapons available to the army quickly caught up with those used in civilian sporting activities. Up until the Crimean war, the army's small arms were about thirty years behind those used in civilian life, this being how long it took for the percussion cap to be accepted by the army after its use was common in civilian weapons. The Army High Command had always had an impressive arsenal of reasons for not upgrading their weapons. But once the administration was reformed, the army was at the forefront in adopting improvements like smokeless powder and metallic cartridges. Technical innovation followed administrative reform. In Nightingale's day the British administration was still used as a model by other countries, and many of them copied these innovations. War soon ceased to be a clash between armies of each country's outcasts, and became instead a conflict between entire populations. Over the next century and a half, a hundred million lives were lost as a direct but unexpected result of the well-meaning efforts of the army reformers, until the monster that they had created was finally brought under control. It almost seems that the Duke of Wellington and Queen Victoria were right after all in trying to keep the army outside the democratic system.

Lord Panmure probably understood better than most the dangers of tinkering with the Duke of Wellington's system. That was why he fought tenaciously against the abolition of the 'purchase' system under which army officer commissions and promotions were sold to the rich. Panmure was not a reformer, as his critics pointed out; he was a civilianiser, and the sale of commissions to civilians ensured that a professional caste of military officer could not emerge. But Panmure failed to stem the tide of reform that he himself had encouraged, and the purchase system was swept away and replaced by promotion on merit. The purchase system had given us officers like Lord George Paget, who rode unarmed into the Valley of Death at the head of the Light Brigade in the suicidal charge and rated it better than the finest fox hunting in Leicestershire. His only participation in the fighting that day was when he stopped his men from killing a Russian who refused to surrender. Officers like this disappeared from the British Army, replaced by professionals who were properly trained to send men to their deaths.

Nightingale had no idea, obviously, that she was helping to promote this expansion of the role of war in society. Nevertheless she would have been able to explain why such a development could happen even in a world in which mankind, according to her, moved continuously towards perfection. Like the disaster at Scutari, she would have called it 'fresh temporary evil' – her phrase for the damage caused accidentally by philanthropists, which eventually must lead to 'fresh permanent good'. In this case, she would say, the permanent good that these horrors brought is a society which, as a result of its experiences, no longer has any appetite for war at all.

Nightingale seems to have had some second thoughts about Lord Panmure and recognised his merits. Did Queen Victoria also forgive him? There is some indirect evidence that she may have done. It is nice to think that during her widowhood and his retirement, when they were neighbours in Scotland, Panmure may have on some occasion presented his humble duty to Her Majesty in a private meeting in which he discussed with his Sovereign his disloyal deceptions and his pandering to Parliament as he could not discuss these matters with anyone else. He could have told her that he and Palmerston had been conducting a training session during which Her Majesty's servants had allowed her to observe the effect of her ideas on the public without exposing her to public criticism.

The Queen knew about the death of Panmure's brother in the war, and also of the family history and the attachment between the brothers, and so she probably understood his personal feelings towards the Army High Command. In their private meeting, he may have pointed out that there was evidence that Her Majesty was being led astray; that he had put his untruths officially in writing to her; that she was bound to discover them, and when she did so she could hold him entirely responsible for any unpleasant consequences. He had made himself a figure of ridicule in her service. He would go down in infamy for his defence of incompetent officers, his dishonourable treatment of McNeill and Tulloch, and his resistance to Florence

Nightingale, all of which courses of action he had pursued only to demonstrate their folly to the Queen. He may have reassured her that he felt no injustice; on the contrary, this was precisely what Her Majesty's barons were *for*. Fortunately, he could tell her, the family name had already been dishonoured by his father's outrageous behaviour. As he was a widower with no heir himself, the Barony of Panmure would become extinct with his death. He had not saddled future generations with his undeserved reputation.

What benefits had been gained by his deceptions? He could have enumerated them to her: a wiser Queen; a stronger army; a more respected Government; a co-operative and productive House of Commons; and a people whose regard for their monarch had risen dramatically since the youthful errors that had exposed her to so much criticism early in her reign. Did this conversation take place, and did she understand? It seems that Her Majesty was quite fond of Panmure, visiting him at his Scottish estate near Balmoral. She wrote sympathetic notes to his bereaved sister when he died. These could easily be acts of normal Royal politeness to a neighbour and former Minister. But her feelings at his death went a little further than normal politeness. She formed the idea that Panmure had died of a chill contracted when he dutifully came to stand at the roadside, as he always did, at the bridge where her Royal carriage entered the Scottish highlands.[37] Her Majesty's sentimental theory of his death may show how much she felt he had sacrificed in life, in fulfilling that 'humble duty'.

Panmure had learned his humble duty from Palmerston in the early days of the latter's premiership, when the two of them had to undo the damage caused by Panmure's confrontational letters to the Generals. Palmerston had been obliged to teach Panmure that a leader can often achieve more by standing in the shadows and facilitating free debate and information flow than by setting himself up as a champion. It was a lesson that Florence Nightingale learned from Palmerston too, when she went back to work after her breakdown.

She eventually came to see through Palmerston's flippant public image: 'Lord Palmerston is a great loss,' she wrote when he died in 1865, still in harness as Prime Minister at over eighty years of age. 'he was a powerful protector to me, especially since Sidney Herbert's death. I never asked him to do anything, but he did it. He did not do himself justice. If the right thing was to be done, he made a joke but he did it.'[38] She had by then discovered that even Palmerston's air of humbug was a humbug. Even so, it seems that she did not know quite how much he had done. She did not know that he had discovered why men were dying in her hospital and had sent the Sanitary Commission to stop it. These secret philanthropists went to astonishing lengths to hide their good deeds, especially from each other.

It must be partly because of her new insight into the methods of politicians like Palmerston, as well as disenchantment with the approach she used at Scutari, that Nightingale's management methods changed radically after her breakdown. For the rest of her life, she adopted an approach that was the extreme opposite of the one she had used during her short nursing career. She set herself a number of difficult objectives in the years after the war. She wanted to reverse the policy she had previously endorsed of making military nurses subordinate to the medical officers. Other objectives included separating sanitary and medical responsibilities in the army, reducing the use of civilian hospitals in favour of community health care delivery, modifying accepted standards of hospital architecture, introducing statistical reporting in them, and bringing commercial sanitary engineering expertise into government. In addition to these public health questions she became actively involved in the administration of India, in education, the relief of poverty, the regulation of prostitution, and many other areas.

Each of her public health objectives could only be achieved by introducing change at every level of military and civilian government. During the war she had insisted on being given a title and authority, and had shunned the hospitals where her authority was not well defined. But after the war she never accepted any title or authority at all. No paid official was ever to report to her, and she refused all requests by organisations that wanted to use her name. She worked with Cabinet Ministers, Viceroys, hospital administrators, senior Government officials, and others simply by meddling sixteen hours a day in their business. She never wanted to superintend nurses again. She lost her youthful desire to enter a competitive profession like a man, and turned against the idea that a woman should have a career. For many years she stopped referring to nursing as a profession, and she opposed the registration of nurses as being the first step in creating a career path. She also naturally opposed the idea of women becoming doctors – she probably did not think it was a worthwhile activity for either sex, but may have thought that the careerist instincts of the male were incorrigible.

At Scutari, in her desire to make a career for herself and others, she had micro-managed the nurses' lives; many of them were so oppressed by her tight control that they escaped to other hospitals, a move which she did her utmost to resist. When she began to take an interest in nursing again later in life, her method of controlling nurses was the exact opposite: empowerment. She monitored probationer nurses' development through written reports from the training school, identified those whom she trusted on the basis of these reports, and then motivated these nurses and ensured that they were given the most important posts. Then she continued to motivate these picked leaders by occasional interviews throughout their career, acting as an employment and information exchange. This hands-off approach to managing nurses may appear to have been chosen by necessity to suit her invalidity. But it may have been simply a deliberate reversal of her Scutari role, and an endorsement of the view of her friend John Stuart Mill that the 'principal business of the central authority should be to give instruction, the local authority to apply it. Power may be localised, but knowledge to be most useful must be centralised.'

Amy Hughes, the district nurse who wrote the book that instructed mothers how to avoid boiling their children's milk, is an example of a nurse whom Nightingale developed in this way. Miss Hughes trained at St Thomas's in 1885, and as was the custom at the end of her training paid a visit on Miss Nightingale. The sage of

South Street lay on her couch and chatted for a while, then suddenly announced that her visitor was to become a 'district nurse' – attending the sick poor in their homes rather than in hospital. Amy Hughes was startled by this news, but as Miss Nightingale went on to describe the necessity for such work with great feeling, Miss Hughes felt that she had no alternative but to agree even though she had worked for her training and had no legal obligation to the Nightingale Fund. Nightingale thereafter interviewed her every year, and twice made her change jobs. After ten years Nightingale revised Amy Hughes' book on district nursing, introducing much new material including the detailed instructions for sterilising milk while retaining its nutrients.

It must have been a source of pride to Nightingale that the woman she selected and commanded to help keep the poor out of hospital should take to it well enough to write an instruction book 'to help my fellow-workers in the service of the poor' as Hughes put it on the title page. As a special mark of favour, Nightingale allowed Hughes to dedicate the book to her 'with permission', although she insisted that Hughes remove a reference to Nightingale's having helped to write it. Hughes, by preserving every single word that Nightingale wrote to her, has now repaid her mistress by posthumously acquitting her of a charge of encouraging milk-borne infections.

A factor which contributed to the disaster in the East had been the failure to use effectively the available means of communication to share information between hospitals and to obtain expert advice. A simple weekly report of deaths sent from her hospital to the military authorities in the Crimea would have saved thousands of lives. Because of this, statistical reporting in hospitals became an obsession of Nightingale's in later life. In addition, she used the Post Office to great effect in maintaining a network of suppliers of public health information.

She is thought to have been the most prolific letter-writer that the world is ever likely to know, rivalling or exceeding Charles Dickens. Approximately 12,000 of her letters are known to survive and many previously unknown ones come to light each year, often preserved as family heirlooms. The number known or suspected to have been deliberately destroyed is also large. Relatively few of her letters were on family and social business. She maintained a nation-wide network of experts, and ensured the diffusion of their information by putting them in touch with Government departments in need of advice and arranging for them to be paid.

The Post Office had stopped charging recipients for the carriage of letters only fifteen years before the Crimean war, when it adopted the pre-paid penny post which encouraged the flow of unsolicited information. The Victorian postal system was by the 1860s a marvel of efficiency, and Nightingale exploited it to the full. In a letter to a chemist who developed techniques for measuring the purity of air and water, she requests him to provide a report on water analysis for the War Office and gives him instructions on how to get paid from public funds. The envelope is consigned simply to 'Dr R Angus Smith Esq. PhD, Manchester' above Nightingale's imperious command 'To be forwarded'. She didn't need to know the address; the Post Office would find it out. Nightingale had discovered the information superhighway. Angus Smith was one of a very few experts whom Nightingale mentioned approvingly by name (twice) in *Notes on Nursing*. He went on to become the country's first salaried environmental protection officer. It is highly unlikely that Nightingale ever met him; he seems to have been typical of the many unassuming and dedicated public servants who benefited from being part of the extensive Nightingale postal network.

She remained completely bed-ridden for eleven years after 1857. Her disability did not interfere with her work, and it has been suggested that it may even have increased her productivity. She was in regular written communication with hundreds of public health administrators, but hardly saw anyone in person except Sutherland, her doctor, for whom she obtained more or less permanent employment in military and civilian public health posts. She preferred not to speak, even to him, and communicated her instructions for the country's sanitary improvements by notes even when he was in her presence.

This was her most intense period of work – those first years after her return from the war, following her discoveries and her recovery from mental and physical collapse. The small army of her collaborators was soon whittled down by early death: Sidney Herbert, Alexis Soyer, the reformer of army kitchens, Arthur Clough, and Thomas Alexander, her nominated head of the Army Medical Department. She toiled on, as if seeking a martyrdom of unseen suffering and slavery, like that of the soldiers abandoned by their country during that first terrible winter above Sebastopol.

Nobody has ever discovered what she achieved for public health, because her way of working makes it hard to measure her success by customary standards. There is a revisionist school of thought that claims that in great reform movements a leader with a dominant and ambitious personality usually slows down the spontaneous organic process of reform within society's institutions. Nightingale's rival John Simon is cited as an example of an apparently charismatic leader who was in reality a parasite attached to one such spontaneous process, diverting a small part of its energy to feed his own career ambitions. The rapid improvement of sanitation and medical education in the 19th century, for both of which Nightingale worked assiduously behind the scenes, are quoted as examples of these organic processes of reform that proceeded more smoothly precisely because they did not have a leader.[39]

7

———

Reputation and myth

HISTORIANS AGREE THAT Nightingale destroyed part of her correspondence during the years after the war. We might expect that she would do this to protect her reputation, but even her worst critics are surprised that she carefully preserved so much that obviously casts her in a bad light, including evidence of her callous treatment of Sidney Herbert and her jibes at Lord Panmure about whom she later admitted she had been mistaken. It is probably true that she preserved the bad as well as the good because she wanted to be historically important, like President Nixon, but that does not explain why she *did* destroy some historically important material. A thorough re-examination of the records in the light of her post-war discovery shows that there is a pattern to the destruction. It concerns the discussion of alternative explanations for the deaths at Scutari before she came to accept Farr's diagnosis in May 1857. The most conspicuous example of her censorship is the destruction of correspondence between her and Farr while she was in the process of conversion to his theories during March and April of that year. A letter has been quoted from William Farr confirming that he had reluctantly destroyed at her request all the letters she wrote him from that period. In her own file of letters *from* William Farr, now in the British Library, there is no correspondence at all between mid-

February and early May 1857, while the periods before and after are filled with letters. This shows clearly where the focus of her destruction lay.

In these destroyed letters she must have continued to promote the theory of her friends McNeill and Tulloch that the men were already dying when they entered her hospital. She must have written many other letters before she met Farr, expounding this view that their previous ill-treatment by the army had killed them. She apparently destroyed nearly all such letters, or persuaded their correspondents to destroy them. Only one is known to have survived – the one already quoted, which she had written to Lord Panmure in August 1855: 'The physically deteriorating effect of the Scutari air has been much discussed but it may be doubted. The men sent down to Scutari in the winter died because they were not sent down till half dead – the men sent down now live and recover because they are sent in time'. The letter shows that she did not believe that Sutherland's Sanitary Commission had made any difference to the death rate at Scutari in the spring of 1855.

Her destruction of the correspondence was so comprehensive that we are only able to date her conversion to Farr's theories by noting when the hole appears in her records, and by picking up fragments from around the rim of the crater, so to speak. One such fragment is the letter that she wrote to McNeill in May 1857 telling him that she had informed Queen Victoria that bad hygiene in her hospitals had killed the soldiers. She destroyed this letter, but she must have been unaware of the fact that her inquisitive sister had made a copy of it. There was a statement in this anxious letter to McNeill that does not appear in any other surviving letter. That statement was of her belief that reducing the overcrowding at Scutari, rather than improving the sanitation, had caused the death rate to fall. This theory was one that she would consistently deny afterwards, because it supported the doctors' argument that the Chadwick-inspired Sanitary Commission had achieved nothing. She later tried to get Dr Sutherland, the head of the Sanitary Commission, to agree with her that the death rate only fell when his sanitary improvements were complete, but he would not do so: 'The mortality at Scutari had fallen off before our Sanitary works – as you will see by the table you have,' wrote Sutherland. 'Our works swept the excess away.'[1]

Nightingale went to extraordinary lengths to track down the originals of letters that she had written during the period when she was, as we would say now, in denial of Farr's theory and just before her breakdown when she was admitting to a change of heart. She persuaded some of her correspondents to destroy them – like Farr – while others returned them to her so that she could selectively destroy them herself. The censorship tended to focus on the correspondence with her closest confidants. Conspicuously missing from the period are letters to her religious adviser Cardinal Manning, to Reverend Mother Mary Clare, her confidante at the Bermondsey Convent, to Colonel Lefroy, to Arthur Clough, and nearly all letters to her family between 13 July and 15 August 1857. In many cases she had to wait until after the recipient's death to recover her letters. This may explain why there are so many original letters *from* Nightingale in her own papers now in the British Library. These include her letters to Sidney Herbert – which she demanded that he return just before her breakdown. On that occasion Herbert replied to his old friend gently and sadly refusing her request: 'I enclose a batch of your papers. But I do not give up my rights of property, our engagement not having been broken off you have no right to have your letters back.'[2] After Herbert died, Nightingale visited his home at Wilton and removed these letters.[3]

In some cases she appears to have been extremely selective, only destroying parts of letters. For example, one of her letters to Herbert in March 1857 says 'I now send you some sanitary figures . . . .' The rest of the letter is missing. The missing figures may have made reference to Farr's new theory, and her denial of it. The absence of a separate leaf may be accidental, but there is a more significantly incomplete letter to Nightingale from Colonel Lefroy, Panmure's Crimean trouble-shooter. In it Lefroy begins to talk about the differences in relative mortality in the Crimea and at Scutari, but just as he does so the remainder of the letter is torn off, which cannot be an accident.[4] Lefroy wrote this letter just after Nightingale returned to England, and it is quite possible that the missing pages contained Nightingale's first glimpse of the mortality figures that Tulloch had prepared and then suppressed at Panmure's request. There may well have been some reference in Lefroy's letter to Nightingale's previous claim to the War Office that 'the Scutari air' was not to blame.

Sir Edward Cook, the first biographer to have access to Nightingale's papers after her death, found that she had carefully organised her papers dating from before 1861, and had obviously destroyed many of them. From that date onwards, she seemed to have preserved virtually everything. This also supports the theory that she had something to hide from the early period. The most obvious explanation would be that she wanted to protect her Crimean reputation, but this doesn't fit with the pattern of destruction. If that had been her objective then she could easily have destroyed much more. She could have destroyed the letters that she had written to Lefroy and Herbert from the Crimea in which she was conspicuously silent on the need for improvements to sewers and ventilation. Destroying these letters would have helped to perpetuate the myth, circulated by Kinglake in his ponderous history of the war, that it was she who had called for the Sanitary Commission to be sent to Scutari. In any case, if she wanted to protect her reputation, why would she print and disseminate against the Government's wishes her Confidential Report, 'Notes on Matters Affecting the Health of the British Army', which remains to this day the only known source of evidence that her hospitals were more than twice as lethal as the hospitals in the Crimea that she had denigrated during the war?

There is one way to explain her very selective destruction of the records: she thought that she was going to die and was worried that after her death some of her letters of criticism of Farr and defence of her hospital could be used by the enemies of sanitary reform to discredit Farr and challenge his theories. This is borne out by the evidence cited in Cope that she asked Farr to destroy her letters in connection with her supposed imminent death. The destruction is that of a woman concerned with a purely operational matter: the successful implementation of sanitary reforms. She could not allow her death to interfere with her purpose.

After the spring of 1857, when Nightingale completed her statistical analysis with Farr, she never spoke of her mission at Scutari in favourable terms. This is in marked contrast to the period before that date, when she was sometimes quite vainglorious about it. One illustration of her later reluctance to express satisfaction with her work at Scutari is in a letter she wrote to her aunt in August 1887 containing a rare retrospective self-congratulation. She conspicuously omits to mention the value of her work up to her breakdown, including her war service and the Royal Commission: 'In this month 34 years ago you lodged me in Harley Street. And in this month, 31 years ago you returned me to England from Scutari. And in this month 30 years ago the first Royal Commission was finished. And since then, 30 years of work often cut to pieces but never destroyed.'[5] She could easily have written, 'In all, 34 years of work often cut to pieces ....' Such omissions are admittedly very inconclusive, and neither Nightingale nor any of the people closest to her left behind any reminiscences confirming that she felt guilt as a result of her failure during the war. Nightingale may not have known, may not have admitted that her feelings of guilt were even important to her. But Farr, Herbert, Tulloch, McNeill, Lefroy, Sutherland, and others could not have failed to understand the reason for her obsessive activity, her illness, and her attacks on her family. Some of them must have felt at least partly responsible for the official blunders that had given her so much responsibility and had led her into a terrible personal disaster. They surrounded her like a bodyguard: tolerant to her whims, impervious to her insults and sarcasm, discreetly carrying out her nagging orders to the letter, and taking their secrets to the grave.

But Nightingale would not be Nightingale is she couldn't find a way to leave behind some trace of her feelings without having to acknowledge them. The obvious places to look for a leakage of her emotions would be in her mystical writings, particularly the collection entitled *Suggestions for Thought*, which she wrote in the months following her breakdown. This was an expanded version, running to 800 pages, of a sixty-nine page work that she had printed in 1852, before she went to the war. She began to write *Suggestions for Thought* as a description of the religious doubts that she attributed to ordinary people, and her answers to them. It started life in 1852 as 'To the Artizans of England', her response to some cynical arguments put to her by working-class men in the villages surrounding her father's estate in Derbyshire. Indignant, and perhaps unable to counter their arguments face to face, she had laboured earnestly over a pamphlet which rebutted their atheistical views. After the war, this pamphlet in its expanded version became *Suggestions for Thought to the Searchers after Truth among the Artisans of England*. Then in its final volume the audience was no longer the artisans; the title became *Suggestions for Thought to Searchers after Religious Truth*.

Who had these searchers become in 1860, if they were no longer the artisans of 1852? Was there now only one searcher after religious truth, and was her name Florence Nightingale? The 1860 version of this book (of which only six printed copies are known to have existed) was only seen by her closest confidants. Her mentor and protector Sir John McNeill, who knew better than anyone what she had been through, was one of them. McNeill pronounced the work totally unsuited for the purpose for which she said it was intended – the conversion of unbelievers. However he added the obscure prediction that it was a 'mine from which one day much precious metal may be drawn.'[6] Such a work should indeed be a goldmine of personal information, because of her claim that it contains her spiritual guidance to a public suffering from religious doubts. When people are suppressing an emotion they are likely to attribute it to others. A psychologist can often explore a subject's own unconscious by giving him an opportunity to make speculative generalisations about other people's emotions.

The book may be one of a common genre: a plea from the emotions to the more rational part of the brain, asking to be let in.

[187]

Suggestions for Thought is a collection of oblique suggestions of things that Florence Nightingale ought to start thinking about without fear. Things like guilt, remorse, suffering and evil. It could be subtitled: *Notes on Matters Affecting the Health of Miss Florence Nightingale, Founded on the Experience of the Russian War.* Virtually everything that is in the 1852 version of her religious testament survives in slightly altered form in the 1860 *Suggestions for Thought.* A comparison of the two documents allows us to study the continuity and change in Nightingale's most private thinking before and after the war and, more important, her post-war discoveries.

The 1852 version was a rather dry and theoretical proof that human nature must be innately good despite the fact that the historical record seems to show the contrary. Nightingale claimed that our recognition of past evil is in itself proof that we can avoid it in future. Human progress will occur purely as a result of our innate ability to recognise evil. Sinners do not need to feel remorse, neither is there any need for God to punish them. What we must do is strive to improve our ability to distinguish good from evil.

The Nightingale philosophy had no room in it for distinctions between sin, ignorance, evil, mistakes, and crime. These were all the result of cause-and-effect relationships which were not properly understood by the perpetrators. Knowledge of God's laws would eventually abolish all of them. Those who make mistakes, she said, are the pioneers: 'The pioneer's is the highest calling, and God calls the highest men to it. But thieves and murderers, who are also His calling, are in some sense His pioneers!'[7] During the war she had told Lord Raglan proudly that 'My father's religious and social ethics make us strive to be the pioneers of the human race.' When she did so she was already including herself in a category that contained thieves and murderers, because she had already defined it thus in the 1852 version of her tract. This gives some idea of the broad-minded philosophy with which her father had equipped her. Oddly, the 1852 version also mentions 'sanitary science', but in its older sense of medical care rather than drainage. She used it in 1852 to argue that minds can be made healthy by following good religious advice in the same way that the body can benefit physically from medical counsel.

One of the most remarkable aspects of Nightingale's thought is that many of her concepts, including the religious ones, survived the shocks of the war and its aftermath. After she found out about her failure at Scutari, we might have expected her to conclude that it had been juvenile arrogance that had dared to disguise itself as the voice of God calling her to work in hospitals. We might have expected her to remark that calls from God are a sign of over-confidence coupled with a lack of basic training. But many private notes show that her faith was unchanged, and God continued to speak to her. Likewise, her belief in the perfectibility of man and the duty of mankind to strive for perfection, was a cornerstone of her beliefs before the war and afterwards. The post-war *Suggestions for Thought* confirms this.

To say that these mental constructions survived intact is only another way of saying that they helped her to survive a shock that would have driven many over the brink. It is to acknowledge that the conceptual framework with which she started was of an exceptionally strong manufacture. One of the concepts that was to stand her in good stead was that of using numeric data to support proposals for social change. We have seen that unfortunately she was not familiar before the war with Farr's use of death statistics in public health. She was, however, familiar with the use of statistics in social science pioneered by Adolphe Quetelet. Even before the war she was fascinated by Quetelet's work. She went considerably further than him in her belief that statistics, by revealing cause and effect relationships which were not visible at the level of the individual, could help administrators to improve society. This belief is at the root of the optimistic advice in her *Suggestions for Thought*. She was much more optimistic than Quetelet himself, who thought that the main benefit of his discoveries would be intellectual satisfaction.

One reason that British workers like Nightingale could be more optimistic about the practical application of Quetelet's theories was that in Britain the industrial revolution had given them practical experience of how numerical approaches could help to increase productivity. Jeremy Bentham's 'greatest happiness for the greatest number' was an attempt to apply the concepts of industrial revolution to social issues, much to the distress of some humanitarians who found it inappropriate to measure human happiness like ingots of pig iron. Edwin Chadwick had begun his career as Bentham's protégé, and Chadwick's unfeeling reliance on numbers and productivity was part of the reason for his inability to mobilise public opinion. After her breakdown Nightingale's religious approach and her emotional commitment may have helped British social science to break out of Bentham's trap.

Nightingale adapted Quetelet's theories to make them more practical and more acceptable to philanthropists. Quetelet's demonstration that statistical methods could predict accurately even something as capricious as the number of twenty-year-old men marrying sixty-year-old women, or the number of murders committed with each type of instrument, made it appear that free will was less important than many philanthropists would like. Nightingale met this problem head on by denying the importance of free will at the individual level, even contradicting Quetelet. In the absence of knowledge, she claimed, the ability of the individual to choose was limited, and in the presence of knowledge any rational being would make the same choice. She wrote in *Suggestions for Thought* how unimportant her supposed 'free will' had been in determining her own actions: 'Could I, when I knew the soldiers were being murdered wholesale, decide otherwise than to give all I had to prevent it?' This was itself a revealingly ambiguous rhetorical question. Was she referring to the murdered soldiers at Scutari, or to the 1200 soldiers a year who she found afterwards were being killed by defective sanitation in their barracks in England? In both cases her free will had been the same but the statistical information at her disposal was different and, therefore, so were her actions.

Nightingale came to believe that Quetelet had discovered in statistics the language that God uses for telling us what to do in order to improve mankind. Quetelet had in fact discovered an empirical proof that 'we are members one of another' – all of us are variations on a theme, something that was by no means understood before. This enables us to use empirical data to predict the effect on society of an administrator's actions. She wrote of 'the application of Quetelet's discoveries to explaining the plan of God in teaching us by these results the laws of progress – to explaining the path on which we must go if we are to discover the laws of the Divine Government.'[8] She used the word 'law' almost as a synonym for cause-and-effect relationship. The world is made up of these causes and effects but they are only gradually being identified by mankind, according to her. The most powerful tool for doing so is the statistical method, which arrays apparently unrelated facts in such a way as to allow man to relate the cause to the effect. The reason that she may have used the concept of law instead of talking of cause and effect is that in her Unitarian way she did not want to attempt complex descriptions of the cause, as the medical profession did. Statistical evidence was more important.

God requires us, therefore, to work by trial and error. Statistics only work after the fact. To learn how to prevent premature death many such deaths must occur in a controlled environment, and someone must wish to make use of the experience gained. That, she now knew, was why God had called her. This optimistic analysis was the positive side of *Suggestions for Thought*, the logical part, the thoughts that she attributes to herself as writer of the book. The book also describes some negative, more emotional, thoughts. These she attributes to the reader, the 'searcher after religious truth,' whom she was trying to help by writing these suggestions. Nightingale's philosophy as expounded in the book will, she hopes, help to drive these bad thoughts out of the reader's mind. The bad thoughts, on examination, turn out to be what one would expect of a well-meaning woman who is tortured by the discovery of her ignorant participation in a slaughter of the innocents.

In her book, Nightingale tells the tormented searcher after religious truth that she should not feel remorse and guilt for past mistakes because these mistakes were a part of God's plan. Nightingale assures the searcher that evil is necessary in God's scheme to achieve perfection, and that in feeling remorse and guilt the searcher is actually obstructing His plan because these negative feelings prevent her from concentrating on the tasks He has given her. The searcher after truth must realise that there will be no forgiveness for her and other criminals because God believes that forgiveness is not only unnecessary but would also be unkind. Throughout the book, Nightingale uses the plural 'we' to express her 'official' beliefs: the optimistic philosophy that she claims to have and which she wishes the reader to adopt. Occasionally, an 'I' appears, usually when expressing a bad thought which needs correcting, as if to get closer to the reader by imagining the reader's individual situation. An example is the following description of counter-productive guilt. There is a sudden change from 'our' to 'I' in the first sentence, and then the closer to her guilt she comes, the more confused the personal pronouns, as Nightingale becomes lost in a hall of verbal mirrors:

> Our belief amounts to this: that I may look back on any particular moment of the past, and truly feel that it was impossible at that moment (God's laws being what they are, and having operated on all preceding that moment as they did) that I should have willed other than as I did. It is therefore untrue and useless for me to cry out 'Oh, how worthy of blame, how deserving of punishment I was.' My good friend, I should rather say to myself 'don't be afraid, you will have suffering enough in what you have done. You exhaust the powers which you have in you for finding out the laws to alter nature or circumstance, by these exclamations.' 'Come back,' I would say kindly to myself, 'I know you could not help it. Let us have patience with ourself, and see what we can do.'[9]

The cure for remorse, according to Nightingale, is extremely simple: it is to realise that it does not exist. 'Remorse is not a true feeling – not a feeling of what really is; for remorse is blame to ourselves for the past. But if the origin of our will, and our will itself, were, as it has been, in accordance with law, there cannot in truth be blame to ourselves personally, individually.'[10]

[192]

In admonishing the searcher after truth not to waste time on remorse, Nightingale uses the official 'our', but does go so far as to admit to having strayed down the forbidden path of remorse herself: 'Our experience is, that to dwell on the past error with feelings of remorse depresses the energy, all of which is wanted to pursue the right in future.'[11] This admission that she has experienced remorse was added after the war. In her earlier 1852 tract we find word for word the quotations above about remorse 'not being a true feeling', one which distracts people from good works. The difference is that in 1852 there is never any mention that the writer might ever have suffered any remorse. No cry from the heart 'Oh, how worthy of blame, how deserving of punishment I was'; no admission that the author has herself been guilty of the sin of remorse. A sentence in the 1860 version: 'To look back on my life is to look back upon a tissue of mistakes,' was not present in 1852.

One reason why remorse is not true feeling is that God himself is the author of all the evil for which men may blame themselves: 'God's laws *are* the origin of moral, as of physical evil – that it is so is part of His righteous rule. Through them, by our mistakes, we find truth; by our errors, knowledge; by our sufferings, happiness; by our evil, good.' In 1852 mankind had to learn how to recognise evil. It was no good relying on remorse to identify evil that we have done, as we have seen, and it was no good thinking God was going to punish us, for example by visiting cholera upon us as was vulgarly supposed. God is more merciful than that. God has given us an innate ability to recognise good and evil so he does not need to use punishments as a deterrent. But in 1860 there is a major departure from the 1852 version. She had discovered that God does need to use punishment after all: 'We find that [i.e. an official Nightingale belief follows] *punishment*, if the word be used in the sense of suffering or privation consequent on sin or ignorance, does exist in God's moral government, and we see it to be right, because its effect will be sooner or later to induce mankind to remedy the evils which incur it.'[12]

Remorse is still not true, but suffering God's punishment for mistakes has now become essential to the learning process. Nightingale seems to have made this fine distinction to disguise the internal nature of her afflictions. She could not admit that her suffering was the result of her own emotional distress. God is, in 1860, inflexible in His punishment, and fortunately is not prone to 'having mercy on His erring children. This mercy would be the height of cruelty. As long as His laws have not inflicted evil consequences on our sin and ignorance till no vestige of either is left in us, mercy means to leave us in sin and consequently in misery.'[13] Punishment can only be useful when applied to the living. Eternal damnation cannot possibly exist, says Nightingale, because it would not be a remedial punishment. It would not serve God's purpose of promoting human progress.

All sin, says Nightingale, arises from ignorance of God's laws. By law, as we have already seen, Nightingale meant something like a cause-and-effect relationship. Because mankind can, by examination of statistics, learn how these laws operate, he can ensure that evil is only 'temporary', i.e. does not affect all future generations. Like a good teacher, God gives us an eternity to answer each of our problems. In this eternity there will always remain some evil unresolved, but 'there will not be always masses of evil, lying untouched, unpenetrated by light and wisdom'. The most important addition to the philosophy in 1860 is an explanation of how philanthropists could cause new evils by their ignorant intervention, and yet still be doing God's work: 'Each advance has always brought evil with good, because each advance must, in some degree, be made upon a hypothesis. But mankind, because men are similar to each other, will more and more speedily turn the evil into good ... there will be a perpetual and rapid change of evil into good; thence fresh temporary evil, thence fresh permanent good.'[14]

An an example of man-made evil she quoted Quetelet's finding that charities which took in abandoned children increased child mortality dramatically by encouraging mothers to abandon them in unhealthy crowded institutions. Although inevitable, such philanthropic evil would be easy to remedy due to the philanthropists' skill at identifying and rectifying their own mistakes. This also explained,

[194]

of course, why the disaster at Scutari should lead to rapid improvements in public health that more than compensated for it.

It may not be too surprising, against this background of the sufferings identified in *Suggestions for Thought*, that Nightingale appeared to identify herself with Christ. Or, it might be more accurate to say that she may have believed that Christ had a similar problem to hers. She dismissed outright the possibility that God might have made Christ suffer for the sins of others[15] – that did not fit in with her scheme of improvement at all. The implication is that Christ suffered for a mistake of his own. Nightingale talked about Christ in a familiar way, as if she thought that she understood him as a human being, and it may be that she imagined that he, too, had been one of God's pioneers: 'Christ's whole life almost was a war upon the family,' she wrote approvingly. She thought him a 'beautiful tender spirit' but criticised his rather off-hand attitude to public health, morals, and education. Some of her private religious writings have caused embarrassment because they seem to equate her sufferings with Christ's, as in the following note written in about 1868:

'I have seen his face
The crown of glory inseparably united with the Crown of Thorns
giving forth the same light
Three times he has called me
once to his service Feb 7 1837
Once to be a Deliverer May 7 1852
Once to the cross July 28 1865
to suffer more even that I have hitherto done
aut pati aut mori [either to suffer or to die]
for on the Cross I shall see his face
Am I being offered to him?
Then this is his answer
the crown of thorns round the light and radiant head
And is it not worth all to see his face?
and may I think that I am another Himself, another like that?
Oh too happy *aut pati aut mori*

[195]

Oh too blessed that He should look upon me as another like that
another in *état de victime* [victimised]
for all perfection is in that'[16]

In another note she refers to God's call to her to be a 'saviour' on
May 7 1852, showing that this word was synonymous with 'deliverer'.
It will be remembered that she referred to Colonel Tulloch as a deliverer for his efforts to feed the starving troops in the Crimea single-
handed. She defines a saviour or deliverer as 'one who saves from
social, from moral error' by finding out one or more of the laws of
God. It is not clear whether she had a theory to explain how Christ
earned the status of saviour, and the right to suffer. In her philosophy a person could suffer for her sins for her whole lifetime, but no
suffering was to be eternal and she did not seem to believe in heaven.
There was only one way out of this intellectual problem, and that was
that the sufferer would have to participate in, and experience the lives
of future, less sinful generations – a state that she called 'continued
identity'. This was in tune with her own consuming interest in the
long-term improvement of society and her disdain for the pursuit of
short-term individual goals.

She did not foresee a heavenly park for disembodied spirits but
rather a future existence in which the dead could continue to exercise their full range of individual and idiosyncratic human capabilities. Mere communication between the dead and the living would not
be sufficient relief for the departed sinners who had suffered so
much in their lifetime. Justice would require that they should be able
to actively participate after their death in the better life on earth that
they helped to create. 'Without the belief in a continued identity,
there is really no belief in [God's] wise and good superintendence,'
she confessed. 'What would we say of a Being who could cause such
sufferings for no future benefit to the sufferer, but for future temporary benefit to some future being?'[17] The continued identity theme is
one that only appeared after the war, in the 1860 version of *Suggestions
for Thought*. It seems that she was hoping for some sort of multiple
and partial reincarnation into the personalities of later generations.

She could presumably help to make this come true, for herself, by devoting all her idiosyncratic individual capabilities in life to the pursuit and promotion of goals that would only be reached in an eternity of man's existence.

If Nightingale planned to live on in future generations, it was not her intention to do so through her public reputation. This is fortunate because the distortion of her reputation that took place after her death was truly astonishing. An examination of the information sources available shows that during her lifetime most people must have known that the sentimental wartime propaganda portrait of her was embarrassingly false. It appears that nobody had the heart to demolish this outdated image while she lived, and after her death various self-seeking organisations and individuals dusted it off and added a varnish of new myths about her role in the training of modern hospital nurses.

A very large number of educated people after 1857 knew the details of Nightingale's theory that her hospital had caused a disproportionate number of the fatalities during the war. Most medical people would also know that she had changed her mind during the Royal Commission, because she had widely canvassed her old theory in letters that she later destroyed. Many influential people in all walks of life had received private copies of her confidential report pointing out how the mortality 'was due to the frightful state of the Hospitals at Scutari; how much it depended on the number which each Regiment was unfortunately enabled to send to those pesthouses'. This allegation appeared in the first few pages, and in an annex there was also a table of data to support it. It is likely that at least a hundred copies of the report went to the most influential citizens in the country. The recipients must have talked of it with others – but obeyed the strict instructions that she gave them not to publish it, leave it lying around, or refer to it publicly. From letters of the time it appears that in those days people could make sensational revelations in confidence to their correspondents under the simple admonition that the revelations were 'private'. People could be trusted, but nevertheless it must be assumed that the revelations in

[197]

the 'confidential report' leaked to a very wide audience by word of mouth, though never in print.

We cannot easily establish what were the opinions of the mass of the population. If we could, we might be able to determine to what extent Nightingale's ideas contributed to the remarkable changes in society that came later in her life. We might also be able to discover whether the one-dimensional public image with which she returned from the East was really all that ordinary people ever knew. Was she always to them simply the merciful angel of Scutari, whose personal purity had silenced the curses in the soldiers' throats and made the rough surgeons gentle? Is it only because of our own supposedly superior modern intellect that the 'real' Florence Nightingale is now emerging? Strangely enough it is probable that between 1857 and 1910 the whole country knew much more about Nightingale's failure and her personal problems than did later generations. The Nightingale myth may be a modern re-invention.

People who were not chosen to receive her confidential report must have heard the inside story from those 'in authority' who were. In addition, some popular books powerfully criticising Nightingale appeared during and just after the war from nurses who had worked under her. An example is Mrs Davis's 1857 autobiography which in an appendix contains the allegation that Nightingale's own 'Barrack Hospital at Scutari continued to present the greatest amount of least alleviated misery of any war hospital belonging to the British Army of the East.'[18] More importantly, Nightingale herself ensured that the mass of the population received information that would counter the wartime propaganda. One of the people to whom she sent her confidential report was Harriet Martineau, a famous and successful popular journalist of the time. Nightingale did not know Martineau very well, and could only have sent the book with the idea of provoking Martineau into print. They agreed that Martineau would do a series of articles and a book, which Nightingale wanted to be published very cheaply to get wide circulation. She volunteered to pay Martineau to write the book, eventually called *England and her Soldiers*.

Nightingale stipulated that Martineau must pretend that the work was based only on extracts from public documents, even though she could use the confidential report for additional background information. (The main difference between the public and confidential documents was the detailed indictment of Nightingale's own hospital.) Martineau must also not attribute any information to Nightingale and Nightingale insisted on revising the proofs, 'to guard against "innocent mistakes" as you say.' The phrase shows that they both knew it was censorship. Nightingale did change the proofs – she made Martineau include additional material about military tactics so that there could be a pretext for putting the book in regimental libraries. She told Martineau she hoped to arrange this with with the help of her friend Colonel Lefroy who had been given the job of founding the Army Educational Corps. Unfortunately Lefroy's absence for two months at the critical time interfered with this plan. The book stated that thousands of soldiers had been killed in hospital, poisoned by a foul atmosphere due to bad ventilation, and that Nightingale's own Barrack Hospital had been the worst-ventilated of all.

Nightingale supplied, for inclusion in the book, copies of the most attractive diagrams from one of her other reports which showed the rise and fall of the mortality in the hospitals at Scutari and in the East as a whole. 'No pesthouse could be more fatal than the Camp, the Transport, and the Hospital,' wrote Martineau, but she did not include the figures from Nightingale's confidential report that would have proved that the Barrack Hospital alone was a more deadly pesthouse than any combination of the three. Unlike previous books this one did not eulogise Nightingale. On the few occasions when it mentions her it describes her as a helpless participant, rather than as a monumental figure for whom the hospital might have been designed as a stage on which to exhibit her greatness. She is shown attending to the personal cleanliness of the victims and 'preparing them for surgery' – one of the recurring nightmares of families must have been the idea that their loved ones died in agony under the amputation saw. No soldiers were described kissing anybody's shadow, or anything remotely similar. There was no indica-

[199]

tion that Nightingale had anything to do with the book's production.

Martineau sent a copy of *England and her Soldiers* to Sidney Herbert, recently returned as Minister of War. She suggested to Herbert it would be a good idea to put a copy in each regimental library. Herbert was not sympathetic to the idea. 'It is a book for the authorities rather than for the men' he told her.[19] When Nightingale's friend Lefroy returned, Nightingale tried to get him to approve the army library scheme, but Lefroy said that someone had already suggested that to Herbert, who had vetoed the idea and that Lefroy could not go against the decision of his chief. Nightingale thereupon donated the fifty copies she had ordered to the lending libraries in 'Mechanics Institutes' throughout the country. There it would be read by the same 'artisans of England' with whom she had discussed her optimistic religious theories before the war.

England and her Soldiers must have had a relatively large popular readership, and was perhaps of more interest to civilians whose sons had died in the hospitals than it would have been to the soldiers. The publisher had not made the edition as cheap as Nightingale wanted, and her donation of copies to the libraries as well as a payment to Martineau to supplement the fee from the publisher may have been essential to ensure that her message reached the public. By the time the book was published in 1859, Nightingale had not been seen or heard of for a while. The contrast between her and Mary Seacole was striking. Mary Seacole was the heroic entrepreneurial nurse who ran her own convivial hotel at the front and clambered over the battlefields with a satchel of bandages. On her return to England, Seacole was awarded the Crimea Medal, an extraordinary departure from the rules. Lord Palmerston tried to award Nightingale a medal too.[20] No record remains of Nightingale's reaction to this proposal, but we can assume it was negative.

Immediately after the war Seacole was sporting her Crimea Medal proudly and living the high life in London, deservedly feted by the war's veterans and publishing to wide acclaim her account of her exploits. But where was Miss Florence Nightingale? She was not recounting her experiences as a lesson to the nation's youth, or basking with Mother Seacole on the music-hall stage. She appeared to be in hiding. Martineau's book, and Nightingale's disappearance, must have changed the general public's perception of Nightingale and her mission to Scutari. So must the publication of her strange and very popular *Notes on Nursing* in early 1860. Perhaps it will never be possible to tell how much the mass of the population knew of the truth about Florence Nightingale between 1860 and 1900. But it seems unlikely that the image of the angel of Scutari survived intact, even with the help of Kinglake's highly romanticised account in his history of the war, published between 1860 and 1881.

By the time Nightingale died in 1910, aged ninety, none of her contemporaries remained to contradict any posthumous distortions of her memory. The significance of her confidential report and the reasons for its suppression had been forgotten. Many of the copies she distributed found their way into medical collections, where the annex containing the secret of Scutari lay unopened for more than a century like the time capsule that she must have intended. The huge volume of papers that Nightingale left behind is impossible to condense into a comprehensive biography, and each biographer has been able to create a different Nightingale by drawing on different material. Sir Edward Cook, the biographer authorised by the family in 1913, created a career woman appropriate to an era that was looking forward to female emancipation. Cecil Woodham-Smith wanted to emphasise the family stresses and strains that her surviving relatives had forbidden Cook to describe and which fascinated 1950s England so much. In emphasising this aspect, Woodham-Smith lent credence to Nightingale's own theory that her breakdown was caused by her relationship with her mother and sister. Woodham-Smith borrowed political and nursing material from Cook and thus perpetuated both his censorship of the conflict with Queen Victoria and the myth of the Nightingale Training School that Cook had embellished to help that institution to survive the loss of its figurehead.

The tendency of biographers to rely almost exclusively on Nightingale's own archives has also obscured some of the extraordinary political storms through which she sailed, unaware as she was (at least before her shipwreck) of the tempests that raged around her. The result is a portrait which is unfair to her because it isolates her and does not give her the full credit she deserves for shaping the future of her nation. Nightingale, by selectively destroying the records of the events that caused her breakdown, also created her own reputation for irrational behaviour. This probably has caused many biographers to not take too seriously her claims that her hospital killed patients rather than cured them. In addition, there was probably a reluctance to examine so macabre a subject. What useful purpose could it serve?

In asking whether it serves a useful purpose now, we should ask how Nightingale would have wanted history to remember her. She was contemptuous of the notion that Sidney Herbert would have wanted to be remembered for saving lives. If she was sincere, she too should shun fame. Would she then prefer to be forgotten as an individual, the better to achieve her ambition of merging her soul into ours? If this were true, it would be unkind to rake over these old stories. But if it were true she would not have hoarded for posterity the huge archives that give such a fascinating insight into her age.

After about ten years of total invalidism, the middle-aged Nightingale appeared to regain some serenity, even happiness, and became more physically mobile. She started to take an interest in the Nightingale Training School, and formed sentimental attachments with some of the more able nurses there. She became very close to her sister and Parthe's husband and step-children, and probably she gained some insight into the real reason for the breakdown that she had previously blamed on her family.

There is evidence that she abandoned her harsh philosophy that philanthropists' mistakes are inevitable and beneficial, perhaps because she was able to stop pretending that she did not suffer remorse and shame for her own imagined blunders. In 1873 she wrote a rambling article entitled 'What will be our religion in 1999?' In it she makes indirect reference to the great blunder of her life and of the improvement she hopes for to the public attitude to such blunders before the millennium: 'There is no public opinion yet, it has to be created, as to not committing blunders for want of knowledge. Good intentions are supposed to be enough. Yet blunders, organised blunders, do more mischief than crimes. Yes, organised carelessness is more hurtful even than actual sin. Until you can create such a public opinion, little good will be done.' This is a clear contradiction of her earlier claim that blunders are beneficial. 'Organised carelessness' is a perfect description of the activity in the Barrack Hospital at Scutari. She now, in 1873, believed that avoiding blunders by foresight would be better than trial and error. She hoped that by 1999, people would have learned to avoid organised blunders like the one in which she participated.

So, if she did not want that old discarded individual identity named Florence Nightingale to be remembered for the good that she accomplished, she might have wanted it to be remembered for this great evil, so that we may learn to recognise 'organised carelessness' in time to avoid it. This may be why she preserved her records, so as not to lose the evidence of a great blunder by someone whose intentions were above reproach. It doesn't seem such a bad thing to go down in history for. How else might she choose to be remembered? As a tyrannical invalid? A neurotic meddler in Government affairs? As the founder of modern secular nursing, whose right to the title is subject to perpetual scholarly dispute? As a case of *Brucella melitensis?* Or as – perish the thought – the Lady with the Lamp?

It seems that she may have wanted history to remember how an ambitious young woman responded to a unique opportunity. How her country called on Florence Nightingale in a great national emergency, and sent her with unlimited power and resources to care for the health of 'the finest army that ever left these shores.' To remind us of the lessons learned she may have wanted history to remember how, through her ignorance and arrogance, she let that army die.

References

The following abbreviations are cited in the Notes, p. 209

Adkin — Adkin, Mark, *The Charge: Why the Light Brigade Was Lost.* Leo Cooper, London 1996

AMNS — Baly, Monica, *As Miss Nightingale Said . . .*, Baillière Tindall, London 1997

Artizans — Nightingale, Florence, 'To the Artizans of England', 1852 (British Library Cup 1247)

Baly — Baly, Monica, *Florence Nightingale and the Nursing Legacy.* (Second Edition) Whurr Publishers, London 1997

Bishop & Goldie — Bishop, W.J. and Sue Goldie, *A Bio-Bibliography of Florence Nightingale*, Dawsons of Pall Mall, London 1962

BLAM — British Library, Additional MSS

Bolster — Bolster, Evelyn, *The Sisters of Mercy in the Crimean War.* Mercier Press, Cork 1964

Bulloch — Bulloch, Vern, ed., *Florence Nightingale and Her Era*, Garland, New York 1990

Calabria — Calabria, Michael, and Janet Macrae, *Suggestions for Thought by Florence Nightingale.* University of Pennsylvania, Philadelphia 1994

Cantlie — Cantlie, Neil, *A History of the Army Medical Department*, Churchill Livingstone, London 1974

Chelsea — 'Report of the Board of General Officers Appointed to Inquire into the Statements Contained in the Reports of Sir John McNeill and Colonel Tulloch'. Chelsea Board, London 1856

Clough — Mulhauser, Frederick L., *The Correspondence of Arthur Hugh Clough*. Clarendon, Oxford 1957

Clough Poems — Lowry, H. F., ed., *The Poems of Arthur Hugh Clough*. Clarendon, Oxford 1951

Contribution — Nightingale, Florence, 'A Contribution to the Sanitary History of the British Army During the Late War With Russia'. John W. Parker, London 1859

Cook — Cook, Sir Edward, *The Life of Florence Nightingale*. Macmillan, London 1913

Cope — Cope, Zachary, *Florence Nightingale and the Doctors*. Museum, London 1958

Davis — Davis, Elizabeth, *The Autobiography of Elizabeth Davis, A Balaclava Nurse*, ed. Jane Williams. 2 vols. Hurst & Blackett, London 1857

Diamond — Diamond, Marion, and M. Stone, 'Nightingale on Quetelet'. Journal of the Royal Statistical Society, 1981

ES — Martineau, Harriet, *England and her Soldiers*. Smith, Elder & Co., London 1859

Eyler — Eyler, John M., *Victorian Social Medicine: The Ideas and Methods of William Farr*. Johns Hopkins, Baltimore 1979

Finlayson — Finlayson, Geoffrey, *The Seventh Earl of Shaftesbury*. Eyre Methuen, London 1981

GBH — *General Board of Health* (Papers relating to, with Introductory Report, by the Medical Officer of the Board, on the Preventability of certain kinds of Premature Death). Eyre and Spottiswoode, London 1858

GCal — Goldie, Sue, 'A Calendar of the Letters of Florence Nightingale'. Oxford Microform, Oxford 1983

Geison — Geison, Gerald L., *The Private Science of Louis Pasteur*. Princeton 1995

GLRO — 'Greater London Record Office'

Goldie Crimea — *'I have Done My Duty': Florence Nightingale in the*

Crimean War, 1854–56, ed. Sue M. Goldie. Manchester University Press, Manchester 1987

Goodman — Goodman, Margaret, *Experiences of an English Sister of Mercy*. Smith, Elder & Co., London 1862

Greville — Greville, Charles, *The Greville Memoirs*. Longmans, London 1874

Harley Street — Verney, H., *Florence Nightingale at Harley Street*. Dent, London 1970

Hibbert — Hibbert, Christopher, *The Destruction of Lord Raglan: A Tragedy of the Crimean War, 1854–55*. Longmans, Green, London 1961

Hodder — Hodder, E., *The Life and Work of the Seventh Earl of Shaftesbury*. Cassell, London 1886

Hopkirk — Hopkirk, Peter, *The Great Game*. Oxford University Press, Oxford 1990

Hospital Reports — 'Copy of all Official Reports of the Hospitals at Scutari, Kululi, Abydos, and Smyrna, since February last'. War Department 31 July 1855. House of Commons No. 449

Jenkins — Jenkins, Roy, *Gladstone*. Papermac, London 1996

Lambert — Lambert, Royston, *Sir John Simon 1816–1904*. Macgibbon & Kee, London 1963

Longmore — Longmore, T., *The Sanitary Contrasts of the British and French Armies During the Crimean War*. Charles Griffin, London 1883

M&T — 'Report of the Royal Commission into the Supplies of the British Army in the Crimea. Vol. XX 1856' (McNeill and Tulloch Report)

McNeill — Macalister, Florence Stewart, *Memoir of the Right Hon. Sir John McNeill, G. C. B. and of his second wife, Elizabeth Wilson. By their granddaughter*. John Murray, London 1910

Marston — Marston, Maurice, *Sir Edwin Chadwick*. Leonard Parsons, London 1925

Martin — Martin, Kingsley, *The Triumph of Lord Palmerston*. Hutchinson, London 1963

Martineau — Martineau, Harriet, *England and Her Soldiers*. Smith, Elder, London 1859

MSH — 'A Medical and Surgical History of The British Army which Served in Turkey and The Crimea During the War Against Russia in The Years 1854–55–56'. London 1858

NoM — *Nightingale, Florence, Notes on Matters Affecting the Health, Efficiency, and Hospital Administration of the British Army, founded chiefly on Experience of the Last War*. Harrison & Sons, London 1858

NoN — Nightingale, Florence, *Notes on Nursing: What It Is and What It is Not*. Harrison, London 1860

Osborne — Osborne, Sidney Godolphin, *Scutari and Its Hospitals*. Dickinson, London 1855

Paget — Paget, Gen. Lord George, *The Light Cavalry Brigade in the Crimea*. John Murray, London 1881

Panmure — Douglas, Sir George and Ramsey, Sir George, *The Panmure Papers*. (2 vols) Hodder & Stoughton, London 1908

Pickering — Pickering, George, *Creative Malady*. Allen & Unwin, London 1974

Portal — Portal, Robert, *Letters from the Crimea*. (Privately printed) Warren & Son, Winchester 1900

Reason Why — Woodham-Smith, Cecil, *The Reason Why*. Constable, London 1987

Ridley — Ridley, Jasper, *Lord Palmerston*. Constable, London 1970

RSC — 'Report of the Commissioners Appointed to Enquire into the Regulations affecting the Sanitary Condition of the Army, the Organization of Military Hospitals, and the Treatment of the Sick and Wounded.' Vol. XVIII (1857–58)

Russell — Russell, W. H., *The War from the Landing at Gallipoli to the Death of Lord Raglan*. Routledge, London 1855

St. Aubyn — St. Aubyn, Giles, *Queen Victoria, A Portrait*. Sceptre, London 1992

Sebastopol — 'Report of the Select Committee on the Army before Sebastopol'. House of Commons, London 1855

Simon — Simon, Sir John, *English Sanitary Institutions*. Cassell, London 1890

SNFN — Nightingale, Florence, 'Subsidiary Notes on Female Nursing'. Harrison & Sons, London 1858

SRO — Scottish Record Office

Shepherd — Shepherd, John, *The Crimean Doctors*. Liverpool University Press, 1991

Skretkowicz — Skretkowicz, Victor, *Florence Nightingale's Notes on Nursing*. Baillière Tindall, London 1996

Smith — Smith, F. B., *Florence Nightingale: Reputation and Power*. Croom Helm, London 1982

Stanmore — Stanmore, Lord Sidney Herbert, *Lord Herbert of Lea*. (2 vols) John Murray, London 1906

Strachey — Stratchey, Lytton, *Eminent Victorians*. Chatto & Windus, London 1924

ST — Nightingale, Florence, *Suggestions for Thought to the Searchers After Truth Among the Artizans of England*. (3 vols) Eyre & Spottiswoode, London 1860 (Privately printed. See also BL Cup 1247 for the 1852 version)

Summers — Summers, Anne, *Angels and Citizens: British Women as Military Nurses, 1854–1914*. Routledge & Kegan Paul, London 1988

Sweetman — Sweetman, John, *War and Administration*. Scottish Academic Press, Edinburgh, 1984

Terrot — Richardson, Robert, ed., *Nurse Sarah Anne*. John Murray, London 1977

Tulloch — Tulloch, Alexander, *The Crimean Commission and the Chelsea Board*. Harrison, London 1857

Vicinus — Vicinus, Martha and Bea Nergaard, *Ever Yours, Florence Nightingale*. Virago, London 1989

Victoria Letters — Benson, A. C. and Viscount Esher, *The Letters of Queen Victoria*. John Murray, London 1907

Wellcome — Wellcome Institute for the History of Medicine, London

WHO — The World Health Report, WHO Geneva, 1996

Woodham-Smith — Woodham-Smith, Cecil, *Florence Nightingale*. Constable, Edinburgh 1950

Notes

2. Early life

1 Vicinus, p 46
2 Vicinus, p 40
3 'I hate an "Order" and am so glad that I was never "let in" to form one' – Vicinus, p 219
4 Bishop & Goldie, p 105
5 Vicinus, p 41–2, p 50
6 Woodham-Smith, p 124
7 Cook, Vol. 1, p 117
8 Artizans, p 13
9 See, for example, the paper by F. G. P. Neison in the British Association proceedings at Oxford in 1847, which Florence and her sister both attended.
10 GCal, August 1854, no. 797
11 Goldie Crimea, p 18

3. War

1 Asa Briggs, *The Age of Improvement*, p 377, 384. London, Longmans, 1955

2 RSC, p 362

3 Goldie Crimea, p 71, 107

4 Cook, p 277

5 Goldie Crimea, p 37

6 Shepherd, pp 281–2. Nobody knows whether Nightingale knew of this criticism; the young surgeon himself died at Scutari and Nightingale sat by him while he died.

7 Goldie Crimea, p 37. This 'surgical' letter is a good example of Nightingale's adaptation to her correspondent. It was written to a surgeon.

8 National Army Museum. 6807-293-8, Burgoyne to Raglan 27 March 1855

9 Terrot, p 100

10 Terrot, p 85, 118

11 Terrot, p 109

12 Goodman, p 140, pp 165–6

13 Terrot p 156

14 Goldie Crimea, p 113

15 Davis, Vol. 2, p 117

16 Letter to Mary Shore Smith, n.d. [1888?]. Author's collection

17 Vicinus, p 110

18 Sweetman, pp 84–96

19 Aristocrats changed their names frequently. Lord Ashley as he was known at this time later became Lord Shaftesbury, Lincoln became Newcastle, Panmure became Dalhousie, Cochrane became Dundonald. In this book, the best-known name is used throughout even where it is anachronistic.

20 Lambert, pp 226–7

21 Simon, p 230

22 Panmure, Vol. 1, p 63

23 Hospital Reports, p 1, 11

24 Hospital Reports, p 20

25 Goldie Crimea, pp 168–9

26 Hospital Reports, p 1

27 Stanmore, vol. 2, p 137

28 Hopkirk, p 180
29 Vicinus, p 189
30 Smith, p 53
31 Goldie Crimea, p 126
32 Goldie Crimea, p 174
33 Goldie Crimea, p 218
34 Goldie Crimea, p 244
35 Panmure, vol. ii, p 356
36 Goldie Crimea, pp 103–4
37 Baly, p 8
38 Cook, vol. 1, p 237
39 Cook, vol. 1, pp 269–70
40 Vicinus, p 136
41 Longmore, p 17

4. Post-mortem

1 Panmure, pp 105–6
2 Victoria Letters, vol. iii, pp 221–2
3 St. Aubyn, p 220
4 Panmure, p 107
5 Panmure, vol. ii, p 108; it is reassuring to see that even seasoned Victorian courtiers sometimes stumbled over the complex modes of address; Panmure should have said 'Your Majesty's condemnation'.
6 Chelsea, pp 112–13
7 Chelsea, p 190
8 Shepherd, p 307
9 SRO/GD 371/255/2
10 BLAM 43402 f161/2
11 BLAM 43401 f300
12 BLAM 45796 f94
13 BLAM 45768 f26
14 LSE Farr Collection, vol. ix, item 5

15 Tulloch, p 3
16 SRO/GD 371/253/8
17 Wellcome Western MSS 8994 f110
18 BLAM 43402 f164
19 McNeill, p 387
20 SRO/GD 371/255/2
21 Vicinus, pp 173–4
22 McNeill, p 391
23 Panmure, vol ii, p 494
24 McNeill, p 292
25 Greville, vol. v, p 109
26 BLAM 50134 f2
27 GLRO NC3 SU 94 16/1/57
28 GLRO NC3 SU 81
29 Tulloch's improved table in *NoM* for October–April shows that of 41,395 patients who stayed in the Crimea, 4522 died i.e. 13%; of 12,518 sent to Scutari, 5341 died i.e. 36%. Using figures from *Contribution* for arrivals November–March, and *RSC* p 363 for arrivals 1 Nov–1 April, about 12,360 arrived at Scutari in five months; from death roll for Scutari and MO reports from Kulali in *Contribution*, it seems about 4513 died, i.e. 37%.
30 Cope, p 103
31 University of British Columbia collection, item B2, copy in Wellcome, 9084 f4
32 Wellcome, 8997 f32
33 BLAM 45768 f33
34 Wellcome, 8997 f42
35 Wellcome RAMC 271/23
36 Woodham-Smith, one of the few writers to touch upon this subject, does not seem to have found the Appendix, because she only quotes the Preface and does not describe the tables. It is Appendix II to Section IX, pages XXIII to XXVII, between pages 332 and 333.
37 Because those who were hospitalised in the Crimea but neither died there nor were sent to Scutari must have survived.

38 Nevertheless, the anonymous pamphlet *Observations of a non-Commissioner* which appeared late in 1858 attributed to Sir John Hall, claimed to prove from these figures that amount of trench duty was the determining factor in mortality.

5. Cover-up

1 Vicinus, p 184
2 BLAM 43394 f116
3 BLAM 45759 f18
4 Shepherd, p 584; MSH pp 269–72; on 10/12/54 Nightingale was trying to obtain choloroform apparatus for Scutari (private information).
5 Lummis File, National Army Museum
6 Adkin, p 207
7 Grey to FN, 29/6/57 Durham University
8 BLAM 45796 f224
9 RSC, p 5
10 Stanmore, p 14
11 Stanmore, p 11
12 Greville, 28/1/45 Second Part, vol. II, pp 267–8
13 Delane to Herbert 6/2/58 quoted Woodham-Smith, p 319
14 Vicinus, p 178
15 Clough, p 529
16 Smith, p 85
17 Woodham-Smith, p 315
18 BLAM 43394 f95, BLAM 45768 f57
19 Clough Poems, p 24
20 Pembroke Papers, 2057, F8/IV/C33
21 Hurd, Commemoration of the Fiftieth Anniversary of the Founding by Florence Nightingale of the First Training School, Carnegie Hall, NY 18/5/10. Quoted in Cook I.345
22 Countway Library, Harvard University, B MS c 11.2
23 See also Goldie Crimea, pp 97, 272–3, 278

24 Tulloch, p xii

25 Tulloch, p 150

26 Reason Why, p 265

27 Claydon, bundle 308

28 Woodham-Smith, p 107

29 AMNS, p 61

30 Baly, p 113

31 Vicinus, pp 177–82; internal evidence indicates this must have been written during or just after her breakdown.

32 National Army Museum. 6807-293-8 Burgoyne to Raglan, 27 March 1855

33 Claydon, bundle 71

6. Vengeance

1 See Lambert for descriptions of the state of England's cities in the 1850s.

2 Lambert, p 68

3 Lambert, p 522

4 Simon said 'Liability to these *other* infections', meaning to exclude small-pox which he admitted was avoidable by vaccination.

5 The Builder, 30/10/58, p 723

6 Lambert, p 48

7 The Builder, 6/11/58, p 740

8 The Builder, 20/11/58, p 770

9 The second volume was 'Subsidiary Notes on Female Nursing'.

10 SNFN, pp128–9. She also listed small-pox even though Simon had excluded it from his list. Simon's expression 'Current contagions' has been replaced by the modern equivalent 'fast-spreading contagions' – see Skretkowicz, p 55.

11 Lambert, p 51. Simon's efforts to find this scientific insight failed, and he eventually repeated Snow's observations and was widely credited with Snow's discovery (see Lambert, p 249).

12 Public Health Reports by John Simon, Edited by Edward Seaton,

1887. The deletions concerning Snow's theory are marked by sequences of four dots on p 443.

13 World Resource Institute estimate, quoted in Scientific American November 1997

14 WHO says that treatment of pneumonia is the world's most common *misuse* of antibiotics – which creates drug-resistant bacteria.

15 It was also an assumption that Alphonse Quetelt believed in. See Diamond, p 185, 205

16 Strachey, p 173

17 NoN, p 6

18 Lambert, p 600, 619

19 Cantlie, vol. 2, p 125

20 See for example Cope, p 15

21 AMNS, p 2; Baly, p 131

22 Wellcome Western MSS 5478 ff8/4–8

23 'Boiled milk is sometimes ordered, and if brought to the boiling-point, not beyond it, the milk undergoes less change . . . In cases where the taste of boiled milk is disagreeable, it may be placed in a closely covered jar and subjected to continued heat without boiling by standing the jar in a sauce-pan of water and letting it simmer for about an hour.' Practical Hints on District Nursing by Amy Hughes, London, The Scientific Press Limited, 1897, pp 53–4

24 British Medical Journal No. 1061, April 2, 1960

25 Quoted in Diamond, Part 1, p 74

26 The Builder, 28/8/58, p 578

27 Baly, p 25

28 Baly, p 121

29 'Hospital Acquired Infection', by Plowman *et al.* Office of Health Economics, London 1997

30 Government Response to 3rd Report of the Health Committee on Breast Cancer Services, 1994–95 Cm 3007

31 Observations of a Non-Commissioner, n.d.

32 Woodham-Smith, p 357, see also BLAM 43396 f306

33 Panmure Papers, vol. 1, p 197. See also Jenkins, p 143, 159
34 BLAM 45763 f29
35 BLAM 43397 f34–71. This draft of Nightingale's is not the same as her published eulogy of 1862, of which a draft is in BLAM 43395 f321. The published version contained less praise of Lord Panmure.
36 F. B. Smith, p 106
37 Panmure, vol. ii, p 495
38 Cook, vol. 2, p 92
39 Lambert, p 460n, 461n

7. Reputation and myth

1 BLAM 45751 ff.44–9
2. BLAM 43394 f.135
3 University of British Colombia, item C30. Letter from Lady Herbert's granddaughter
4 BLAM 43397 f238
5 Cook, vol. 2, p 353
6 Calabria, p xxxviii
7 ST, vol. 3, p 71
8 Diamond, p 73
9 ST, vol. 2, p 18
10 ST, vol. 3, p 68
11 ST, vol. 3, p 71
12 ST, vol. 1, p 155
13 ST, vol. 1, p 148
14 ST, vol. 1, p 95
15 ST, vol. 3, p 71
16 BLAM 45844 f7
17 ST, vol. 3, p 119
18 Davis, vol. 2, p 247
19 Letter from Herbert to Martineau, July 1859, author's collection
20 Ridley, pp 479–80

Index